W9-ANV-809

THE
OXFORD BOOK OF
PARODIES

THE
OXFORD BOOK
OF
PARODIES

Edited by
JOHN GROSS

OXFORD

UNIVERSITY PRESS

Great Clarendon Street, Oxford OX2 6DP

Oxford University Press is a department of the University of Oxford.
It furthers the University's objective of excellence in research, scholarship,
and education by publishing worldwide in

Oxford New York

Auckland Cape Town Dar es Salaam Hong Kong Karachi
Kuala Lumpur Madrid Melbourne Mexico City Nairobi
New Delhi Shanghai Taipei Toronto

With offices in

Argentina Austria Brazil Chile Czech Republic France Greece
Guatemala Hungary Italy Japan South Korea Poland Portugal
Singapore Switzerland Thailand Turkey Ukraine Vietnam

Oxford is a registered trade mark of Oxford University Press
in the UK and in certain other countries

British Library Cataloguing in Publication Data

Data available

Library of Congress Cataloging-in-Publication Data

Library of Congress Control Number: 2009938374

Typeset by RefineCatch Limited, Bungay, Suffolk
Printed in Great Britain by
Clays Ltd., St Ives plc.

ISBN 978–0–19–954882–8

3

CONTENTS

PART TWO

INTRODUCTION

A PARODY is an imitation which exaggerates the characteristics of a work or a style for comic effect. Such is the broad definition on which most dictionaries or reference books agree. It all seems plain enough. But when we move on to consider individual cases, the whole thing becomes more complicated. Does the borrowed style of a parody have to be sustained throughout its full length, for instance? And must mimicry always constitute the main point of a parodist's art? What about those occasions when the real function of the work which he or she is imitating is to provide the parodist with a framework or a launching pad—with the means of getting at a target, rather than the target itself?

Parodies come in many shapes and sizes, and many different degrees of subtlety or its reverse. There are mocking parodies and affectionate parodies, parodies which are exquisitely accurate, and parodies which are rough-edged but effective. There are light skits, boisterous send-ups, and savage lampoons. Parody can be the most entertaining form of criticism, and one of the most delicate. It can be erudite and allusive, but it is also a folk art—a favourite with children, a natural resource for popular humour. Swift's poem 'A Description of a City Shower' is a parody, after a fashion. (To appreciate it to the full you have to realize, or be shown, that it is based on a passage from Virgil's *Georgics* and two brief scenes from the *Aeneid*.) 'While shepherds washed their socks by night' is also a parody, after another fashion.

It simplifies the question of classification if one thinks of parody as being flanked on the one side by pastiche and on the other by burlesque. A pastiche is a composition in another artist's manner, without satirical intent—an *exercice de style*. Burlesque fools around with the material of high literature and adapts it to low ends: it takes serious characters and thrusts them into pantomime situations.

We are not dealing with hard-and-fast distinctions, however. A good deal of burlesque could equally well be classified as parody (provided you do not think that it is simply too crude, that 'parody' is a term that should be reserved for higher things). Nor is the dividing-line between parody and pastiche absolutely clear-cut. A pastiche, after all, is not a forgery. It positively advertises the fact that it is an imitation: it has the charm of deliberate artifice. And so do many of the very best parodies—Max Beerbohm's, say, or C. S. Calverley's. We marvel at the author's *trompe l'œil* technique, even as we share the underlying joke.

It would be a mistake for anyone writing about parodies to become entangled in a search for exact definitions. They are not a form of writing that is meant to be taken too seriously: they exist primarily in order to amuse. And an anthologist who tried to limit a selection of parodies to perfect specimens would be cutting himself off from too much valuable material. The impulse to parody is too deep, too widespread, and too many-sided to be confined to a fixed format or a rigid set of rules.

Most of the pieces in the present collection are none the less parodies in the most obvious sense. They are imitations which are exaggerated for comic effect. But the book also contains variants, oddities, semi-parodies, and many items which would be at least as much at home in an *Oxford Book of Burlesques*.

Exposing the limitations of other writers is not, in itself, a particularly noble task, and if that were the principal benefit which parodists had to offer their trade would surely be regarded as a fairly dismal one. In reality, however, the corrective aspects of parody are only secondary—and in many cases, not even that. Parody is an art, and like any other art it calls for both imagination and technical skill. It is not enough for a parodist to detect absurdity in others. He must create something absurd himself—something deliberately, enjoyably absurd.

A few critics have gone further, and argued that good parody is always based on affection. The idea is that you have to be fond of a writer before you can enter into his spirit, as opposed to merely aping his mannerisms. But this is too sunny a view of the matter. Many excellent parodies are undoubtedly motivated by exasperation or contempt. They are designed to annihilate.

What is true, on the other hand, is that the killer-parodies are in a small minority. Most parodies are relatively benign, especially the ones with staying power. And although parody is the nearest literary equivalent of caricature, its connotations are more playful. In his poem 'The Donkey' G. K. Chesterton introduces the creature—of which he finally wants us to take a sympathetic, indeed a spiritually elevated view—as 'the devil's walking parody | On all four-footed things'. Describing it as a walking caricature would have been too harsh.

Whether or not most parodists are affectionate, they certainly tend to rejoice in the styles they are making fun of. They are not telling us that we should not write like Robert Browning (or George Crabbe or Henry James or Muriel Spark), still less that Browning should not write like Browning. Their message, rather, is a mixture of astonishment and satisfaction. How extraordinary, they imply, that *anyone* should write like Browning—that he should choose to apprehend the universe in this one peculiar fashion. And how gratifying that he should keep it up—that he can always be relied on to be Browningesque.

Much of the pleasure of parody comes from contemplating the rival worlds that authors inhabit, each incurably idiosyncratic, each revolving on its own axis. It is a pleasure intensified by two of the parodist's stock devices, the variations on a theme (ten different ways of looking at 'Old King Cole') and the transposition of material from one author to another—so that Elizabeth Bennet and her sisters find themselves in Llaregyb, and Miss Joan Hunter Dunn is celebrated by Chaucer. The point of such juxtapositions lies less in any sharpening of satirical focus than in the joy of incongruity.

The finest parodists are masters of the slight stylistic distortion, the barely visible tweak. Did Kipling actually write a poem with the refrain 'An' it's trunch trunch truncheon does the trick'? No; but you feel that he stopped himself just in time—and then Beerbohm stepped in and did the job for him. Or take the line in Henry Reed's parody of a poem by Thomas Hardy—'It were better should such unbe'. The only thing that persuades you that it is not a genuine bit of Hardy is that you do not believe he could have compressed quite so much of himself into a mere six words. It took a parodist to do it.

Outright jokes are often a mistake in parodies. They can so easily tear through the fabric of mock-seriousness. But it very much depends on the context and on the parodist's judgement (and also, of course, on whether the jokes are funny). Malcolm Bradbury's parody of Iris Murdoch is set in a country house called Bishop's Breeches. It does not augur well—it looks like altogether too much of a good thing—when we learn that there is another country house nearby called Buttocks. But our doubts are soon dispelled. It turns out that the humour of the piece depends on playing off a daydream of fine feelings and gracious living against a succession of outrageous gags. The balance between the two is brilliantly maintained.

Again and again parody pushes out beyond its strict boundaries, and what started out as mimicry turns into independent fantasy. This is particularly true in the case of fiction. From *Don Quixote* (which transcended its burlesque origins) onwards, parody played a notable role in the rise of the novel. Two writers in this volume exemplify the process—Fielding, with an extract from *Shamela* (which was already halfway along the path which led to his first true novel, *Joseph Andrews*), and Jane Austen, with extracts from her teenage skits (which pointed forward to *Northanger Abbey*).

A parody is no longer worthy of the name, however, if it loses sight of its target. (*Readers* may be unaware of the parody-element in a work—the poems in Lewis Carroll's *Alice* books are a celebrated case in point—but that is not the same thing.) And parodists can throw light on the parodied in any number of ways, social or psychological as well as artistic. Take the extraordinary parody of Swinburne called 'Octopus' which Arthur Clements Hilton was moved to write in 1872, after visiting an aquarium. At first sight the joke turns on the mismatch between the poet's luxuriant style and a highly unsuitable subject. But essentially the poem is about Swinburne's sexuality.

Ope thy mouth to its uttermost measure
And bite us again!

You wonder how much Hilton knew. (He was only an undergraduate at the time.) A few years before this, Swinburne's friend, the redoubtable equestrienne Adah Mencken, had complained to Dante Gabriel Rossetti that Swinburne was not up to the mark as a lover: 'I can't make him understand that biting's no good.'

Parodists provide insight as well as entertainment. Their humour can range from the cheerfully scurrilous to the bittersweet, and there is room in their world for both anger and pathos. (One parodist in these pages jeers at Christopher Robin as a money-spinner, another asks us to contemplate him in lonely old age.) Finally, over and above their other qualities, they offer—or should—those artistic satisfactions which I have already mentioned. In the words of John Updike (an admirable parodist himself), 'a parody is not a piece of patient verbal construction like a crossword puzzle or a palindrome; it must be an inspired thing. It must have a grace, a pleased unfolding, of its own.'

Not every parody, needless to say, lives up to this ideal. But many of them do. Kenneth Koch's parody of William Carlos Williams radiates selfishness in a manner that is little less than sublime. The John Buchanesque villains in Alan Bennett's *Forty Years On* are evoked to thrilling perfection (especially the white-haired old man 'with a nervous habit of moving his lips as he talks'). And among the countless writers who have ridiculed Wordsworth in his simplistic mode, Catherine Maria Fanshawe (who was one of the earliest) stands out by virtue of her ability to make you see *why* the poet should have written in this way:

> There is a river clear and fair
> 'Tis neither broad nor narrow;
> It winds a little here and there—
> It winds about like any hare;
> And then it holds as straight a course
> As, on the turnpike road, a horse,
> Or through the air an arrow.

That ought to be utterly plodding. But it is curiously soothing as well, even idyllic, like a homely but serene Dutch landscape. And somehow all the more idyllic for being comic.

A history of parody in English would have to begin by considering the mass of medieval burlesque directed at the Church (parodies of religious services were commonplace) or at the conventions of chivalry and courtly love. An anthologist, however, is under no such obligation, any more than he is obliged to pick his way through the scraps of parody scattered around Elizabethan and Jacobean drama, or to hunt for possible gems among the minor classical burlesques of the seventeenth century. He can reasonably assume that most of his readers will be happy to leave such material to the specialists.

The acknowledged masterpieces of Augustan and Georgian satire might seem much more in an anthologist's line. They have retained their power, and many of them—*The Rape of the Lock*, for example, or *The Beggar's Opera*—have an obvious parodic element. But 'parody' doesn't seem an adequate label for works of this scope. It suggests a smaller, more compact art.

The first English writer whom anyone could describe as primarily a parodist was Isaac Hawkins Browne (1705–60)—wealthy, worldly, an MP (who never made a speech), and, as far as one can judge, a contented man. In 1736 Browne published *A Pipe of Tobacco*, a slim volume containing six poetic tributes to tobacco purportedly written by six leading poets of the day, including Swift and Pope. It is accomplished and agreeable, without packing much of a punch; the fact that it was still being fondly recalled seventy or eighty years later—it is mentioned in *Mansfield Park*—is a reflection of its novelty value, and also an index of how slowly things had advanced in the interim. It was not until the very end of the eighteenth century that formal parody achieved anything like its full power, with the squibs by George Canning and his colleagues in the *Anti-Jacobin*—to be followed in 1812 by a collection of variations on a theme that put Hawkins Browne in the shade, the *Rejected Addresses* of James and Horace Smith.

The nineteenth century saw a prodigious outpouring of parody, which continued undiminished into the twentieth. There were parodists of every variety, from hack humorists beyond number to virtuoso performers such as C. S. Calverley and J. K. Stephen. The same writer could work at very different levels, too. Lewis Carroll's best parodies are pure poetry, but he was also capable of routine Victorian jocosity—of producing a parody of Swinburne entitled (with a nod towards *Atalanta in Calydon*) 'Atalanta in Camden Town'.

One thing to which the popularity of parodies bears witness is the major role played by literature in Victorian and post-Victorian culture. They would never have had the appeal they did if large numbers of people had not had at least some acquaintance with what was being parodied. It is true that this was no guarantee of quality. The parodists' favourite targets were inevitably anthology-pieces, sentimental classics, and the kind of poems that were regularly assigned as school-work or chosen for recitation. This in turn ensured that many of them were specimens of what Chesterton called 'good-bad poetry'. (According to an expert, Carolyn Wells, writing in 1904, the most frequently parodied poem in the nineteenth century was the now-forgotten 'My Mother', by Ann Taylor.) But good-bad poetry has its good side, as you might say, while some familiar favourites were good without qualification. It is a stirring thought that it was once widely assumed—if parodies are any guide—that there was nothing esoteric about Gray's 'Elegy' or *The Rubáiyát of Omar Khayyám*.

The legacy of the Victorian schoolroom lived on well into the twentieth century. It crops up in unexpected places—in Noël Coward, for instance. One of Coward's finest songs is built around a ringing affirmation:

> The stately homes of England,
> How beautiful they stand

—lines lifted straight from a poem written *circa* 1830 by Felicia Hemans (who also wrote what was once one of the popular parodist's greatest stand-bys, 'The boy stood on the burning deck'). But Mrs Hemans continued:

> Amidst their tall ancestral trees,
> O'er all the pleasant land

while the Coward version proceeds

> To prove the upper classes
> Have still the upper hand . . .

The same song also contains an echo of Walter Savage Landor's 'Rose Aylmer'—'Ah what avails the sceptred race!' One wonders how many of Coward's audience, in the 1930s, actually picked up these references. But it does not much matter. The main thing is that the words lent the song a touch of class.

The best twentieth-century parodies impress by their sophistication. There was a strong impulse towards parody in many of the leading masters of modernism, from Joyce to Nabokov. (A relatively simple example of the genre is embedded in the most celebrated of modernist poems, *The Waste Land*—a sardonic version of Oliver Goldsmith's lines 'When lovely woman stoops to folly'.*) At a less Olympian level, the parodies which were a staple of the competition pages in the *New Statesman* and the *Spectator* maintained a remarkably high standard, especially around the middle years of the century. And in America some notable masters of the craft were at their peak around the same time—among them E. B. White and S. J. Perelman. Many of them were associated with the *New Yorker*.

---

* For Goldsmith's lovely woman, the only way of hiding her shame is to die. Eliot's lovely woman, after it is all over, 'smooths her hair with automatic hand, | And puts a record on the gramophone.'

There is a more light-hearted variation on Goldsmith by Mary Holtby:

> When lovely woman stoops to folly
> The prospect can be awfully jolly.

Parodists today operate in a world in which it is hard to avoid the effects of dumbing down. They cannot rely on as many common literary reference points as their predecessors did, or take advantage of as many shared allusions. And there are plenty of other forces in contemporary society that make for cruder humour, just as they make for cruder language and cruder manners.

Fortunately there are also satirists at hand to anatomize such faults, along with our other failings. Parody remains one of their most effective weapons; and even the less aggressive forms of parody are still cultivated with some success. What is striking, in fact, is not how much has been lost but how much survives. You will not have any trouble finding debased parodists if you search the lower depths, but the best of today's practitioners would have been outstanding in any period.

Traditionally, anthologies of parodies have been anthologies of literary parodies. That is largely true of this one. It is, I think, what most readers would expect. But I have also tried to range further afield—to provide some reminders that parody's scope extends well beyond poetry, fiction, and the world of letters.

The first and longer of the book's two parts is devoted to English-language authors, arranged in chronological order, along with parodies that they have inspired. The second part includes sections on more general literary topics, on aspects of individual authors which would not have fitted comfortably into the format of the first part, and on a handful of foreign writers. But it also looks beyond literature—at politics, journalism, the theatre, the law, and a sampling of other pursuits.

In making my selection, my guiding principle has been to choose items that I enjoy. In a few minor cases material has been included primarily on grounds of historical interest, but even then only when that interest struck me as exceptional. My choices are also designed to reflect the parodies that were available, rather than the stature of those parodied. The fact that Sir Henry Newbolt has two parodies devoted to him does not mean that I think he is twice as significant as Milton, who has only one, still less that I find him infinitely superior to Keats, who does not have any.

The allocation of space none the less proved a recurrent problem, as it must surely do with most anthologies. There is a convention that anthologists do not go into details about items which they would have included if only they had had room, and I shall abide by it; but it is perhaps not out of order to mention that I found myself facing some particularly hard choices in respect of fiction.

There are many excellent parodies of novelists in English. Some of them are brief. (In recent years the 'digested reads' of John Crace in the *Guardian* have made compression virtually a form of parody in itself.) But the best of them, beginning with the unsurpassed parodies by Beerbohm in *A Christmas Garland*, tend to be quite long, and for good reason. You can capture a novelist's style in a few lines, but you generally need space if you are going to do justice to his substance—to the working out of the story and the development of character. And in Anthologyland, alas, it is the law of the jungle. Space given to Smith means space denied to Jones. A lot of space given to Smith can mean space denied to several Joneses.

A question which came up from the outset was how much information should be supplied (if any) about the originals of parodies—the works on which they were based. The prevailing view in conversations I had was that, whatever may have been the case in the past, readers today need help: we live in a less literary world, 'familiar quotations' are no longer any such thing, et cetera. My own feeling is that this line of argument tends to idealize the past and underrate the present. But I can recognize its force, and I was soon persuaded that some indication of the originals was called for.

My biggest initial doubt was an old one. Where would we find all the extra space? Someone had spoken jokingly of the anthology ending up like a volume of translations, with the original on the facing page—and the image lingered. But then I realized that space was going to be much less of a problem than I had feared.

The chief reason is that a high proportion of parodies (quite possibly—I have not done any statistical research—a majority of good parodies) are aimed at a writer's general style rather than a specific work. When such a work is targeted, moreover, its relationship with the parody is often a fairly loose one; and when it is well known and easily accessible, it has generally seemed to me enough to point readers towards it, rather than providing them with a text.

I have therefore adopted a mixed policy. Where a parody is based on a specific work, I have indicated what that work is (except where the title of the parody makes it obvious). In some cases I also add a brief quotation from the original, either to suggest its flavour or point up some feature of the parody; occasionally I have judged it worth quoting it in its entirety. Finally, I have tried to supply any details about the background of a parody that are needed to ensure that the reader has at least a good general idea of what is going on.

JOHN GROSS

Acknowledgements

I OWE a particular debt to Christopher and Judith Ricks, who first suggested that I undertake this book, and who offered encouragement at a discouraging moment. Among other friends, Martin Dodsworth was especially helpful. I am also indebted for assistance and advice to Michael Holroyd, Alan Jenkins, John Kerrigan, Jim McCue, David Miller, Edward Mirzoeff, and Anthony Thwaite. At Oxford, Judith Luna has yet again proved an exemplary editor.

J. G.

PART ONE

ANGLO-SAXON AND MEDIEVAL

OLD-SAXON FRAGMENT

Syng a song of Saxons
In the Wapentake of Rye
Four and twenty eaoldormen
Too eaold to die . . .

W. C. SELLAR and
R. J. YEATMAN

BEOLEOPARD, OR THE WITAN'S WAIL

Whan Cnut Cyng the Witan wold enfeoff
Of infangthief and outfangthief
Wonderlich were they enwraged
And wordwar waged
Sware Cnut great scot and lot
Swingë wold ich this illbegotten lot.

Wroth was Cnut and wrothword spake.
Well wold he win at wopantake.
Fain wolde he brakë frith and crackë heads
And than they shold worshippe his redes.

Swinged Cnut Cyng with swung sword
Howled Witanë hellë but hearkened his word
Murie sang Cnut Cyng
Outfangthief is Damgudthyng.

W. C. SELLAR and R. J. YEATMAN

VARIATIONS ON 'SUMER IS ICUMEN IN'

I. 'Ancient Music'

Winter is icummen in,
Lhude sing Goddamm,
Raineth drop and staineth slop,
And how the wind doth ramm!
         Sing: Goddamm.
Skiddeth bus and sloppeth us,
An ague hath my ham.

Freezeth river, turneth liver,
    Damn you, sing: Goddamm.
Goddamm, Goddamm, 'tis why I am, Goddamm,
    So 'gainst the winter's balm.
Sing goddamm, damm, sing Goddamm,
Sing goddamm, sing goddamm, DAMM.

EZRA POUND

2. 'An Antient Poem'

Wynter ys i-cumen in;
Lhoudly syng *tish-ù*!
Wyndës blo and snoeth sno,
    And all ys icë nu.
      (Syng *tish-ù*!)

Leggës trembel after bath,
    And fingrës turneth blu,
Wisker freseth, nosë sneseth—
    Merie syng *tish-ù-*
      -tish-ù-
      -tish-ù-
Wel singest thou *tish-ù*;
Ne stop thou never nu!

FRANK SIDGWICK

3. 'The Runnymede Song'

Fredome ys icumen ynn
    Lhude syng hura
Kynge du sine, Baronnes wyn
Magna Carta duth begyne
    Syng hura hura.

Sune shal cum democracie
    Lhude syng hura
Lette alle tirantes qwale an cowar
We shal hav ye peeplys powre.
    Hura, hura hura.

Thynges be wurs than tymes afor
    Softe syng goddam
Pesants ar ye slawterd lam
Magna Carta ys a sham

Fer Baronnes ruin we crie goddam
Softe syng goddam.

E. O. PARROTT

4. 'Murie Sing'

Plumber is icumen in;
Bludie big tu-du.
Bloweth lampe and showeth dampe,
And dripth the wud thru.
Bludie hel, boo-hoo!

Thawth drain, and runneth bath;
Saw sawth, and scruth scru;
Bull-kuk squirteth, leakë spurteth;
Wurry springeth up anew,
Boo-hoo, boo-hoo.

Tom Pugh, Tom Pugh, well plumbës thu, Tom Pugh;
Better job I naver nu.
Therefore will I cease boo-hoo,
Woorie not, but cry pooh-pooh,
Murie sing pooh-pooh, pooh-pooh,
Pooh-pooh!

A. Y. CAMPBELL

5. 'Baccalaureate'

Summa is i-cumen in,
    Laude sing cuccu!
Laddes rede and classes lede,
Profesor bemeth tu—
    Sing cuccu!

Scholour striveth after Aye,
    Bleteth after sheepskin ewe;
Writë theseth, honoure seazeth,
    Murie sing cuccu!

Cuccu, cuccu, wel singes A-B cuccu;
    Ne flunke thu naver nu;
Sing cuccu, nu, cuccu,
Sing cuccu, Phye Betta Cappe, nu!

DAVID McCORD

GEOFFREY CHAUCER · 1343?–1400

IMITATION OF CHAUCER

Women ben full of Ragerie,
Yet swinken not sans secresie
Thilke Moral shall ye understand,
From Schoole-boy's Tale of fayre Ireland:
Which to the Fennes hath him betake,
To filch the gray Ducke fro the Lake.
Right then, there passen by the Way
His Aunt, and eke her Daughters tway.
Ducke in his Trowses hath he hent,
Not to be spied of Ladies gent.
'But ho! our Nephew,' (crieth one)
'Ho,' quoth another, 'Cozen John';
And stoppen, and laugh, and callen out,—
This sely Clerk full low doth lout:
They asken that, and talken this,
'Lo here is Coz, and here is Miss.'
But, as he glozeth with Speeches soote,
The Ducke sore tickleth his Erse-root:
Fore-piece and buttons all-to-brest,
Forth thrust a white neck, and red crest.
'Te-he,' cry'd Ladies; Clerke nought spake:
Miss star'd; and gray Ducke crieth Quake.
'O Moder, Moder' (quoth the daughter)
'Be thilke same thing Maids longen a'ter?
'Bette is to pyne on coals and chalke,
'Then trust on Mon, whose yerde can talke.'

ALEXANDER POPE

One of a series of imitations of earlier English poets, written in Pope's youth.

Pope also parodied Chaucer in what were probably the last lines of verse he wrote. While lying on his sickbed, about a month before he died, he learned of the death of his pet dog Bounce, who had been entrusted to the care of his friend Lord Orrery. 'I doubt not', he wrote to Orrery, 'how much Bounce was lamented: They might say as the Athenians did to Arcite, in Chaucer [in The Knight's Tale],

Ah Arcite! gentle Knight! Why would'st thou die
When thou had'st Gold enough, and Emilye!—

Ah Bounce! Ah gentle Beast! Why would'st thou die?
When thou had'st Meat enough, and Orrery?'

THE TALE OF MISS HUNTER DUNN

[Geoffrey Chaucer rewrites Sir John Betjeman]

A Mayde ther was, y-clept Joan Hunter Dunn,
In all of Surrie, comelier wench was none,
Yet wondrous greet of strength was she with-alle,
Ful lustily she smote the tenis-balle.
And whether lord or lady she wolde pleye,
With thirtie, fortie love wolde winne the day.
A Squyer eke ther was, in horseless carriage,
And he wolde fayn have sought her hand in marriage,
Though he coude songes make, with mery rime,
At tennis she out-pleyed him every time;
To make her wyf he saw but little chaunce,
But then be-thought to take her to a daunce
In gentil Camberlee, where after dark
They held long daliaunce in the carriage park;
Eftsoons, Cupide had the twain in thralle,
And this they found the beste game of alle.

STANLEY J. SHARPLESS

EDMUND SPENSER · 1552–1599

from THE SCHOOLMISTRESS: A POEM IN IMITATION OF SPENSER'S STYLE

In evrich mart that stands on British ground,
In evrich village less y-known to fame,
Dwells there in cot uncouth, afar renowned,
A matron old, whom we school-mistress name,
Who wont unruly brats with birch to tame:
They grieven sore in durance vile y-pent,
Awed by the pow'r of uncontroulèd dame;
And oft-times, on vagaries idly bent,
For task unconned or unkempt hair are sore y-shent.

Nar to this dome is found a patch so green,
On which the tribe their gambols do display:
Als at the door impris'ning board is seen,

Lest weakly wights of smaller size should stray,
Eager, perdie, to bask in sunshine day.
The noises intermixed, which thence resound,
Do learning's little tenement betray,
Where sits the dame, disguised in look profound,
And eyes her fairy throng, and turns her wheel around.

Right well knew she each temper to descry,
To thwart the proud and the submiss to raise,
Some with vile copper prize exalt on high,
And some entice with pittance small of praise:
And other sorts with baleful sprigs affrays.
Eke in her absence she command doth hold,
While with quaint arts the thoughtless crowd she sways;
Forewarned, if little bird their tricks behold,
'Twill whisper in her ear, and all the scene unfold.

Lo! now with state she utters the command.
Eftsoons the urchins to their tasks repair;
Their books of stature small take they in hand,
Which with pellucid horn securèd are,
To save from finger wet the letters fair:
The work so quaint, that on their backs is seen,
St. George's high achievements does declare;
On which thilk wight that has y-gazing been
Kens the forthcoming rod, unpleasing sight, I ween!

But ah! what pen his woeful plight can trace,
Or what device his loud laments explain,
The form uncouth of his disguisèd face,
The pallid hue that dyes his looks amain,
The plenteous show'r that does his cheek distain,
When he in abject wise implores the dame,
Nor hopeth aught of sweet reprieve to gain;
Or when from high she levels well her aim,
And through the thatch his cries each falling stroke proclaim.

The other tribe, aghast, with sore dismay
Attend, and con their tasks with mickle care:
By turns, astonied, evrich twig survey,
And from their fellow's furrowed bum beware,
Knowing, I wist, how each the same may share:
Till fear has taught 'em a performance meet,

And to the well-known chest the dame repair,
Whence oft with sugared cates she doth 'em greet,
And gingerbread y-rare, now, certes, doubly sweet . . .

WILLIAM SHENSTONE

The eighteenth century teemed with imitations and burlesques of Spenser; of the burlesques, Shenstone's—first published in 1742—was the most popular.

WILLIAM SHAKESPEARE · 1564–1616

IN A HIGH STYLE

According to John Aubrey, in Brief Lives, *Shakespeare's father was a butcher—'and I have been told heretofore by some of the neighbours, that when he was a boy he exercised his father's trade, but when he killed a calf he would do it in a high style, and make a speech'. This is a supposed version of one of these early flights.*

Thou bleeding piece of meat, can it be meet
That thou shouldst die, to feed the appetite
Of some tun-bellied Stratford alderman?
Was it for this my sharp intrusive knife
Did pierce thy throat and force thee to the change
From lusty bullock to unfeeling veal?
Oh I could weep, but that a second thought
Comes hasty on the footsteps of the first.
That alderman will gobble down his share,
(And more besides) but others too will taste
The bounty of thy flesh, thy blood, thy tripes.
Yes, worthier folks will gain good nourishment
From this thy rich, though most unwilling gift.
For what's at stake is steak; your steaks will feed
A poet's fancy, build a poet's frame.
Calves die, but I shall live, and live in fame.

GEORGE SIMMERS

IMITATION

Therefore do thou, stiff-set Northumberland,
Retire to Chester, and my cousin here,
The noble Bedford, hie to Glo'ster straight

And give our Royal ordinance and word
That in this fit and strife of empery
No loss shall stand account. To this compulsion
I pledge my sword, my person and my honour
On the Great Seal of England: so farewell.
Swift to your charges: nought was ever done
Unless at some time it were first begun.

HILAIRE BELLOC

from 'SAVONAROLA' BROWN

[a moment of comic relief in 'Savonarola: A Tragedy']

(*Enter the Borgias'* FOOL)
                  Well, Fool, what's thy latest?
FOOL: Aristotle's or Zeno's, Lady—'tis neither latest nor last. For, marry, if the cobbler stuck to his last, then were his latest his last *in rebus ambulantibus*. Argal, I stick at nothing but cobble-stones, which, by the same token, are stuck to the road by men's fingers.
LUCREZIA: How many crows may nest in a grocer's jerkin?
FOOL: A full dozen at cock-crow, and something less under the dog-star, by reason of the dew, which lies heavy on men taken by the scurvy.
LUCREZIA (*to* FIRST APPRENTICE): Methinks the Fool is a fool.
FOOL: And therefore, by auricular deduction, am I own twin to the Lady Lucrezia!

MAX BEERBOHM

from MODIFIED SONNETS

['a group of poems dedicated to adapters, abridgers, digesters and condensers everywhere']

'Shall I Compare Thee to a Summer's Day?'

Who says you're like one of the dog days?
You're nicer. And better.
Even in May, the weather can be gray,
And a summer sub-let doesn't last forever.
Sometimes the sun's too hot;
Sometimes it is not.
Who can stay young forever?
People break their necks or just drop dead!

But you? Never!
If there's just one condensed reader left
Who can figure out the abridged alphabet,
    After you're dead and gone,
    In this poem you'll live on!

HOWARD MOSS

BEN JONSON · 1572–1637

A RETORT

Ben Jonson's 'Ode to Myself' was prompted by the failure of his play The New
Inn *in 1629—a failure made all the more painful by the fact that he was 57 at the
time, an old man by the standards of the day:*

      Come, leave the loathèd stage,
      And the more loathsome age,
  Where pride and impudence in faction knit,
      Usurp the chair of wit:
Indicting and arraigning every day,
      Something they call a play.
    Let their fastidious, vain
    Commission of the brain,
Run on, and rage, sweat, censure, and condemn:
They were not made for thee, less thou for them . . .

*The Ode is a fine poem, which transcends the occasion which gave rise to it. But at
least one of Jonson's literary contemporaries was unimpressed by his angry pride:*

      Come leave this saucy way
      Of baiting those who pay
Dear for the sight of thy declining wit.
      'Tis known it is not fit,
That a stale poet, just contempt once thrown,
      Should cry up thus his own.
    I wonder by what dower
    Or patent you had power,
From all to rape a judgment. Let 't suffice
Had you been modest, you'd been granted wise . . .

OWEN FELLTHAM

Felltham was thirty years younger than Jonson. He is best known for his collection of essays, Resolves *(1628).*

There are many touches of parody in Jonson's plays. Most of them have been obscured by the passage of time, but one of them provokes a memorable comment. In Every Man in His Humour, *Jonson makes fun of some overblown lines by the poet Samuel Daniel. A character recognizes the allusion, and exclaims: 'A parody, a parody, with a kind of miraculous gift to make it absurder than it was.'*

JACOBEAN PROSE

1. EPITAPH ON THE INVENTOR OF THE WATER CLOSET

Here lyeth the bodye
of
Sir John Harington, Knight
Whose deare Renowne it was (boldlye presuming to impute to Majestie the Necessities of oure weake Fleshe yet by Soe greate a Condescension not being putt downe) to contrive for a Queene such a THRONE as no other Monarque (Noe, not Solyman in all hys Glorie) did heretofore bestride.

L. E. JONES

2. A FLEA AND HIS FOREBEAR

'A Descendant of John Donne's Original Flea is
Speaking, Over Twenty Years later, to His Host'

'What, sir, are we in the waie to Paules Crosse, to heere the Deane preach of the paines of hell? Hee maketh moe men to lie awake, to seeke out and sigh for their sinnes; thanne I and all my race of rest-robbers and night-annoyes, to seeke & scratche by candlelight. Hee is a grete disturber of the peace of this citie of London. And yet I love him well (for I & my people have ever loved sanctity, & habited with holy men); as my ancestor loved him (that dyed in his service and liveth in his verse).

'This famous flea, sir, was Jacke Donnes faytheful freende & fellow, xx yeeres agoe. They sorted well together; being both lads of metile & foes to quietnesse, good bedde-men & haunters of hostelries; & as the one was nimble of his limbes, so the other of his wittes, and bothe prodigious leapers in their owne kinde, soe that a man might not know where to have them next.

'Jacke Donne (thate is nowe the Dean) woulde have had his faithfull flea doe the office of a bedde for him & his mistresse (since shee would meete with him in no other). If you would know how this illustrious flea (pulex illustrissimus) dyed, having performed a service of soe great weighte; reade Jacke Donne's lines.

'Fare you well, sir. In so greate a presse as crowdeth aboute the Crosse you are like to lose me (and find a dozen moe). If I may come to him through the throng of sermon swallowers, I will seek entertainment with the Dean; and as my ancestor laboured to serve his youth in the gratification (though slight) soe will I his age in the mortification of the flesh.'

ANON.

An entry for a competition in the New Statesman, *submitted under the pseudonym 'Pulex' (the Latin for a flea). Donne's poem 'The Flea' records the union of two lovers through fleabites:*

> *It suck'd me first, and now sucks thee,*
> *And in this flea, our two bloods mingled be . . .*

ROBERT HERRICK · 1591–1674

'UPON JULIA'S CLOTHES'—SOME VARIATIONS

> *Whenas in silks my Julia goes*
> *Then, then (methinks) how sweetly flows*
> *That liquefaction of her clothes.*
>
> *Next, when I cast mine eyes and see*
> *That brave vibration each way free;*
> *O how that glittering taketh me!*

Whenas in furs my Julia goes,
Of slaughtered vermin goodness knows,
What tails depend upon her clothes!

Next, when I cast my eyes and see
The living whelp she lugs to tea,
Oh, how their likeness taketh me!

E. V. KNOX

Whenas galoshed my Julia goes,
Unbuckled all from top to toes,
How swift the poem becometh prose!

And when I cast mine eyes and see
Those arctics flopping each way free,
Oh, how that flopping floppeth me!

BERT LESTON TAYLOR

Whenas in jeans my Julia crams
Her vasty hips and mammoth hams,
And zips-up all her diaphragms,

Then, then, methinks, how quaintly shows
(Vermilion-painted as the rose)
The lacquefaction of her toes.

PAUL DEHN

Whenas in slacks my Julia goes,
Then, then, methinks, how adipose
Her tissue grows.

Next, when I cast mine eyes and see
That undulation, each way free;
O how that movement taketh me!

MICHAEL BARSLEY

ON LADY A——

[after 'To the Virgins, to make much of Time']

Gather ye rosebuds while ye may,
~~Old Time is still a-flying,~~
Despite the pads, the whale-bone stay,
The rougeing and the dyeing.

That glorious lamp of heaven, the moon,
   Is usually a-setting
While to Cole Porter's latest tune
   Ye still are seen curvetting.

That age is best which is the first,
   When looks and limbs are younger;
'Tis past recall, although ye thirst
   And amorously hunger.

NICOLAS BENTLEY

Nicolas Bentley also drew the accompanying picture.

JOHN MILTON · 1608–1674

MR SMITH TRIES IN VAIN TO TELEPHONE

               Soe hee
His eager Steps pursu'd, with Purpose clere
And unfulfill'd Intent, nor turn'd, nor stay'd
His onward Course, impatient to inspire
With urgent Speech the Engin sensible
To Breath articulate. Yet al in vaine:
Him of his swift Converse unequall Fate
Bereft, and in the silent solitary Street
Left impotent. His angry Eyes aflame
Like living Coales the glassy Tower transfix'd
Where unrepentant, careless, unashamed,
A son of *Belial* to the ekkoing Wire
Outpour'd his foolish love, with sweet Delay
Entranc'd, al els forgot. He long in Hope
Kept faithfull watch, though vaine; as once of old
The hapless Mother from her Casement gaz'd
Al unavailing, for his glad Return
Whom in her Tent the avenging *Kenite* pierc'd
With sharp and bitter Nail; or *Ceres* fair
Awaited long her deare *Persephone*
By *Pluto's* guile ensnar'd. In deep Despaire,
And by Frustration rack'd, at last he turn'd
Unsatisfied away; what time the Other, stirr'd
By garrulous Emotion, straight renew'd

Interminable Speech and soft Discourse
Unending . . .

G. H. VALLINS

ANDREW MARVELL · 1621–1678

TO HIS FAR FROM COY MISTRESS

Had I but Strength enough, and time
Thy boldness Lady were no crime.
We would sit down, and think which way
Next to disport us in love's Fray.
But thou, sweet hot impetuous Wench
Has't cull'd cruel lessons from the *French*;
No vast *Atlantick* could produce
Those Tydes thou seeks't of am'rous Juice.
Hi thee to *Lesbos*; there to sport
With Baubles of a sturdier sort,
Whose vibrant Aires fair nymphs adore.
Cool thus thy needes: make mine less sore.
E'en yet, wilde Tumult in thine eyes
Calls from soft Ease my Sword to rise,
Who, tristely swathed in *Stygian* glooms,
Anew his nuptial Toil resumes.

CHARLES ROBINSON

JOHN AUBREY · 1626–1697

A BRIEF LIFE

This account of a once-notorious Oxford don formed part of a series of newsletters contributed to the Spectator *by 'Mercurius Oxoniensis' between 1968 and 1971.*

R. H. Dundas, of Ch: Ch:, Oxon, was Scotch by birth, his father sheriff of Duns, Berwickshire (whence also Duns Scotus, the Subtile Doctor; but others deduce him from Embleton in Northumberland). He was bred up in England, at Eaton coll., and afterwards at New Coll., Oxon; then, for the rest of his days, Student (as they call their Fellows) at Ch: Ch. But he remained *patriae memor*, as those of that nation do, even when transplanted

to more civil societies. He once went so far as to introduce haggis (a bar-
barous dish) to the High Table at Ch: Ch:, who rightly rejected it and never
suffered it to return. He kept a fair house in Scotland, in Stirling, all his
life and would invite his pupills thither in vacation. His sister made them
welcome—at least such as did not guffle their soup, which she would in no
wise suffer (as —— —— did: *quaere plus de hoc*).

As a scholler he was no great shakes. The examiners at Oxon put
him in the first class, but he was not puffed up thereby. 'Twas absurd,
he would say, there should be but one class for himself and Jack Beazley
(Sir J. B., the great pot-critick). He was a Grecian, taught the history of
the Greeks, and especially their diseases (clap, haemorrhoids, etc.), to
which he ascribed much of their publick acts; but in general he despised
deep researches, holding to the good old view that dons should drink port
and mind the boyes, as he did himself, perhaps too much. In the second
of our great warres he lost his notes, wherefrom he taught; which loss
(occasioned by some misdirection by the publick carrier) mightily discouraged him. It was magnified by his pupills (*Mem.* never believe undergraduates), until some supposed that a *magnum opus* had perished; but 'twas only
a parcel of old jottings made by himself as an undergraduate, filled out
with trifles.

He served in the first warre in Mesopotamia and corresponded almost
daily with the Lady Mary Murray; who however afterwards, in a huff,
sent back all his letters. The reason unknown: some suppose that he had
grumped to her (as he did to others) that her husband, Gilbert Murray, then
Regius Professor of Greek (and so of Ch: Ch:), would not join in college
port-bibbing; which she, being a furious water-drinker, no doubt resented.
N.B. She was the daughter of that Countess of Carlisle who emptied his
Lordship's claret into the moat at Naworth: a horrid fact.

Returning to Ch: Ch:, he held the office of Censor, which he prized
mightily. Would say that once a man had been censor of Ch: Ch: there
was nothing left for him to do: 'twas the *acme* or zenith of human life. He
maintained that he was the best censor that coll. had ever had; which others
doubted. He had a mysticall notion of the censorship, not shared by his
successors, on whom he made sharp animadversions, as they on him; but
'tis a matter of opinion only.

He had a dry, laconicall way of expressing himself, more apophtheg-
maticall than profound, but useful to rebuke the impertinency of youth.
His correspondence was terse, by post-card. He also wrote comments
on undergraduates, grading 'em like cattle, *alpha, beta, gamma*, whether
plump or no, pink-faced or exsuccous, etc. These comments he writ in a
neat, exiguous hand on backs of envelopes, which he would then preserve
(his rooms a very jackdaw's nest) and bring up thirty years later to discon-
cert 'em.

He was *Paederastes*, but Platonick: assured the world he was a virgin *quoad corpus*: at most a viewer. He would question the young men curiously, and *de pudendis*; which they, being ingenuous youths, and forewarned by their fellows, took in good part. Sometimes, I fear, they pulled the old boy's leg. One only took it amiss and complained to his parents, and they to others, and so it was objected to him; whereupon he, in umbrage, took leave of absence for a year and sailed round the world, viewing naked boys, brown, black and yellow, diving for sponges etc.; which pleased him mightily. His other observations on the world were very trivial (no cosmopolite, no delight in art or letters). Then he returned to his old tricks, and viewed again in Parson's Pleasure.

He would visit schools also, for the same purpose, till deflected by headmasters, and would give passage in his car to stable-boys, who told him of strange doings in the bedstraw of Lambourn and Newmarket (*quaere*, whether unsollicited?). On Friday nights he would—as allowed by the rules of that society—invite youths from other colls. to the High Table of Ch: Ch: and question them over the snuff. Would sometimes, when *inter pocula*, forget himself. I have heard him quiz one of His late Majesty's learned judges, whether circumciz'd or no. I forget the judge's answer.

These curious indagations he somehow persuaded himself were right and useful: a publick duty wrongly neglected by others and left to him, as alone sustaining antique morality. 'Tis marvellous how men deceive themselves about their own motives; for I would impute hypocrisy to no man.

He was generous and would do good by stealth. By his prying, how impertinent soever, he would sometimes discover the needs of the young men, and privately relieve them, or see them relieved; which won him gratitude and caused all his faults (which at worst were venial) to be forgotten.

He believed—'tis the *naeve* of Ch: Ch: men—that Ch: Ch: was the centre of the world. He kept its annual record, marvellously complete (he had the eye of a hawk for detail) and maintained all the old traditions, sometimes adding new: e.g. that of emptying the residue of the port-decanter into his own glass as unfit for keeping; which did no good to his liver.

He died in Edinburgh, *anno* 1960, *aetatis suae* 76. After his death there was much ado to recover a curious illustrated book which he had borrowed (through a Minister of the Kirk) from a Scotch noblewoman, and not yet returned. 'Twas run down at last, in the hands of a fellow collegian, like him a batchelour. 'Tis now safe in Bodley's library, reserved to be read only by Heads of Houses, Bishops, etc. 'Tis best in such hands, for 'tis of rare indecency.

His life has now been writ by Master Roger Venables, and is printed by Sir B. Blackwell, in octavo, and to be bought at his shop in Broad-street; but 'tis very taedious. The lives of these old collegians should be writ briefly. Theirs are vegetable virtues, to be distilled, not dilated, and without a

grain of salt hardly to be saved from insipidity. 'Twould have tickled the
old rogue to see himself eterniz'd in this bumbling litany. But 'tis a work
of piety, so let it pass.

'MERCURIUS OXONIENSIS' (H. R. TREVOR-ROPER)

naeve] *A blemish.*

JOHN DRYDEN · 1631–1700

from ABSOLUTE AND ABITOFHELL

Based on Dryden's Absalom and Achitophel, *'Absolute and Abitofhell' is a
satirical response to* Foundations, *a collection of essays by leading members of
the modernist wing of the Anglican Church which was published in 1912. The
opening section of the poem traces what the author sees as the dilution of religious
faith among Anglicans over previous centuries.*

> In former times, when Israel's ancient Creed
> Took Root so widely that it ran to Seed;
> When Saints were more accounted of than Soap,
> And *Men* in happy Blindness serv'd the *Pope;*
> Uxorious *Jeroboam,* waxen bold,
> Tore the Ten Tribes from *David's* falt'ring Hold,
> And, spurning Threats from Salem's Vatican,
> Set gaiter'd Calves in Bethel and in Dan.
> So, Freedom reign'd; so, Priests, dismay'd by naught,
> Thought what they pleas'd; and mention'd what they thought.
> Three hundred years, and still the Land was free'd,
> And Bishops still, and Judges disagree'd,
> Till men began for some Account to call,
> What we believ'd, or why believ'd at all?
> The thing was canvass'd, and it seem'd past doubt
> Much we adher'd to could be done without;
> First, *Adam* fell; the *Noah's* Ark was drown'd,
> And *Samson* under close inspection bound;
> For *Daniel's* Blood the Critick Lions roar'd,
> And trembling Hands threw *Jonah* overboard . . .

RONALD KNOX

Jonathan Swift · 1667–1745

from A NEW VOYAGE TO THE COUNTRY OF THE HOUYHNHNMS

Gulliver sets out on his travels again. In the country of the Houyhnhnms, he finds a situation in some ways curiously suggestive of the 1960s, and especially of American universities at that time. The Yahoos are increasingly in revolt against Houyhnhnm rule. Many younger Houyhnhnms, including the group led by Skewbald, admire and even identify with them; many of the older ones, including such senior figures as the Chestnut, are anxious to appease them. One result of this crisis-ridden atmosphere is that there are frequent special meetings of the Houyhnhnm general assembly.

At that moment the Heralds began to summon all the Houyhnhnms to yet another Meeting of the Assembly. The younger Set cantered off to the Meeting-place in high Spirits, and I followed as quickly as I might. The Motion before the Houses was as follows: that the Assembly should be held every Day. This was proposed by the Chestnut, who argued, with some Show of Logick, that since special Meetings were being called with increasing Frequency, in these critical Times, it would be more reasonable to keep the Assembly in permanent Session, with Adjournments from Time to Time; and seconded by the Skewbald, who urged that every Matter of *Concern* to them all, and especially their Dealings with the Yahoos, should be kept under continual Review, and discussed by every Member of the Community; he was cheered by his young Comrades. Opposing the Motion, the Dapple-Grey objected that such daily Meetings would leave little Time for any other Work, and in View of the Depletion of their Asses and Working Yahoos, they could ill afford to neglect their Cattle and Crops by spending Hours every Day in Committee. The Debate continued, with much being said on both Sides, when suddenly some fifty Yahoos rushed into the Meeting-Place and squatted on the Ground. The Dapple-Grey at once asked the Master, who was in the Chair, to have the Ushers eject them; he replied that he considered such Action to fall outside his Prerogative, and requested that the Matter be put to a Vote. By a Small Minority it was resolved that the Yahoos be allowed to remain until the End of the Session. The Master said that he welcomed this Decision, since it would give the Yahoos an Opportunity to be educated in the Procedures of the Assembly.

When the Debate was resumed on the first Question, the Yahoos took an increasingly active Part in the Proceedings. They crudely imitated the oratorical Gestures of the Speakers, as when one would raise a Hoof to the Sky, or lay it across his Heart. They raised Shrieks of Applause, shaking their clenched Fists, when the Piebald spoke in Denunciation of the rigid and out-moded Customs of the Assembly; and when Iron-Grey, a friend of the Dapple-Grey's, tried to make a speech in defence of Tradition and the Laws of Reason, they howled him down, drumming on their Chests until he could no longer be heard, and even trying to lay their Paws on him. It soon became apparent that there was no longer any Freedom of Speech for any but the more extream of the Houyhnhnms, so loudly did the Yahoos intervene, grunting 'Ut, Ut, Ut,' hissing, making lascivious Gestures and throwing Showers of Dirt. I could not understand how it was that the Brutes, who had neither Speech nor the Understanding of Speech, could know which Orators to cheer and which to objurgate, until I saw the Skewbald making secret Signs behind his Back to prompt them; waving in the Air what I took to be small bundles of fragrant, or bitter Herbs, that their keen Muzzles could not fail to snuff, at the appropriate Moments. Suddenly the Brutes got up in a Body and scrambled out, leaving their customary Tokens behind them on the Ground. A Resolution was then put by the Chestnut to the Effect that the Yahoos be asked to send permanent Representatives to the Assembly; he felt that this Afternoon had been a remarkable Occasion for all of them, and that much Progress had been made towards mutual Understanding.

MATTHEW HODGART

AMBROSE PHILIPS · 1674–1749

from NAMBY-PAMBY: OR, A
PANEGYRIC ON THE NEW VERSIFICATION

Naughty-paughty Jack-a-Dandy,
Stole a piece of sugar candy
From the grocer's shoppy-shop,
And away did hoppy-hop.

   All ye poets of the age,
All ye witlings of the stage,
Learn your jingles to reform,
Crop your numbers and conform.
Let your little verses flow
Gently, sweetly, row by row;
Let the verse the subject fit,
Little subject, little wit.
Namby-Pamby is your guide,

Albion's joy, Hibernia's pride.
Namby-Pamby Pilly-piss,
Rhimy pimed on Missy-Miss;
Tartaretta Tartaree,
From the navel to the knee;
That her father's gracy-grace
Might give him a placy-place.
He no longer writes of Mammy
Andromache and her lammy,
Hanging-panging at the breast
Of a matron most distressed.
Now the venal poet sings
Baby clouts and baby things,
Baby dolls and baby houses,
Little misses, little spouses,
Little playthings, little toys,
Little girls and little boys.
As an actor does his part,
So the nurses get by heart
Namby-Pamby's little rhymes,
Little jingle, little chimes,
To repeat to little miss,
Piddling ponds of pissy-piss;
Cacking-packing like a lady,
Or bye-bying in the crady.
Namby-Pamby ne'er will die
While the nurse sings lullaby.
Namby-Pamby's doubly mild,
Once a man, and twice a child;
To his hanging-sleeves restored,
Now he foots it like a lord;
Now he pumps his little wits,
Sh——ing writes, and writing sh——ts,
All by little tiny bits.
Now methinks I hear him say,
Boys and girls, come out to play!
Moon does shine as bright as day. . . .

                                    HENRY CAREY

---

*Philips wrote a number of short poems addressed to children. They are sentimental
('Dimply damsel, sweetly smiling . . .') but not unpleasant.*

EDWARD YOUNG · 1683–1765

from NEW NIGHT THOUGHTS ON DEATH: A PARODY

What's life?—What's death?—thus coveted and feared:
Life is a fleeting shadow:—death no more!
Death's a dark lantern, life a candle's end
Stuck on a save-all, soon to end in stink.
The grave's a privy; life the alley green
Directing there—where 'chance on either side
A sweetbriar hedge, or shrubs of brighter hue,
Amuse us, and their treach'rous sweets dispense.
Death chases life, and stops it ere it reach
The topmost round of Fortune's restless wheel.
Wheel! Life's a wheel, and each man is the ass
That turns it round, receiving in the end
But water or rank thistles for his pains!
And yet, Lorenzo, if considered well,
A life of labour is a life of ease;
Pain gives true joy, and want is luxury.
Pleasure not chaste is like an opera tune.
Makes man not man, and castrates real joy.
Would you be merry? Search the charnel-house,
Where Death inhabits,—give the king of fears
A midnight ball, and lead up Holben's dance.
How weak, yet strong, how easy, yet severe,
Are Laughter's chains! which thrall a willing world.
The noisy idiot shakes her bells at all,
Nor e'en the Bible or the poet spares.
Fools banter heav'n itself, O Young!—and thee!

WILLIAM WHITEHEAD

Young's blank-verse poem Night Thoughts on Life, Death and Immortality *(1742–5) enjoyed a European reputation for several generations: it was praised by Johnson, admired by Diderot, and illustrated by William Blake. Whitehead, who wrote his parody in 1747, was poet laureate between 1757 and 1785.*

Alexander Pope · 1688–1744

IF POPE HAD WRITTEN TENNYSON'S 'BREAK, BREAK, BREAK'

Fly, Muse, thy wonted themes, nor longer seek
The consolations of a powder'd cheek;
Forsake the busy purlieus of the Court
For calmer meads where finny tribes resort.
So may th' Almighty's natural antidote
Abate the worldly tenour of thy note,
The various beauties of the liquid main
Refine thy reed and elevate thy strain.

See how the labour of the urgent oar
Propels the barks and draws them to the shore.
Hark! from the margin of the azure bay
The joyful cries of infants at their play.
(The offspring of a piscatorial swain,
His home the sands, his pasturage the main.)
Yet none of these may soothe the mourning heart,
Nor fond alleviation's sweets impart;
Nor may the pow'rs of infants that rejoice
Restore the accents of a former voice,
Nor the bright smiles of ocean's nymphs command
The pleasing contact of a vanished hand.
So let me still in meditation move,
Muse in the vale and ponder in the grove,
And scan the skies where sinking Phoebus glows
With hues more rubicund than Cibber's nose. . . .
(After which the poet gets into his proper stride.)

J. C. SQUIRE

Samuel Richardson · 1689–1761

Richardson's novel Pamela (1740–1) enjoyed enormous success from the first. Set down in a series of letters, it tells the story of an innocent young servant who resists her master's attempts on her honour, and eventually reduces him to offering her his hand, which she accepts. (The book's notorious subtitle is 'Virtue Rewarded'.)

Not long after its appearance, Henry Fielding published Shamela, *which purports to lay bare the true facts of the case.* Shamela *(who affects the name 'Pamela' when it suits her) is the very opposite of her predecessor. A coarse but cunning schemer, she targets her employer and manipulates her way ruthlessly into marriage with him. (In Richardson he was known simply as 'Mr B.'; in Fielding the 'B' turns out to stand for 'Booby'.)*

Shamela *can be read and enjoyed in its own right, as a piece of broad comedy. But its deeper appeal lies in the skill, and the healthy scorn, with which Fielding turns Richardson's material inside out. The extract below, part of a letter from Shamela to her mother, is based on chapter XXV of* Pamela. *Mrs Jervis is the housekeeper (and—in Fielding—the heroine's co-conspirator); Parson Williams is the hypocritical divine who becomes Shamela's lover.*

Thursday Night, Twelve o'Clock

Mrs Jervis and I are just in bed, and the door unlocked; if my master should come—Odsbobs! I hear him just coming in at the door. You see I write in the present tense, as Parson Williams says. Well, he is in bed between us, we both shamming a sleep; he steals his hand into my bosom, which I, as if in my sleep, press close to me with mine, and then pretend to awake.—I no sooner see him, but I scream out to Mrs Jervis, she feigns likewise but just to come to herself; we both begin, she to becall, and I to bescratch very liberally. After having made a pretty free use of my fingers, without any great regard to the parts I attacked, I counterfeit a swoon. Mrs Jervis then cries out, O sir, what have you done! you have murthered poor Pamela: she is gone, she is gone.—

O what a difficulty it is to keep one's countenance, when a violent laugh desires to burst forth!

The poor Booby, frightened out of his wits, jumped out of bed, and, in his shirt, sat down by my bed-side, pale and trembling, for the moon shone, and I kept my eyes wide open, and pretended to fix them in my head. Mrs Jervis applied lavender water, and hartshorn, and this for a full half hour; when thinking I had carried it on long enough, and being likewise unable to continue the sport any longer, I began by degrees to come to myself.

The squire, who had sat all this while speechless, and was almost really in that condition which I feigned, the moment he saw me give symptoms of recovering my senses, fell down on his knees; and O Pamela, cried he, can you forgive me, my injured maid? by heaven, I know not whether you are a man or a woman, unless by your swelling breasts. Will you promise to forgive me? I forgive you! D—n you, says I; and d—n you, says he, if you come to that. I wish I had never seen your bold face, saucy sow—and so went out of the room.

O what a silly fellow is a bashful young lover!

He was no sooner out of hearing, as we thought, than we both burst into a violent laugh. Well, says Mrs Jervis, I never saw anything better acted than your part: but I wish you may not have discouraged him from any future attempt; especially since his passions are so cool, that you could prevent his hands going further than your bosom. Hang him, answered I, he is not quite so cold as that, I assure you; our hands, on neither side, were idle in the scuffle, nor have left us any doubt of each other as to that matter.

CLARISSA HARLOWE ONLINE

Subject: R U Kidding?

From: Clarissa Harlowe <claha@virtue.com>

To: Robert Lovelace <lovelaceandlovegirlz@vice.com>

hi bob, TAH. if u think im gonna run off w/ u, :-F. do u really think im that kind of girl?? if your looking 4 a trollop, CLICK HERE NOW: http://www.hotpix.com. TTFN.

ANNE FADIMAN

LORD CHESTERFIELD · 1694–1773

DEAR FATHER

Lord Chesterfield's letters to his son are famous for their emphasis on urbanity and the social graces. This is one of his son's replies.

Westminster School, May 1745

Dear Father,

Thank you for the several letters which have reached me from you recently. It is very good of you to be at such pains to instil in me every detail of all the correct modes of thought and behaviour. I look forward to your letters with keen anticipation, and frequently read the passages of instruction to my schoolfellows, who envy me such a distinguished, wise, solicitous and learned parent. In their view, as in mine, you should be the King's first minister at least.

I am a little short of funds at present due to excessive expenditure on copies of Plato, Aristotle, etc. Could you forward me some more, as I am anxious not to fall behind your expectations of me?

I will terminate this letter now, as I am eager to return to my Demosthenes, which has reached a particularly exciting stage.

Your respectful son,
Philip Stanhope

NOEL PETTY

SAMUEL JOHNSON · 1709–1784

A GLOSSARY OF THE VULGAR TONGUE

In his Life of Johnson, *Boswell observes that 'the ludicrous imitators of Johnson's style'—the parodists—'are innumerable', but he scorns their efforts. He does make a grudging exception, however, for 'A Letter from Lexiphanes; containing Proposals for a Glossary or Vocabulary of the Vulgar Tongue: intended as a supplement to a larger Dictionary'.*

This was the work of the dramatist and theatrical manager George Colman the Elder, who was a fellow-member of Johnson's famous club (and one of the pall-bearers at his funeral). Boswell says, somewhat sniffily, that it was 'evidently meant as a sportive sally of ridicule', but he concedes—as the extract which he quotes demonstrates—that its mimicry of Johnson's style is not 'grossly overcharged'.

It is easy to foresee, that the idle and illiterate will complain that I have increased their labours by endeavouring to diminish them; and that I have explained what is more easy by what is more difficult—*ignotum per ignotius*. I expect, on the other hand, the liberal acknowledgments of the learned. He who is buried in scholastic retirement, secluded from the assemblies of the gay and remote from the circles of the polite, will at once comprehend the definitions, and be grateful for such seasonable and necessary elucidation of his mother-tongue.

Colman appended to his Proposal some specimens of the intended work:

Hodge-podge—a culinary mixture of heterogeneous ingredients; applied metaphorically to all discordant combinations.
Tit for Tat—Adequate retaliation.
Shilly Shally—hesitation and irresolution.
Fee! Fo! Fum!—Gigantic intonations.
Ding dong—Tintinnabulary chimes, used metaphorically to signify dispatch and vehemence.

IN THE SHADES

The caption for a caricature of Johnson and Boswell, drawn in 1915, which hangs in Johnson's former house in Gough Square, off Fleet Street.

BOSWELL: Are you not pleased, Sir, that your house in Gough Square is to be presented to the Nation? JOHNSON: Why, no, Sir. You are to consider that the purpose of a house is to be inhabited by some one. If a house be

not fit for tenancy by Tom or Dick, let it be demolished or handed over without more ado to the rats, which, by frequentation, will have acquired a prescriptive right there. I conceive that in Gough Square a vast number of rats will have been disturbed and evicted. (Puffing, and rolling himself from side to side.) Sir, I am sorry for the rats. Sir, the rats have a just grievance. BOSWELL: Nevertheless, Sir, is it not well that the house of the great Samuel Johnson be preserved? Will it not tend to diffuse happiness and to promote virtue? JOHNSON: Nay, Sir, let us have no more of this foppishness. The house is naught. Let us not *sublimify* lath and plaster. I know not whether I profited the world while I was in it. I am very sure that my mere tenement will not be profitable now that I am out of it. Alas, Sir, when 'tempus edax' has swallowed the yolk of the egg, there is no gain to be had by conservation of the egg-shell.

... or, so very much was Lexiphanes a man of moods, the dialogue might run thus ...

BOSWELL: Are you not glad, Sir, that your house in Gough Square is to be presented to the Nation? JOHNSON: Why, yes, Sir. (In a solemn, faltering tone.) Nothing has pleased me half so well since the *Rambler* was translated into the Russian tongue and read on the banks of the Wolga.

MAX BEERBOHM

'tempus edax'] *Time the devourer*

Beerbohm was appointed one of the governors of Johnson's house when it was first opened to the public. The reference to Johnson's periodical The Rambler *being read on 'the banks of the Wolga' is taken more or less directly from a passage in Boswell's* Life.

'I AM DOCTOR JOHNSON'

The Johnsonian scholar S. C. Roberts wrote a learned survey of parodies of Johnson. He also wrote a number of parodies of him himself, of which the briefest is the most pointed:

'Sir,' we can hear Boswell saying, 'you will never allow merit to a parodist.' JOHNSON: What, Sir, a fellow who claps a 'Sir' on the beginning of his sentence and a Latin derivative on the end of it and cries '*I am Doctor Johnson*'?

EIGHTEENTH-CENTURY VERSE

I. LINES FROM THE ART OF SINKING

Examples of the 'Cumbrous' and 'Buskin' styles of writing, from the treatise The Art of Sinking in Poetry. *They seem to have been specially manufactured for the occasion.*

Who Knocks at the Door?

For whom thus rudely pleads my loud-tongu'd Gate,
That he may enter?——

Shut the Door

The wooden Guardian of our Privacy
Quick on its Axle turn.——

Bring my Cloaths

Bring me what Nature, Taylor to the *Bear*,
To *Man* himself deny'd: She gave me Cold,
But would not give me Cloaths.——

Light the Fire

Bring forth some Remnant of *Promethean* theft,
Quick to expand th' inclement Air congeal'd
By *Boreas*'s rude breath.——

Snuff the Candle

Yon Luminary Amputation needs,
Thus shall you save its half-extinguish'd Life.

Uncork the Bottle and Chip the Bread

Apply thine Engine to the spungy Door,
Set *Bacchus* from his glassy Prison free,
And strip white *Ceres* of her nut-brown Coat.

ALEXANDER POPE

2. TO A GENTLEMAN, WHO DESIRED
PROPER MATERIALS FOR A MONODY

Flowrets—wreaths—thy banks along—
Silent eve—th'accustomed song—
Silver-slippered—whilom—lore—
Druid—Paynim—mountain hoar—
Dulcet—eremite—what time—
('Excuse me—here I want a rhyme.')
Black-browed night—Hark! screech-owls sing!
Ebon car—and raven wing—
Charnel-houses—lonely dells—
Glimmering tapers—dismal cells—
Hallowed haunts—and horrid piles—

Roseate hues—and ghastly smiles—
Solemn fanes—and cypress bowers—
Thunder-storms—and tumbling towers—
   Let these be well together blended—
Dodsley's your man—the poem's ended.

                  ANON. (PUBLISHED 1763)

'Dodsley's your man'—Robert Dodsley was the leading publisher of poetry in the mid-eighteenth century.

THOMAS GRAY · 1716–1771

IF GRAY HAD HAD TO WRITE HIS ELEGY IN THE CEMETERY OF SPOON RIVER INSTEAD OF IN THAT OF STOKE POGES

In the poems which make up the Spoon River Anthology *(1915), by Edgar Lee Masters, the inhabitants of a small town in the Midwest present their own epitaphs—many of them records of sorrow or disaster—from beyond the grave.*

The curfew tolls the knell of parting day,
   The whippoorwill salutes the rising moon,
And wanly glimmer in her gentle ray,
   The sinuous windings of the turbid Spoon.

Here where the flattering and mendacious swarm
   Of lying epitaphs their secrets keep,
At last incapable of further harm
   The lewd forefathers of the village sleep.

The earliest drug of half-awakened morn,
   Cocaine or hashish, strychnine; poppy-seeds
Or fiery produce of fermented corn
   No more shall start them on the day's misdeeds.

For them no more the whetstone's cheerful noise,
   No more the sun upon his daily course
Shall watch them savouring the genial joys,
   Of murder, bigamy, arson and divorce.

Here they all lie; and, as the hour is late,
    O stranger, o'er their tombstones cease to stoop,
But bow thine ear to me and contemplate
    The unexpurgated annals of the group.

There are two hundred only: yet of these
    Some thirty died of drowning in the river,
Sixteen went mad, ten others had D.T.s,
    And twenty-eight cirrhosis of the liver.

Several by absent-minded friends were shot,
    Still more blew out their own exhausted brains,
One died of a mysterious inward rot,
    Three fell off roofs, and five were hit by trains.

One was harpooned, one gored by a bull-moose,
    Four on the Fourth fell victims to lock-jaw,
Ten in electric chair or hempen noose
    Suffered the last exaction of the law.

Stranger, you quail, and seem inclined to run;
    But, timid stranger, do not be unnerved;
I can assure you that there was not one
    Who got a tithe of what he had deserved.

Full many a vice is born to thrive unseen,
    Full many a crime the world does not discuss,
Full many a pervert lives to reach a green
    Replete old age, and so it was with us.

Here lies a parson who would often make
    Clandestine rendezvous with Claflin's Moll,
And 'neath the druggist's counter creep to take
    A sip of surreptitious alcohol.

And here a doctor, who had seven wives,
    And, fearing this *ménage* might seem grotesque,
Persuaded six of them to spend their lives
    Locked in a drawer of his private desk.

And others here there sleep who, given scope,
    Had writ their names large on the Scrolls of Crime,
Men who, with half a chance, might haply cope,
    With the first miscreants of recorded time.

Doubtless in this neglected spot is laid
    Some village Nero who has missed his due,
Some Bluebeard who dissected many a maid,
    And all for naught, since no one ever knew.

Some poor bucolic Borgia here may rest
    Whose poisons sent whole families to their doom
Some hayseed Herod who, within his breast,
    Concealed the sites of many an infant's tomb.

Types that the Muse of Masefield might have stirred,
    Or waked to ecstasy Gaboriau,
Each in his narrow cell at last interred,
    All, all are sleeping peacefully below.

                              *

Enough, enough! But, stranger, ere we part,
    Glancing farewell to each nefarious bier,
This warning I would beg you to take to heart,
    'There is an end to even the worst career!'

                                        J. C. SQUIRE

THOMAS PERCY · 1729–1811

VARIATIONS ON A BALLAD

Three impromptu parodies of Percy's imitation ballad 'The Hermit of Warkworth'.

I put my hat upon my head,
    And walk'd into the Strand,
And there I met another man
    Whose hat was in his hand.

                              *

The tender infant, meek and mild,
    Fell down upon the stone;
The nurse took up the squealing child,
    But still the child squeal'd on.

                              *

I therefore pray thee, Renny dear,
  That thou wilt give to me,
With cream and sugar soften'd well
  Another dish of tea.

Nor fear that I, my gentle maid,
  Shall long detain the cup.
When once unto the bottom I
  Have drunk the liquor up.

Yet hear, alas! this mournful truth
  Nor hear it with a frown—
Thou canst not make the tea so fast
  As I can gulp it down.
                              SAMUEL JOHNSON

Bishop Percy is best remembered for his pioneering collection Reliques of Ancient
English Poetry. *The first and third of these parodies were improvised at tea-
parties given by Frances Reynolds ('Renny') while Percy was present.*

GEORGE CRABBE · 1754–1832

THE THEATRE

Interior of a Theatre described.—Pit gradually fills.—The Check-taker.—
Pit full.—The Orchestra tuned.—One Fiddle rather dilatory.—Is
reproved—and repents.—Evolutions of a Play-bill.—Its final Settlement
on the Spikes.—The Gods taken to task—and why.—Motley Group of
Play-goers.—Holywell Street, St Pancras.—Emanuel Jennings binds his
Son apprentice—not in London—and why.—Episode of the Hat.

  'Tis sweet to view, from half-past five to six,
  Our long wax-candles, with short cotton wicks,
  Touch'd by the lamplighter's Promethean art,
  Start into light, and make the lighter start;
  To see red Phoebus through the gallery-pane
  Tinge with his beam the beams of Drury Lane;
  While gradual parties fill our widen'd pit,
  And gape, and gaze, and wonder, ere they sit.

At first, while vacant seats give choice and ease,
Distant or near, they settle where they please;
But when the multitude contracts the span,
And seats are rare, they settle where they can.

Now the full benches to late-comers doom
No room for standing, miscall'd *standing room*.

Hark! the check-taker moody silence breaks,
And bawling 'Pit full!' gives the check he takes;
Yet onward still the gathering numbers cram,
Contending crowders shout the frequent damn,
And all is bustle, squeeze, row, jabbering, and jam.

See to their desks Apollo's sons repair—
Swift rides the rosin o'er the horse's hair!
In unison their various tones to tune,
Murmurs the hautboy, growls the hoarse bassoon;
In soft vibration sighs the whispering lute,
Tang goes the harpsichord, too-too the flute,
Brays the loud trumpet, squeaks the fiddle sharp,
Winds the French-horn, and twangs the tingling harp;
Till, like great Jove, the leader, figuring in,
Attunes to order the chaotic din.
Now all seems hush'd—but, no, one fiddle will
Give, half-ashamed, a tiny flourish still.
Foil'd in his crash, the leader of the clan
Reproves with frowns the dilatory man:
Then on his candlestick thrice taps his bow,
Nods a new signal, and away they go.

Perchance, while pit and gallery cry, 'Hats off!'
And awed Consumption checks his chided cough,
Some giggling daughter of the Queen of Love
Drops, 'reft of pin, her play-bill from above:
Like Icarus, while laughing galleries clap,
Soars, ducks, and dives in air the printed scrap;
But, wiser far than he, combustion fears,
And, as it flies, eludes the chandeliers;
Till, sinking gradual, with repeated twirl,
It settles, curling, on a fiddler's curl;
Who from his powder'd pate the intruder strikes,
And, for mere malice, sticks it on the spikes.

Say, why these Babel strains from Babel tongues?
Who's that calls 'Silence!' with such leathern lungs?
He who, in quest of quiet, 'Silence!' hoots,
Is apt to make the hubbub he imputes.

What various swains our motley walls contain!—
Fashion from Moorfields, honour from Chick Lane;
Bankers from Paper Buildings here resort,
Bankrupts from Golden Square and Riches Court;
From the Haymarket canting rogues in grain,
Gulls from the Poultry, sots from Water Lane;
The lottery-cormorant, the auction-shark,
The full-price master, and the half-price clerk;
Boys who long linger at the gallery-door,
With pence twice five—they want but twopence more;
Till some Samaritan the twopence spares,
And sends them jumping up the gallery-stairs.

Critics we boast who ne'er their malice balk,
But talk their minds—we wish they'd mind their talk;
Big-worded bullies, who by quarrels live—
Who give the lie, and tell the lie they give;
Jews from St Mary Axe, for jobs so wary,
That for old clothes they'd even axe St Mary;
And bucks with pockets empty as their pate,
Lax in their gaiters, laxer in their gait;
Who oft, when we our house lock up, carouse
With tippling tipstaves in a lock-up house.

Yet here, as elsewhere, Chance can joy bestow,
Where scowling Fortune seem'd to threaten woe.

John Richard William Alexander Dwyer
Was footman to Justinian Stubbs, Esquire;
But when John Dwyer listed in the Blues,
Emanuel Jennings polish'd Stubbs's shoes.
Emanuel Jennings brought his youngest boy
Up as a corn-cutter—a safe employ;
In Holywell Street, St Pancras, he was bred
(At number twenty-seven, it is said),
Facing the pump, and near the Granby's Head:
He would have bound him to some shop in town,
But with a premium he could not come down.
Pat was the urchin's name—a red-hair'd youth,
Fonder of purl and skittle-grounds than truth.

Silence, ye gods! to keep your tongues in awe,
The Muse shall tell an accident she saw.

Pat Jennings in the upper gallery sat,
But, leaning forward, Jennings lost his hat:
Down from the gallery the beaver flew,
And spurn'd the one to settle in the two.
How shall he act? Pay at the gallery-door
Two shillings for what cost, when new, but four?
Or till half-price, to save his shilling, wait,
And gain his hat again at half-past eight?
Now, while his fears anticipate a thief,
John Mullins whispers, 'Take my handkerchief.'
'Thank you,' cries Pat; 'but one won't make a line.'
'Take mine,' cried Wilson; and cried Stokes, 'Take mine.'
A motley cable soon Pat Jennings ties,
Where Spitalfields with real India vies.
Like Iris' bow, down darts the painted clue,
Starr'd, striped, and spotted, yellow, red, and blue,
Old calico, torn silk, and muslin new.
George Green below, with palpitating hand,
Loops the last 'kerchief to the beaver's band—
Upsoars the prize! The youth, with joy unfeign'd,
Regain'd the felt, and felt what he regain'd;
While to the applauding galleries grateful Pat
Made a low bow, and touch'd the ransom'd hat.

JAMES SMITH

*Both this parody and those of William Cobbett on p. 41 and Tom Moore on p. 53
come from the most celebrated collection of parodies of the nineteenth century,*
Rejected Addresses *(1812), by the brothers James and Horace Smith.*

*In 1809 Drury Lane Theatre burned down. In 1812, as the building which
replaced it was nearing completion, a competition was announced for an Address
to be recited at the opening ceremony. None of the efforts that were submitted
satisfied the judges, and while the situation remained unresolved James Smith (a
solicitor) and his brother Horace (a stockbroker) stepped in with a collection of
spoof 'rejected addresses', purportedly by leading poets of the day (and by two
prose-writers, Cobbett and—incongruously—the long-dead Samuel Johnson). The
volume, which was a success from the first, was presented as though the brothers
had written it in close collaboration throughout, but in fact they divided their
labours between them, and the parodies of both Crabbe and Cobbett were the
single-handed work of James.*

WILLIAM BLAKE · 1757–1827

WILLIAM BLAKE REWRITES T. S. ELIOT'S 'THE HOLLOW MEN'

[after 'Auguries of Innocence']

A Scarecrow with his Head of Straw
Is fill'd with Nothing evermore.
The Blind Man's dreams are full at Night
Of those in Heaven still with Sight.
The Dullard wakening to Despair
Has Thoughts compos'd of empty Air.
The Fools that by a Cactus pray
Shall never kiss at Break of Day.
The Crowd upon the hopeless Beach
See Rose & Star they ne'er can reach.
He who hears the Five Bells chime
Shall chant a final Nursery Rhyme.
A Shadow falling here & there
Defeats Man's Memory of Prayer.
A quiet not a violent Noise
Proves the end of this world's Joyes.

BILL GREENWELL

ROBERT BURNS · 1759–1796

LINES ON THE DEATH OF SAMUEL JOHNSON, ESQ.

Ye louns wha lust for mortal fame,
See how the Gods your heroes claim:
Great Samuel is gangin' hame
    Tae tak' his rest.
An' God help those wha bear that frame
    In oaken chest.

For tho' yon deep an' mightie mind
Was crammed wi' wisdom o' mankind,
His body too was sair inclin'd

To lay up store.
An' Samuel's girth is weel enshrined
   In London lore.

Yon couthie Boswell oft he'd tease
An' nothing Scotch cuid e'er him please
Till, journeying tae the Hebrides,
   He seem'd tae thaw,
When plied wi' barley broth an' peas
   An' usquebaugh.

Ane service fine he did for Ayr:
This Boswell's mind he did ensnare,
Which did the young laird keep doon there
   In London's lap,
An' Auchinleck's braw lasses spare
   Fra' Jamie's clap.

An' as for me, I own my due.
When told yon Diction'ry had grew
To hold all words that poets knew
   In sober print,
I made a vow tae use a few
   That were nae in't.

                              NOEL PETTY

RIGID BODY SINGS

[after 'Comin' thro' the Rye']

Gin a body meet a body
   Flyin' through the air,
Gin a body hit a body,
   Will it fly? and where?
Ilka impact has its measure,
   Ne'er a' ane hae I,
Yet a' the lads they measure me,
   Or, at least, they try.

Gin a body meet a body
   Altogether free,

How they travel afterwards
 We do not always see.
Ilka problem has its method
 By analytics high;
For me, I ken na ane o' them,
 But what the waur am I?

JAMES CLERK MAXWELL

rigid body] *in physics, 'an idealized extended solid whose size and shape are definitely mixed and remain unaltered when forces are applied'.*

James Clerk Maxwell (1831–79) was one of the greatest of physicists. He wrote a good deal of serio-comic verse, including skilful parodies of Shelley, Tennyson, and Swinburne. His only other parody of Burns, based on 'John Anderson', is a squib prompted by the departure of an officious senior dean who got on his nerves when he was a student:

John Alexander Frere, John,
 When first we were acquent,
You lectured us as Freshmen
 In the holy term of Lent;
But now you're getting bald, John,
 Your end is drawing near,
And I think we'd better say 'Goodbye,
 John Alexander Frere' . . .

WILLIAM COBBETT · 1763–1835

IN THE CHARACTER OF A HAMPSHIRE FARMER

[a celebration of the reopening of the Drury Lane Theatre: from Rejected Addresses*—see p. 38]*

MOST THINKING PEOPLE,
When persons address an audience from the stage, it is usual, either in words or gesture, to say, 'Ladies and Gentlemen, your servant.' If I were base enough, mean enough, paltry enough, and *brute beast* enough, to follow that fashion, I should tell two lies in a breath. In the first place, you are *not* Ladies and Gentlemen, but I hope something better, that is to say, honest men and women; and in the next place, if you were ever so much ladies, and ever so much gentlemen, I am not, *nor ever will be*, your humble

servant. You see me here, *most thinking people*, by mere chance. I have not been within the doors of a playhouse before for these ten years; nor, till that abominable custom of taking money at the doors is discontinued, will I ever sanction a theatre with my presence. The stage-door is the only gate of *freedom* in the whole edifice, and through that I made my way from Bagshaw's in Brydges Street, to accost you. Look about you. Are you not all comfortable? Nay, never slink, mun; speak out, if you are dissatisfied, and tell me so before I leave town. You are now, (thanks to *Mr Whitbread*), got into a large, comfortable house. Not into a *gimcrack palace*; not into a *Solomon's temple*; not into a frost-work of Brobdignag filigree; but into a plain, honest, homely, industrious, wholesome, *brown brick playhouse*. You have been struggling for independence and elbow-room these three years; and who gave it you? Who helped you out of Lilliput? Who routed you from a rat-hole, five inches by four, to perch you in a palace? Again and again I answer, *Mr Whitbread*. You might have sweltered in that place with the Greek name till doomsday, and neither *Lord Castlereagh*, *Mr Canning*, no, nor the *Marquess Wellesley*, would have turned a trowel to help you out! Remember that. Never forget that. Read it to your children, and to your children's children! And now, *most thinking people*, cast your eyes over my head to what the builder, (I beg his pardon, the architect), calls the *proscenium*. No motto, no slang, no popish Latin, to keep the people in the dark. No *veluti in speculum*. Nothing in the dead languages, properly so called, for they ought to die, ay and be *damned* to boot! The Covent Garden manager tried that, and a pretty business he made of it! When a man says *veluti in speculum*, he is called a man of letters. Very well, and is not a man who cries O. P. a man of letters too? You ran your O. P. against his *veluti in speculum*, and pray which beat? I prophesied that, though I never told any body. I take it for granted, that every intelligent man, woman, and child, to whom I address myself, has stood severally and respectively in Little Russell Street, and cast their, his, her, and its eyes on the outside of this building before they paid their money to view the inside. Look at the brickwork, *English Audience!* Look at the brickwork! All plain and smooth like a quakers' meeting. None of your Egyptian pyramids, to entomb subscribers' capitals. No overgrown colonnades of stone, like an alderman's gouty legs in white cotton stockings, fit only to use as rammers for paving Tottenham Court Road. This house is neither after the model of a temple in Athens, no, nor a *temple* in *Moorfields*, but it is built to act English plays in; and, provided you have good scenery, dresses, and decorations, I daresay you wouldn't break your hearts if the outside were as plain as the pikestaff I used to carry when I was a sergeant. *Apropos*, as the French valets say, who cut their masters' throats—*apropos*, a word about dresses. You must, many of you, have seen what I have read a description of, Kemble and Mrs Siddons in Macbeth, with more gold and silver plastered on their doublets than would have kept an honest family in butcher's meat and flannel from year's end to year's end! I am informed, (now mind, I do not vouch for the fact), but I am informed that all such extravagant idleness is to be done away with here. Lady Macbeth is to have a plain quilted petticoat, a cotton gown, and a *mob cap* (as the court parasites call it;—it will be well for them, if, one of these days, they don't wear a mob cap—I mean a *white cap*, with a *mob* to look at them); and Macbeth is to appear in an honest yeoman's drab coat, and a pair of black calamanco breeches. Not *Salamanca*; no, nor *Talavera* neither, my most Noble Marquess; but plain, honest, black calamanco stuff breeches. This is right; this is as it should be. *Most thinking people*, I have heard you much abused. There is not a compound in the language but is strung fifty in a rope, like onions, by the Morning Post, and hurled in your teeth. You are called the mob; and when they have made you out to be the mob, you are called the *scum* of the people, and the *dregs* of the people. I should like to know how you can be both. Take a basin of broth—not *cheap soup, Mr Wilberforce*—not soup for the poor, at a penny a quart, as your mixture of horses' legs, brick-dust, and old shoes, was denominated—but plain, wholesome, patriotic beef or mutton broth; take this, examine it, and you will find—mind, I don't vouch for the fact, but I am told—you will find the dregs at the bottom, and the scum at the top. I will endeavour to explain this to you: England is a large *earthenware pipkin*; John Bull is the *beef* thrown into it; taxes are the *hot water* he boils in; rotten boroughs are the *fuel* that blazes under this same pipkin; parliament is the *ladle* that stirs the hodge-podge, and sometimes——. But, hold! I don't wish to pay *Mr Newman* a second visit. I leave you better off than you have been this many a day: you have a good house over your head; you have beat the French in Spain; the harvest has turned out well; the comet keeps its distance; and red slippers are hawked about in Constantinople for next to nothing; and for all this, *again and again* I tell you, you are indebted to *Mr Whitbread!!!*

JAMES SMITH

Bagshaw] *the publisher of Cobbett's journal* The Weekly Register.

Mr Whitbread] *Samuel Whitbread, moving spirit on the committee for the rebuilding of the Drury Lane Theatre.*

that place with the Greek name] *the Lyceum Theatre, where the Drury Lane company performed while their own theatre was being rebuilt.*

veluti in speculum] *'as though in a mirror'— a traditional motto for a theatre, inscribed over the proscenium in Covent Garden.*

O. P.] *'Old Prices'—the cry of rioters when the Covent Garden Theatre raised the price of admission in 1809.*

Newman] *the keeper of Newgate prison at the time.*

WILLIAM WORDSWORTH · 1770–1850

FRAGMENT IN IMITATION OF WORDSWORTH

There is a river clear and fair,
'Tis neither broad nor narrow;
It winds a little here and there—
It winds about like any hare;
And then it holds as straight a course
As, on the turnpike road, a horse,
Or, through the air, an arrow.

The trees that grow upon the shore
Have grown a hundred years or more;
So long there is no knowing:
Old Daniel Dobson does not know
When first those trees began to grow;
But still they grew, and grew, and grew,
As if they'd nothing else to do,
But ever must be growing.

The impulses of air and sky
Have reared their stately heads so high,
And clothed their boughs with green;
Their leaves the dews of evening quaff,—
And when the wind blows loud and keen,
I've seen the jolly timbers laugh,
And shake their sides with merry glee—
Wagging their heads in mockery.

Fixed are their feet in solid earth
Where winds can never blow;
But visitings of deeper birth
Have reached their roots below.
For they have gained the river's brink,
And of the living waters drink.

There's little Will, a five years' child—
He is my youngest boy;
To look on eyes so fair and wild,
It is a very joy.
He hath conversed with sun and shower,

And dwelt with every idle flower,
As fresh and gay as them.
He loiters with the briar-rose,—
The blue-bells are his play-fellows,
That dance upon their slender stem.

And I have said, my little Will,
Why should he not continue still
A thing of Nature's rearing?
A thing beyond the world's control—
A living vegetable soul—
No human sorrow fearing.

It were a blessed sight to see
That child become a willow-tree,
His brother trees among.
He'd be four times as tall as me,
And live three times as long.

CATHERINE MARIA FANSHAWE

*Catherine Fanshawe (1765–1834) was five years Wordsworth's senior. She lived a
quiet life but had a wide circle of literary friends, including Walter Scott and Mary
Russell Mitford.*

HE LIVED AMIDST TH'UNTRODDEN WAYS

[*after 'She dwelt among th'untrodden ways . . .'*]

He lived amidst th' untrodden ways
    To Rydal Lake that lead;
A bard whom there were none to praise,
    And very few to read.

Behind a cloud his mystic sense,
    Deep hidden, who can spy?
Bright as the night when not a star
    Is shining in the sky.

Unread his works—his 'Milk White Doe'
    With dust is dark and dim;

It's still in Longmans' shop, and oh!
The difference to him!

HARTLEY COLERIDGE

A SONNET

[based on the sonnet 'Thought of a Briton on the Subjugation of Switzerland'—

Two voices are there: one is of the Sea,
One of the Mountains; each a mighty voice . . .]

Two voices are there: one is of the deep;
It learns the storm-cloud's thunderous melody,
Now roars, now murmurs, with the changing sea,
Now bird-like pipes, now closes soft in sleep:
And one is of an old half-witted sheep
Which bleats articulate monotony,
And indicates that two and one are three,
That grass is green, lakes damp, and mountains steep:
And Wordsworth, both are thine: at certain times
Forth from the heart of thy melodious rhymes,
The form and pressure of high thoughts will burst:
At other times—good Lord! I'd rather be
Quite unacquainted with the A. B. C.
Than write such hopeless rubbish as thy worst.

J. K. STEPHEN

The closing lines echo some lines in another Wordsworth sonnet, 'The world is
too much with us'—

Great God! I'd rather be
A Pagan suckled in a creed outworn . . .

EXAMINATION QUESTION

O! Cuckoo, shall I call thee Bird
Or but a wandering Voice?
State the alternative preferred
With reasons for your choice.

ANON.

A WORDSWORTHIAN SONNET FOR ARNOLD FEINSTEIN, WHO MENDED MY SPECTACLES IN YUGOSLAVIA

Feinstein, artificer of proven worth!
O Saviour of my spectacles! Thou didst know
Exactly where that tiny screw should go
And how to place it there! Of all on earth
I honour thee! Of such men there is dearth—
Great Scientists that yet will stoop so low,
To rude *Mechanics*! Our Life cannot show
A truer Nobleness, or of such pure birth!
Yet thou, by Struga, in that moving coach,
Spinoza-like didst work upon the lens
With aptitude more great than other men's,
Reintroducing it! O dread approach
Of bookish blindness! From which I was set free
When Fate ordained that thou sat'st next to me!

GAVIN EWART

SIR WALTER SCOTT · 1771–1832

LOCHINVAR

[*Scott's poem, illustrated by James Thurber*]

O, young Lochinvar is come out of the west,
Through all the wide Border his steed was the best;
And, save his good broadsword, he weapon had none,
He rode all unarmed, and he rode all alone.
So faithful in love, and so dauntless in war,
There never was knight like the young Lochinvar.

But, ere he alighted at Netherby gate,
The bride had consented, the gallant came late;
For a laggard in love, and a dastard in war,
Was to wed the fair Ellen of brave Lochinvar.

So boldly he entered the Netherby Hall,
Among bridesmen, and kinsmen, and brothers, and all.
Then spoke the bride's father, his hand on his sword
(For the poor craven bridegroom said never a word),
'O come ye in peace here, or come ye in war,
Or to dance at our bridal, young Lord Lochinvar?'

'I long wooed your daughter, my suit you denied—
Love swells like the Solway, but ebbs like its tide—
And now I am come, with this lost love of mine,
To lead but one measure, drink one cup of wine.
There are maidens in Scotland more lovely by far,
That would gladly be bride to the young Lochinvar.'

The bride kissed the goblet; the knight took it up,
He quaffed off the wine, and threw down the cup.
She looked down to blush, and she looked up to sigh.
With a smile on her lips, and a tear in her eye.

He took her soft hand, ere her mother could bar—
'Now tread we a measure,' said young Lochinvar.

So stately his form, and so lovely her face,
That never a hall such a galliard did grace;
While her mother did fret, and her father did fume,
And the bridegroom stood dangling his bonnet and plume . . .

One touch to her hand, and one word in her ear,
When they reached the hall door, and the charger stood near;
So light to the croupe the fair lady he swung,
So light to the saddle before he sprung;
'She is won! we are gone! Over bank, bush, and scaur;
They'll have fleet steeds that follow,' quoth young Lochinvar.

There was mounting 'mong Graemes of the Netherby clan;
Forsters, Fenwicks, and Musgraves, they rode and they ran;
There was racing and chasing on Cannobie Lee,
But the lost bride of Netherby ne'er did they see.
So daring in love, and so dauntless in war,
Have ye e'er heard of gallant like young Lochinvar?

Samuel Taylor Coleridge · 1772–1834

MR FLOSKY

In Thomas Love Peacock's novel Nightmare Abbey *(1818), Coleridge appears in the guise of Mr Flosky, a middle-aged philosopher who has abandoned his youthful radicalism and taken refuge in impenetrable clouds of metaphysics. He bewails the degenerate state of the world, and at one point he informs a fellow-guest at the Abbey, the Honourable Mr Listless, that it is all the result of 'tea, late dinners and the French Revolution':*

The Honourable Mr Listless: Tea, late dinners, and the French Revolution. I cannot exactly see the connection of ideas.

Mr Flosky: I should be sorry if you could; I pity the man who can see the connection of his own ideas. Still more do I pity him, the connection of whose ideas any other person can see. Sir, the great evil is, that there is too much commonplace light in our moral and political literature; and light is a great enemy to mystery, and mystery is a great friend to enthusiasm. Now the enthusiasm for abstract truth is an exceedingly fine thing, as long as the truth, which is the object of the enthusiasm, is so completely abstract as to be altogether out of the reach of the human faculties; and in that sense, I have myself an enthusiasm for truth, but in no other, for the pleasure of metaphysical investigation lies in the means, not in the end; and if the end could be found, the pleasure of the means would cease. The mind, to be kept in health, must be kept in exercise. The proper exercise of the mind is elaborate reasoning. Analytical reasoning is a base and mechanical process, which takes to pieces and examines, bit by bit, the rude material of knowledge, and extracts therefrom a few hard and obstinate things called facts, every thing in the shape of which I cordially hate. But synthetical reasoning, setting up as its goal some unattainable abstraction, like an imaginary quantity in algebra, and commencing its course with taking for granted some two assertions which cannot be proved, from the union of these two assumed truths produces a third, and so on in infinite series, to the unspeakable benefit of the human intellect. The beauty of this process is, that at every step it strikes out into two branches, in a compound ratio of ramification; so that you are perfectly sure of losing your way, and keeping your mind in perfect health, by the perpetual exercise of an interminable quest; and for these reasons I have christened my eldest son Emanuel Kant Flosky.

Coleridge's two eldest children were named after the philosophers David Hartley and Bishop Berkeley.

THOMAS MOORE · 1779–1852

Oh! ever thus from childhood's hour,
I've seen my fondest hopes decay;
I never loved a tree or flower,
But 'twas the first to fade away.
I never nursed a dear gazelle,
To glad me with its soft black eye,
But when it came to know me well,
And love me, it was sure to die!

Few passages of early nineteenth-century verse were as widely known as these lines from Tom Moore's Lalla Rookh, *and few were as cheerfully burlesqued:*

'*'twas ever thus*'

I never rear'd a young gazelle,
(Because, you see, I never tried);
But had it known and lov'd me well,
No doubt the creature would have died.

My rich and aged Uncle John
Has known me long and loves me well,
But still persists in living on—
I would he were a young gazelle.

H. S. LEIGH

Lewis Carroll played more elaborate games with the gazelle in his poem 'Tema Con Variazioni':

I never loved a dear Gazelle—
    Nor anything that cost me much:
High prices profit those who sell,
    But why should I be fond of such?

To glad me with his soft black eye
    My son comes trotting home from school;
He's had a fight but can't tell why—
    He always was a little fool!

But, when he came to know me well,
    He kicked me out, her testy sire:

And when I stained my hair, that Belle
   Might note the change, and thus admire

And love me, it was sure to dye
   A muddy green, or staring blue:
Whilst one might trace, with half an eye,
   The still triumphant carrot through.

Carroll prefaces this parody with an explanatory note: 'Why is it that Poetry has never been subjected to the process of Dilution which has proved so advantageous to her sister-art Music? The Diluter gives us first a few notes of some well-known Air, then a dozen bars of his own, then a few more notes of the Air, and so on alternately: thus saving the listener, if not from all risk of recognising the melody at all, at least from the too-exciting transports which it might produce in a more concentrated form. The process is termed "setting" by Composers, and anyone, that has ever experienced the emotion of being unexpectedly set down in a heap of mortar, will recognise the truthfulness of this happy phrase.'

from 'THE LIVING LUSTRES'

[*a celebration of the reopening of the Drury Lane Theatre: from* Rejected Addresses—*see p. 38*]

When woman's soft smile all our senses bewilders,
   And gilds while it carves her dear form in our heart,
What need has new Drury of carvers and gilders,
   With Nature so bounteous why call upon Art?

How well would our actors attend to their duties,
   Our house save in oil and our authors in wit,
In lieu of yon lamps if a row of young beauties
   Glanced light from their eyes between us and the pit?

HORACE SMITH

AFTER TOM MOORE

When the white rose of theft and the red rose of arson
Shall fade in the gardens they bloom in to-day,
The sun will avail not to wither the grass on
The grave of the lovely Amanda O'Shea!

Her eyes were so blue and her lips were so trustful,
And her heart was so like to the heart of a dove,
That men in her presence were pure and not lustful
And kissed but the kid of her lily-white glove.

She was fairest of all the fair daughters of Erin,
With the grace that the maids of Circassia possess;
And her eye there was always a spark or a tear in—
A spark of amusement, a tear of distress.

She sat on a rout-seat when first I espied her,
The lights of the ballroom less bright than her brow,
And I thought not of Time, the relentless divider:
She lies in the vault of her ancestors now.

Were ever such bandeaux of raven-black tresses
As framed so divinely that oval, her face?
She wore the most perfect of evening dresses
A dream of white satin—a triumph of grace!

That satin, alas, now is sere and is yellow,
The grave that she lies in is dark as her hair;
Tho' years have evanished, there's naught can make mellow
The sorrow I feel and the grief that I bear.

No matter!—I'll see her, an angel with pinions
As white as the robe that she wore at the ball,
On a seat of pure gold in celestial dominions—
The fairest of any, the blandest of all!

                                        MAX BEERBOHM

Beerbohm had previously used the words 'the white rose of theft and the red rose of arson' in one of his essays, 'The Crime'. In a note on the manuscript of the parody, he explained that the phrase 'sounds like a quotation from a poem by Tom Moore but I can't verify the poem, and so I have to write it, if possible'.

LEIGH HUNT · 1784–1859

JENNY KISS'D ME

[after 'Rondeau']

Jenny kiss'd me when we met,
  Jumping from the chair she sat in,
Time, you thief, who love to get
  Sweets into your list, put that in!
Say I'm weary, say I'm old,
  Say that health and wealth have miss'd me,
Say I've had a filthy cold
  Since Jenny kiss'd me.

PAUL DEHN

LORD BYRON · 1788–1824

MR CYPRESS

In Thomas Love Peacock's Nightmare Abbey *(1818), the character of Mr Cypress is based on Byron—Byron in the full romantic, pessimistic, self-dramatizing mode of* Childe Harold. *Cypress is about to go into exile, and on the evening of his departure from England his host at Nightmare Abbey persuades him to entertain the assembled guests with a song:*

There is a fever of the spirit,
  The brand of Cain's unresting doom,
Which in the lone dark souls that bear it
  Glows like the lamp in Tullia's tomb:
Unlike that lamp, its subtle fire
  Burns, blasts, consumes its cell, the heart,
Till, one by one, hope, joy, desire,
  Like dreams of shadowy smoke depart.

Then hope, love, life itself, are only
  Dust—spectral memories—dead and cold—
The unfed fire burns bright and lonely,
  Like that undying lamp of old:
And by that drear illumination,

Till time its clay-built home has rent,
Thought broods on feeling's desolation—
The soul is its own monument.

This is almost too good for Peacock's parodic purpose.

A GRIEVANCE

[*in the manner of* Don Juan]

DEAR MR EDITOR: I wish to say—
     If you will not be angry at my writing it—
But I've been used, since childhood's happy day,
     When I have thought of something, to inditing it:
I seldom think of things: and, by the way,
     Although this metre may not be exciting, it
Enables one to be extremely terse,
Which is not what one always is in verse.

I used to know a man,—such things befall
     The observant wayfarer through Fate's domain:
He was a man, take him for all in all,
     We shall not look upon his like again:
I know that statement's not original:
     What statement is, since Shakspere? or, since Cain,
What murder? I believe 'twas Shakspere said it, or
Perhaps it may have been your Fighting Editor.

Though why an Editor should fight, or why
     A Fighter should abase himself to edit,
Are problems far too difficult and high
     For me to solve with any sort of credit:
Some greatly more accomplished man than I
     Must tackle them: let's say then Shakspere said it:
And, if he did not, Lewis Morris may
(Or even if he did). Some other day,

When I have nothing pressing to impart,
     I should not mind dilating on this matter:
I feel its import both in head and heart,
     And always did,—especially the latter:
I could discuss it in the busy mart

Or on the lonely housetop: hold! this chatter
Diverts me from my purpose. To the point:
The time, as Hamlet said, is out of joint,

And I perhaps was born to set it right;
    A fact I greet with perfect equanimity;
I do not put it down to 'cursed spite':
    I don't see any cause for cursing in it: I
Have always taken very great delight
    In such pursuits since first I read divinity:
Whoever will may write a nation's songs
As long as I'm allowed to right its wrongs.

What's Eton but a nursery of wrong-righters,
    A mighty mother of effective men,
A training-ground for amateur reciters,
    A sharpener of the sword as of the pen,
A factory of orators and fighters,
    A forcing-house of genius? Now and then,
The world at large shrinks back, abashed and beaten,
Unable to endure the glare of Eton.

I think I said I knew a man: what then?
    I don't suppose such knowledge is forbid:
We nearly all do, more or less, know men,—
    Or think we do: nor will a man get rid
Of that delusion, while he wields a pen:
    But who this man was, what, if aught, he did,
Nor why I mentioned him, I do not know:
Nor what I 'wished to say' a while ago.

                                    J. K. STEPHEN

Lewis Morris] *sub-Tennysonian mid-Victorian poet.*

THOMAS HOOD · 1799–1845

YOUNG SAMUEL

Young Samuel's wedding breakfast
With rationed meats was spread;
The Sergeant said 'Black Market'
And marked it down in red.

The Beak, who stood for justice,
(Tho' just sat down to sup)
Said: 'We must put these people down,
So you must take Sam up.'

Poor Sammy was beside himself,
Besides beside his bride,
When someone, stepping out, stepped in
And said, 'Please step outside.'

There Constable X claimed him
While Samuel exclaimed:
'A Sargent and a Constable!'
—But Sam it was got framed.

L. E. JONES

RALPH WALDO EMERSON · 1803–1882

BRAHMA

[after Emerson's 'Brahma'—'If the red slayer think he slays . . .']

If the wild bowler thinks he bowls,
   Or if the batsman thinks he's bowled,
They know not, poor misguided souls,
   They too shall perish unconsoled.
I am the batsman and the bat,
   I am the bowler and the ball,
The umpire, the pavilion cat,
   The roller, pitch, and stumps, and all.

ANDREW LANG

HENRY WADSWORTH LONGFELLOW · 1807–1882

THE MODERN HIAWATHA

He killed the noble Mudjokivis.
Of the skin he made him mittens,
Made them with the fur side inside,

Made them with the skin side outside,
He, to get the warm side inside,
Put the inside skin side outside;
He, to get the cold side outside,
Put the warm side fur side inside.
That's why he put the fur side inside,
Why he put the skin side outside.
Why he turned them inside outside.

GEORGE A. STRONG

LONGFELLOW'S VISIT TO VENICE

(To be read in a quiet New England accent)

Near the celebrated Lido where the breeze is fresh and free
Stands the ancient port of Venice called the City of the Sea.

All its streets are made of water, all its homes are brick and stone,
Yet it has a picturesqueness which is justly all its own.

Here for centuries have artists come to see the vistas quaint,
Here Bellini set his easel, here he taught his School to paint.

Here the youthful Giorgione gazed upon the domes and towers,
And interpreted his era in a way which pleases ours.

A later artist, Tintoretto, also did his paintings here,
Massive works which generations have continued to revere.

Still to-day come modern artists to portray the buildings fair
And their pictures may be purchased on San Marco's famous Square.

When the bell notes from the belfries and the campaniles chime
Still to-day we find Venetians elegantly killing time

In their gilded old palazzos, while the music in our ears
Is the distant band at Florians mixed with songs of gondoliers.

Thus the New World meets the Old World and the sentiments expressed
Are melodiously mingled in my warm New England breast.

JOHN BETJEMAN

*Betjeman's parody was inspired by such early 'sightseeing' poems of Longfellow as
'The Belfry of Bruges' and 'Nuremberg'.*

ALFRED, LORD TENNYSON · 1809–1892

A CANCELLED STANZA

It has been claimed that Tennyson originally intended to open In Memoriam *with the following stanza, but changed his mind:*

> The sun goes down upon the west
> And ever rises in the east;
> That much, we know, is true, at least,
> And hope and trust 'tis for the best.

ANON.

THE HIGHER PANTHEISM IN A NUTSHELL

[after 'The Higher Pantheism']

One, who is not, we see; but one, whom we see not, is:
Surely this is not that: but that is assuredly this.

What, and wherefore, and whence? for under is over and under:
If thunder could be without lightning, lightning could be without
    thunder.

Doubt is faith in the main: but faith, on the whole, is doubt:
We cannot believe by proof: but could we believe without?

Why, and whither, and how? for barley and rye are not clover:
Neither are straight lines curves: yet over is under and over.

Two and two may be four: but four and four are not eight:
Fate and God may be twain: but God is the same thing as fate.

Ask a man what he thinks, and get from a man what he feels:
God, once caught in the fact, shows you a fair pair of heels.

Body and spirit are twins: God only knows which is which:
The soul squats down in the flesh, like a tinker drunk in a ditch.

More is the whole than a part: but half is more than the whole:
Clearly, the soul is the body: but is not the body the soul?

One and two are not one: but one and nothing is two:
Truth can hardly be false, if falsehood cannot be true.

Once the mastodon was: pterodactyls were common as cocks:
Then the mammoth was God: now is He a prize ox.

Parallels all things are: yet many of these are askew:
You are certainly I: but certainly I am not you.

Springs the rock from the plain, shoots the stream from the rock:
Cocks exist for the hen: but hens exist for the cock.

God, whom we see not, is: and God, who is not, we see:
Fiddle, we know, is diddle: and diddle, we take it, is dee.

ALGERNON CHARLES SWINBURNE

Tennyson's 'The Higher Pantheism' is a short poem—shorter than Swinburne's 'nutshell' version. It was recited at the inaugural meeting of the Metaphysical Society, a discussion group which numbered Gladstone, T. H. Huxley, and other distinguished figures among its members, in 1869.

from 'TENNYSONIANA'

[*after* 'The splendour falls on castle walls', *from* The Princess—'The long light shakes aross the lakes . . .']

The splendour falls from castle walls;
    We sell our only genuine Titian
The old duke shakes among the fakes.
    And charges five-and-six admission.
Blow, coach-horns, blow! Set the wild echoes flying!
Blow coach-horns! Answer, echoes, 'Dying, dying, dying!'

PAUL DEHN

THE BT HISTORY OF ENGLAND IN VERSE

The Charge of the Light Brigade*

Half a league, half a league,
Half a league onward
All in the valley of Death

* 8op a minute at peak rate

Phoned the six hundred.
'Forward the Light Brigade!
Charge for the guns!' they said.
Across the valley the touchphone blew:
'Welcome to the Crimea
You are being held in a queue.'
'Forward, the Light Brigade!'
'Thanks for calling—we're afraid
Our lines are busy, but for a cannon or gun
Please press star button, then One.'
Theirs not to reason why,
Theirs but to curse and sigh.
Across the valley the touchphone blew:
'For all other queries, please press Two.'
'Forward the Light Brigade!'
Was there a man dismayed?
Not though the soldiers knew
For Customer Care, you just press Two.
Theirs not to make reply
Theirs but to chirrup: 'Hi!
Welcome to Information Hotline!
For further queries, please press Nine!'
Touchphone to the right of them
Touchphone to the left of them
Touchphone in front of them
All playing Stevie Nicks.
'Our service team is currently engaged
But should you wish to be further enraged
Please press Star then Hash then Six.'
When can their patience fade?
O the vast bill they paid!
All the world wondered
At the charges they made!
'If you wish to be held in a queue
Please now press button Two!'
Into the valley of debt they blundered,
The nobbled six hundred!

CRAIG BROWN

VERS NONSENSIQUES

[a partial translation of 'Break, break, break']

'Cassez-vous, cassez-vous, cassez-vous,
    O mer, sur vos froids gris cailloux!'
        Ainsi traduisait Laure
        Au profit d'Isadore,
(Beau jeune homme, et son future époux).

GEORGE DU MAURIER

EDGAR ALLAN POE · 1809–1849

THE AMATEUR FLUTE

[after 'The Bells']

Hear the fluter with his flute,
        Silver flute!
Oh, what a world of wailing is awakened by its toot!
    How it demi-semi quavers
        On the maddened air of night!
    And defieth all endeavors
        To escape the sound or sigh
    Of the flute, flute, flute,
        With its tootle, tootle, toot;
With reiterated tooteling of exasperating toots,
The long protracted tootelings of agonizing toots
        Of the flute, flute, flute, flute,
            Flute, flute, flute,
And the wheezings and the spittings of its toots.
        Should he get that other flute,
            Golden flute,
Oh, what a deeper anguish will his presence institoot!
    How his eyes to heaven he'll raise,
            As he plays,
            All the days!
        How he'll stop us on our ways
            With its praise!
        And the people—oh, the people,
        That don't live up in the steeple,

But inhabit Christian parlors
Where he visiteth and plays,
   Where he plays, plays, plays
   In the cruellest of ways,
  And thinks we ought to listen,
  And expects us to be mute,
Who would rather have the earache
  Than the music of his flute,
   Of the flute, flute, flute,
   And the tootings of his toot,
Of the toots wherewith he tooteleth its agonizing toot,
   Of the flute, flewt, fluit, floot,
   Phlute, phlewt, phlewght,
And the tootle, tootle, tooting of its toot.

ANON.

MARTIN TUPPER · 1810–1889

The rhythmical musings and maxims of Tupper's Proverbial Philosophy were immensely popular for a time, and a favourite target for Victorian parodists.

OF PROPRIETY

Study first Propriety: for she is indeed the Pole-star
Which shall guide the artless maiden through the mazes of
   Vanity Fair;
Nay, she is the golden chain which holdeth together Society;
The lamp by whose light young Psyche shall approach unblamed
   her Eros.
Verily Truth is as Eve, which was ashamed being naked;
Wherefore doth Propriety dress her with the fair foliage of
   artifice:
And when she is drest, behold! she knoweth not herself
   again.—
I walked in the Forest; and above me stood the Yew,
Stood like a slumbering giant, shrouded in impenetrable shade;
Then I past into the citizen's garden, and marked a tree clipt
   into shape

(The giant's locks had been shorn by the Delilah-shears of
     Decorum;)
And I said, 'Surely nature is goodly; but how much goodlier
     is Art!'
I heard the wild notes of the lark floating far over the blue sky,
And my foolish heart went after him, and lo! I blessed him as
     he rose;
Foolish! for far better is the trained boudoir bullfinch,
Which pipeth the semblance of a tune, and mechanically
     draweth up water:
And the reinless steed of the desert, though his neck be clothed
     with thunder,
Must yield to him that danceth and 'moveth in the circles' at
     Astley's.
For verily, oh my daughter, the world is a masquerade,
And God made thee one thing, that thou mightest make thyself
     another:
A maiden's heart is as champagne, ever aspiring and struggling
     upwards,
And it needeth that its motions be checked by the silver cork of
     Propriety:
He that can afford the price, his be the precious treasure,
Let him drink deeply of its sweetness, nor grumble if it tasteth
     of the cork.

C. S. CALVERLEY

THE NEW BELFRY OF CHRIST CHURCH, OXFORD

'Look on the Quadrangle of Christ, squarely, for is it not a
     Square?
And a Square recalleth a Cube; and a Cube recalleth the Belfry;
And the Belfry recalleth a Die, shaken by the hand of the
     gambler;
Yet, once thrown, it may not be recalled, being, so to speak,
     irrevocable.
There it shall endure for ages, treading hard on the heels of the
     Sublime—
For it is but a step, saith the wise man, from the Sublime unto
     the Ridiculous:
And the Simple dwelleth midway between, and shareth the
     qualities of either.'

LEWIS CARROLL

CHARLES DICKENS · 1812–1870

from THE HAUNTED MAN

Part I

Don't tell me that it wasn't a knocker. I had seen it often enough, and I ought to know. So ought the three o'clock beer, in dirty highlows, swinging himself over the railing, or executing a demoniacal jig upon the doorstep; so ought the butcher, although butchers as a general thing are scornful of such trifles; so ought the postman, to whom knockers of the most extravagant description were merely human weaknesses, that were to be pitied and used. And so ought, for the matter of that, etc., etc., etc.

But then it was *such* a knocker. A wild, extravagant, and utterly incomprehensible knocker. A knocker so mysterious and suspicious that Policeman X 37, first coming upon it, felt inclined to take it instantly in custody, but compromised with his professional instincts by sharply and sternly noting it with an eye that admitted of no nonsense, but confidently expected to detect its secret yet. An ugly knocker; a knocker with a hard, human face, that was a type of the harder human face within. A human face that held between its teeth a brazen rod. So hereafter in the mysterious future should be held, etc., etc.

But if the knocker had a fierce human aspect in the glare of day, you should have seen it at night, when it peered out of the gathering shadows and suggested an ambushed figure; when the light of the street lamps fell upon it, and wrought a play of sinister expression in its hard outlines; when it seemed to wink meaningly at a shrouded figure who, as the night fell darkly, crept up the steps and passed into the mysterious house; when the swinging door disclosed a black passage into which the figure seemed to lose itself and become a part of the mysterious gloom; when the night grew boisterous and the fierce wind made furious charges at the knocker, as if to wrench it off and carry it away in triumph. Such a night as this . . .

BRET HARTE

THE CRATCHIT FACTOR

'Tiny' Tim was legless, to begin with. There is no doubt whatever about that. It was the fifth time in the space of half an hour that the Group Public Relations Adviser had lurched to his feet to propose a toast.

'God bleh, sev one,' slurred the popular 'Tiny', and slid under the top table.

Robert ('Bob') Cratchit, chairman and managing director, rose to reply.

'Viable product . . .' droned Cratchit. 'Cost-effective . . . marketing operation . . . retail outlets . . . growth rate potential . . . export thrust . . .'

The applause was thunderous.

What a sales conference it had been! What concepts, what projections,
what plastic name-tags, what folders stuffed full of background briefing,
what working breakfasts! What a sinking of double Scotches when the day's
labours were over, what a sending to London for the prettiest secretaries
to come down at once with this or that important file, what a tipping of
Jenks (the Gatwick Coach-house International's amiable night-porter) to
turn a blind eye! Such a-goings-on, such Rib Room dinings and Fisherman's
Platter buffet luncheonings, such speechifying, such a-picking-up of Iberian
air hostesses in Ye Post-horn Coffee Shoppe, had never taken place since
the Cratchit Group had gone public.

Only Scrooge looked melancholy. Scrooge had been heard to say that the
Psychology Seminar, wherein the reps had learned how to improve their
sales by copying 'Tiny' Tim's limp, was humbug.

Alone among his colleagues, Scrooge did not sport a plastic name-tag.
Oh no! Plastic name-tags were not for the likes of Scrooge! Scrooge had
been born into this world without a label, was recognised on 'Change
without a label, and would not suffer a label to adorn his person until that
day came when a label was chiselled out for him in stone. Therefore few in
the Cratchit Group knew exactly how Scrooge had been occupying himself ever since, following his nervous breakdown many years ago, he had
turned up at his counting-house to find no counting-house there, and the
warehouse turned into a wine-bar, and the firm of Scrooge and Marley
taken over by his nephew.

There were those who said that Scrooge was retained as the office nark.

'Still having the bad dreams, Uncle?' asked Cratchit as he resumed his
seat, signalling to the waiter to leave 'Tiny' Tim out of the next round of
brandies.

'On and off, nephew,' responded Scrooge gloomily. 'The Ghost of
Christmas Yet To Come still troubles me, especially after one of these
office thrashes. It is a solemn Phantom, draped and hooded, that comes
out of the mist towards—'

'Ever thought of having a check-up?' asked Cratchit hastily. 'There's a
top-hat screening programme these days, you know—the full bit. Blood
pressure, cardiograph, bronchoscope, liver tests, the lot. It's an in-house
facility—why not use it?'

Scrooge was understood to remark that such arrangements were a waste
of the company's money, and that he could not be doing with them and
that they were humbug.

'The Ghost of Christmas Yet To Come was making an interesting
performance projection analysis the other night,' Scrooge added. 'It was

foreseeing the day when capital diverted to fringe benefits, added to your already soaring overheads plus your inability to claw back the cost of all these three-day promotional jags in four-star hotels, and bearing in mind the downward curve of profit-input, would—'

'Or,' interrupted Cratchit, 'there is always the Early Redundancy Plan. Nice golden handshake, index-linked pension, write off your company car—'

'While these rheumy old eyes can see,' said Scrooge firmly, pointing a quavering finger, 'I shall continue to serve the Company in that capacity to which I am most—'

'I've been meaning to talk to you about that, Uncle,' said Cratchit. 'Change of policy. We don't mind anyone fiddling his swindle-sheet any more. In fact, with conventional incentives taxed out of existence, we encourage it. Top executives don't grow on trees, you know.'

'Nevertheless, nephew, I think you should be made aware to what extent your son "Tiny" Tim, is dipping into the petty cash float lately.'

'I told him to, you silly old muffin! Listen, he was offered £5,000 a year more by Dombey and Son (UK) Ltd. On his tax-band, that would have been £750 in his hot little hand. So instead of matching it, we gave him the key to the petty-cash box, and everyone's happy.'

'Belinda Cratchit, your daughter,' pursued Scrooge, consulting a small black notebook, 'is having it off rotten with the Finance Director.'

'Keeps him happy. Dodson & Fogg, the investment advisers, are after him for their Wall Street office. Salary in dollars. I renegotiated his contract to include an office penthouse, a Panther De Ville 4.2 convertible, five weeks a year in Bermuda, and the use of Belinda. He'll stay.'

'Master Peter Cratchit,' mouthed Scrooge, shielding his face from the assembled merry-makers with a glossy brochure, 'has a black secretary.'

'Perk,' said Cratchit.

Scrooge, lips pursed in disapproval, put away his notebook. 'I had a visit from old Marley the other night,' he said. 'He wore the chains he had forged in life, made link by link, and yard by—'

'You told me,' said Cratchit, snapping his fingers for the bill.

'But did I tell you that he conducted me to a certain counting-house, where clerks were content to work for wages their masters gave them, and where there was no such thing as a company car, or a mortgage assistance scheme, or a suit of clothes that technically belonged to the firm but was rented to the employee for a nominal sum; and where executives' wives were not put on the pay-roll to provide a hidden salary increase; and where credit cards were not strewn about like confetti? Times,' said Scrooge, 'have changed.'

'I'll drink to that,' said Cratchit, doing so.

At this point, there was a commotion, as a tall young stranger in a soiled green coat that had evidently once adorned a much shorter man, pushed his way into the room, and he begged the company's leave, and that they would excuse him for taking the liberty, but he would insist upon having a word with the chairman and managing director, and wouldn't take no for an answer.

'Thousand pardons, sir,' commenced the stranger, approaching Cratchit. 'Forgive unwarrantable intrusion—realise am in completely wrong novel—but like your way of doing business, sir—temporarily disengaged—would be grateful for employment, very.'

Cratchit regarded the stranger coldly.

'Are there no Job Centres?' asked Cratchit.

'Plenty of Job Centres, sir—but—'

'And the unemployment benefits? Are they still in full vigour?'

'Believe so, sir.'

'Then sod off,' said Cratchit.

Meantime Scrooge was glumly examining the luncheon bill for £740 plus VAT and service charge, to which Cratchit had carelessly appended his signature.

'No good will come of this,' uttered Scrooge, to no-one in particular. 'The company is living beyond its means. Annual input twenty pounds, annual output nineteen pounds ninety-nine pee, result solvency. Annual input twenty pounds, annual output twenty pounds, one pee—'

Cratchit, having disposed of the stranger, turned to his sales director, David Copperfield.

'There's another one who doesn't know what bloody book he's living in,' he murmured. 'Now you're a bright spark, Dave: what do *you* think of the way I'm running this outfit?'

'It's a far, far better thing that you do, than you have ever done,' said the sales director.

KEITH WATERHOUSE

ROBERT BROWNING · 1812–1889

IMITATION OF ROBERT BROWNING

Birthdays? yes, in a general way;
For the most if not for the best of men.
You were born (I suppose) on a certain day,
So was I; or perhaps in the night, what then?

Only this: or at least, if more
You must know, not think it, and learn, not speak;
There is truth to be found on the unknown shore,
And many will find where few will seek.

For many are called and few are chosen,
And the few grow many as ages lapse.
But when will the many grow few; what dozen
Is fused into one by Time's hammer-taps?

A bare brown stone in a babbling brook,—
It was wanton to hurl it there, you say,—
And the moss, which clung in the sheltered nook
(Yet the stream runs cooler) is washed away.

That begs the question; many a prater
Thinks such a suggestion a sound 'stop thief!'
Which, may I ask, do you think the greater,
Sergeant-at-arms or a Robber Chief?

And if it were not so? Still you doubt?
Ah! yours is a birthday indeed, if so.
That were something to write a poem about,
If one thought a little. I only know.

               P. S.

There's a Me Society down at Cambridge,
Where my works, *cum notis variorum*,
Are talked about; well, I require the same bridge
That Euclid took toll at as Asinorum.

And, as they have got through several ditties
I thought were as stiff as a brick-built wall,
I've composed the above, and a stiff one it is,
A bridge to stop asses at, once for all.

                        J. K. STEPHEN

THE COCK AND THE BULL

[*a response to* The Ring and the Book]

You see this pebble-stone? It's a thing I bought
Of a bit of a chit of a boy i' the mid o' the day.
I like to dock the smaller parts o' speech,
As we curtail the already cur-tail'd cur—
(You catch the paronomasia, play 'po' words?)
Did, rather, i' the pre-Landseerian days.

Well, to my muttons. I purchased the concern,
And clapt it i' my poke, having given for same
By way o' chop, swop, barter or exchange—
'Chop' was my snickering dandiprat's own term—
One shilling and fourpence, current coin o' the realm.
O-n-e one, and f-o-u-r four
Pence, one and fourpence—you are with me, sir?—
What hour it skills not: ten or eleven o' the clock,
One day (and what a roaring day it was
Go shop or sight-see—bar a spit o' rain!)
In February, eighteen sixty-nine,
Alexandria Victoria, Fidei ——
Hm—hm—how runs the jargon? being on the throne.

Such, sir, are all the facts, succinctly put,
The basis or substratum—what you will—
Of the impending eighty thousand lines.
'Not much in 'em either,' quoth perhaps simple Hodge.
But there's a superstructure. Wait a bit.
Mark first the rationale of the thing:
Hear logic rivel and levigate the deed.
That shilling—and for matter o' that, the pence—
I had o' course upo' me—wi' me say—
(*Mecum*'s the Latin, make a note o' that)
When I popp'd pen i' stand, scratch'd ear, wiped snout,
(Let everybody wipe his own himself)
Sniff'd—tch!—at snuff-box; tumbled up, ne-heed,
Haw-haw'd (not hee-haw'd, that's another guess thing),
Then fumbled at, and stumbled out of, door.
I shoved the timber ope wi' my omoplat;
And *in vestibulo*, i' the lobby to wit
(Iacobi Facciolati's rendering, sir),
Donn'd galligaskins, antigropeloes,
And so forth; and, complete with hat and gloves,
One on and one a-dangle i' my hand,
And ombrifuge (Lord love you!), case o' rain,
I flopp'd forth, 'sbuddikins! on my own ten toes
(I do assure you there be ten of them),
And went clump-clumping up hill and down dale
To find myself o' the sudden i' front o' the boy.
But case I had n't 'em on me, could I ha' bought
This sort-o'-kind-o'-what-you-might-call toy,
This pebble thing, o' the boy-thing? Q. E. D.

That's proven without aid from mumping Pope,
Sleek porporate or bloated Cardinal.
(Is n't it, old Fatchaps? You're in Euclid now.)
So, having the shilling—having i' fact a lot—
And pence and halfpence, ever so many o' them,
I purchased, as I think I said before,
The pebble (*lapis, lapidis, -di, -dem, -de*—
What nouns 'crease short i' the genitive, Fatchaps, eh?)
O' the boy, a bare-legg'd beggarly son of a gun,
For one and fourpence. Here we are again.

Now Law steps in, bigwigg'd, voluminous-jaw'd;
Investigates and re-investigates.
Was the transaction illegal? Law shakes head.
Perpend, sir, all the bearings of the case.

At first the coin was mine, the chattel his.
But now (by virtue of the said exchange
And barter) *vice versa* all the coin,
Per juris operationem, vests
I' the boy and his assigns till ding o' doom;
(*In saecula saeculo-o-o-rum;*
I think I hear the Abate mouth out that.)
To have and hold the same to him and them.
Confer some idiot on Conveyancing.

Whereas the pebble and every part thereof,
And all that appertaineth thereunto,
Quodcunque pertinet ad eam rem
(I fancy, sir, my Latin's rather pat),
Or shall, will, may, might, can, could, would or should
(*Subaudi caetera*—clap we to the close—
For what's the good of Law in a case o' the kind),
Is mine to all intents and purposes.
This settled, I resume the thread o' the tale.
Now for a touch o' the vendor's quality.
He says a gen'lman bought a pebble of him
(This pebble i' sooth, sir, which I hold i' my hand),
And paid for't, *like* a gen'lman, on the nail.
'Did I o'ercharge him a ha'penny? Devil a bit.
Fiddlepin's end! Get out, you blazing ass!
Gabble o' the goose. Don't bugaboo-baby *me!*
Go double or quits? Yah! tittup! what's the odds?'
There's the transaction view'd i' the vendor's light.

Next ask that dumpled hag, stood snuffling by,
With her three frowsy blowsy brats o' babes,
The scum o' the kennel, cream o' the filth-heap—Faugh!
Aie, aie, aie, aie! ὀτοτοτοτοτοῖ
('Stead which we blurt out Hoighty toighty now),
And the baker and candlestickmaker, and Jack and Jill,
Blear'd Goody this and queasy Gaffer that.
Ask the schoolmaster. Take schoolmaster first.

He saw a gentleman purchase of a lad
A stone, and pay for it *rite*, on the square,
And carry it off *per saltum*, jauntily,
Propria quae maribus, gentleman's property now
(Agreeably to the law explain'd above),
In proprium usum, for his private ends,
The boy he chuck'd a brown i' the air, and bit
I' the face the shilling; heaved a thumping stone
At a lean hen that ran cluck clucking by
(And hit her, dead as nail i' post o' door),
Then *abiit*—what's the Ciceronian phrase?—
Excessit, evasit, erupit—off slogs boy;
Off like bird, *avi similis*—you observed
The dative? Pretty i' the Mantuan!)—*Anglice*
Off in three flea skips. *Hactenus*, so far,
So good, *tam bene. Bene, satis, male,*—
Where was I with my trope 'bout one in a quag?
I did once hitch the syntax into verse:
Verbum personale, a verb personal,
Concordat—ay, 'agrees,' old Fatchaps—*cum*
Nominativo, with its nominative,
Genere, i' point o' gender, *numero*,
O' number, *et persona*, and person. *Ut*,
Instance: *Sol ruit*, down flops sun, *et*, and,
Montes umbrantur, out flounce mountains. Pah!
Excuse me, sir, I think I'm going mad.
You see the trick on 't though, and can yourself
Continue the discourse *ad libitum*.
It takes up about eighty thousand lines,
A thing imagination boggles at;
And might, odds-bobs, sir! in judicious hands,
Extend from here to Mesopotamy.

                                   C. S. CALVERLEY

EDWARD LEAR · 1812–1888

THERE WAS AN OLD MAN WITH A BEARD

There was an old man with a beard,
A funny old man with a beard.
He had a big beard,
A great big old beard,
That amusing old man with a beard.

JOHN CLARKE

The author is Australian, and this is perhaps best read with an Australian accent.

WALT WHITMAN · 1819–1892

SINCERE FLATTERY OF W.W. (AMERICANUS)

The clear cool note of the cuckoo which has ousted the
    legitimate nest-holder,
The whistle of the railway guard dispatching the train to the
    inevitable collision,
The maiden's monosyllabic reply to a polysyllabic proposal,
The fundamental note of the last trump, which is presumably
    D natural;
All of these are sounds to rejoice in, yea to let your very ribs
    re-echo with:
But better than all of them is the absolutely last chord of the
    apparently inexhaustible pianoforte player.

J. K. STEPHEN

CAMERADOS

Everywhere, everywhere, following me;
Taking me by the buttonhole, pulling off my boots, hustling me
    with the elbows;
Sitting down with me to clams and the chowder-kettle;
Plunging naked at my side into the sleek, irascible surges;
Soothing me with the strain that I neither permit nor prohibit;

Flocking this way and that, reverent, eager, orotund,
    irrepressible;
Denser than sycamore leaves when the north-winds are
    scouring Paumanok;
What can I do to restrain them? Nothing, verily nothing.
Everywhere, everywhere, crying aloud for me;
Crying, I hear; and I satisfy them out of my nature;
And he that comes at the end of the feast shall find
    something over.
Whatever they want I give; though it be something else, they
    shall have it.
Drunkard, leper, Tammanyite, small-pox and cholera patient,
    shoddy and codfish millionaire,
And the beautiful young men, and the beautiful young
    women, all the same,
Crowding, hundreds of thousands, cosmical multitudes,
Buss me and hang on my hips and lean up to my shoulders,
Everywhere listening to my yawp and glad whenever they
    hear it;
Everywhere saying, say it, Walt, we believe it:
Everywhere, everywhere.

BAYARD TAYLOR

MATTHEW ARNOLD · 1822–1888

MATTHEW ARNOLD WRITES TO *THE LISTENER*

[after 'Philomela']

On the night of May 31st 1942 the broadcast of the nightingale was accompanied by the sound of the thousand bombers setting out for Cologne.

    Hark! ah, the nightingale,
    Somewhere in Surrey!
    Listen, Eugenia, to the radio!
    What melody!—what else?

    O wanderer from classic times,
    Still dost thou harp on that antique event,
    Thy mythological metamorphosis
    In lonely Daulis and the Thracian wild—

Ignoring time and change,
This English garden-copse,
The leaf-hung microphone,
The trellised 'cellist nigh,
Thine audience unseen?
Dost thou not hear to-night
Metallic Furies in mechanic flight,
The brazen-bowelled harpies overhead,
Stretched wings, unfeathered breasts,
With open throttles roaring out above
Thy relatively sequestered solitude?
Can'st thou mourn on,
Embroidering thine old-world threnody,
Oblivious of their note, as they of thine,
While my racked nerves and brain,
Disturbed in cultivated meditation
By this cacophonous phenomenon,
Apotheosis of our modern life,
Can find no balm?
Thou canst! again—Eugenia!
What bursts! what drones! what incongruity!
Eternal fixity!
Eternal flux!

'SAGITTARIUS' [OLGA KATZIN]

The Listener *was a weekly magazine published by the BBC from 1929 to 1991.*
Broadcasts of birdsong were a popular feature of BBC radio during the Second
World War.

THE DOVER BITCH

A Criticism of Life: for Andrews Wanning

So there stood Matthew Arnold and this girl
With the cliffs of England crumbling away behind them,
And he said to her, 'Try to be true to me,
And I'll do the same for you, for things are bad
All over, etc., etc.'
Well now, I knew this girl. It's true she had read
Sophocles in a fairly good translation
And caught that bitter allusion to the sea,
But all the time he was talking she had in mind
The notion of what his whiskers would feel like

On the back of her neck. She told me later on
That after a while she got to looking out
At the lights across the channel, and really felt sad,
Thinking of all the wine and enormous beds
And blandishments in French and the perfumes.
And then she got really angry. To have been brought
All the way down from London, and then be addressed
As a sort of mournful cosmic last resort
Is really tough on a girl, and she was pretty.
Anyway, she watched him pace the room
And finger his watch-chain and seem to sweat a bit,
And then she said one or two unprintable things.
But you mustn't judge her by that. What I mean to say is,
She's really all right. I still see her once in a while
And she always treats me right. We have a drink
And I give her a good time, and perhaps it's a year
Before I see her again, but there she is,
Running to fat, but dependable as they come.
And sometimes I bring her a bottle of *Nuit d'Amour.*

ANTHONY HECHT

WILLIAM JOHNSON CORY · 1823–1892

THE SUICIDE OF SIR FRANCIS HINSLEY

[*based on 'Heraclitus'—'They told me, Heraclitus, they told me you were dead | They brought me bitter news to hear and bitter tears to shed . . .'*]

They told me, Francis Hinsley, they told me you were hung
With red protruding eye-balls and black protruding tongue.
I wept as I remembered how often you and I
Had laughed about Los Angeles and now 'tis here you'll lie;
Here pickled in formaldehyde and painted like a whore,
Shrimp-pink incorruptible, not lost nor gone before.

EVELYN WAUGH

Sir Francis Hinsley is a character in Evelyn Waugh's novel The Loved One—*an old-fashioned English literary man who settles in Hollywood and achieves success as a publicist and scriptwriter, but commits suicide after his career goes into decline. The young colleague (a fellow-expatriate) who is deputed to write a poem for his funeral jots down the lines inspired by 'Heraclitus', and also finds himself recalling Tennyson's ode on the death of the Duke of Wellington:*

Bury the great Knight
With the studio's valediction.
Let us bury the great Knight
Who was once the arbiter of popular fiction . . .

DANTE GABRIEL ROSSETTI · 1828–1882

CIMABUELLA

*[Cimabuella—a figure in the manner of the thirteenth-century
Florentine painter Cimabue]*

Fair-tinted cheeks, clear eyelids drawn,
    In crescent curves above the light
Of eyes, whose dim, uncertain dawn
    Becomes not day: a forehead white
Beneath long yellow heaps of hair:
She is so strange she must be fair.

Had she sharp, slant-wise wings outspread,
    She were an angel; but she stands
With flat dead gold behind her head,
    And lilies in her long thin hands:
Her folded mantle, gathered in,
Falls to her feet as it were tin.

Her nose is keen as pointed flame;
    Her crimson lips no thing express;
And never dread of saintly blame
    Held down her heavy eyelashes:
To guess what she were thinking of,
Precludeth any meaner love.

An azure carpet, fringed with gold,
    Sprinkled with scarlet spots, I laid
Before her straight, cool feet unrolled:
    But she nor sound nor movement made
(Albeit I heard a soft, shy smile,
    Printing her neck a moment's while);

And I was shamed through all my mind
    For that she spake not, neither kissed,

But stared right past me. Lo! behind
　　Me stood, in pink and amethyst,
Sword-girt and velvet-doubleted,
A tall, gaunt youth, with frowzy head,

Wide nostrils in the air, dull eyes,
　　Thick lips that simpered, but, ah me!
I saw, with most forlorn surprise,
　　He was the Thirteenth Century!
I but the Nineteenth: then despair
Curdled beneath my curling hair.

O, Love and Fate! How could she choose
　　My rounded outlines, broader brain,
And my resuscitated Muse?
　　Some tears she shed, but whether pain
Or joy in him unlocked their source,
I could not fathom which, of course.

But I from missals, quaintly bound,
　　With cither and with clavichord
Will sing her songs of sovran sound:
　　Belike her pity will afford
Such faint return as suits a saint
So sweetly done in verse and paint.

BAYARD TAYLOR

EMILY DICKINSON · 1830–1886

SHE SEES ANOTHER DOOR OPENING

My fortitude is all awry
To sit upon this chair
And, idly lifting up my eye,
To glimpse the door ajar there.

Through that door could come what bother
In what undreamed of pelts
A cat, a dog, or God the Father,
Or—gulp—somebody else!

FIRMAN HOUGHTON

from EMILY DICKINSON IN SOUTHERN CALIFORNIA—I

> I called one day—on Eden's strand
> But did not find her—Home—
> Surfboarders triumphed in—in Waves—
> Archangels of the Foam—
>
> I walked a pace—I tripped across
> Browned couples—in cahoots—
> No more than Tides need shells to fill
> Did they need—bathing suits—
>
> From low boughs—that the Sun kist—hung
> A Fruit to taste—at will—
> October rustled but—Mankind
> Seemed elsewhere gone—to Fall—

from EMILY DICKINSON IN SOUTHERN CALIFORNIA—II

> I bore Hope's candle farthest West—
> And now—obliged to halt—
> Hear Asia's rumor of despair
> Behind a wall of Salt—
>
>   X. J. KENNEDY

WILLIAM MORRIS · 1834–1896

RONDEL

> Behold the works of William Morris,
>   Epics, and here and there wall-papery,
>   Mild, mooney, melancholy vapoury
> A sort of Chaucer *minus* Horace.
>
> Spun out like those of William Loris,
>   Who wrote of amorous red-tapery,
> Behold the works of William Morris,
>   Epics, and here and there wall-papery!

Long ladies, knights, and earls and choris-
    ters in the most appropriate drapery,
Samite and silk and spotless napery,
Sunflowers and apple blossoms and orris,
Behold the works of William Morris!

ANON.

William Loris] *Guillaume de Lorris, medieval French poet.*

BALLAD

Part I

The auld wife sat at her ivied door,
    (*Butter and eggs and a pound of cheese*)
A thing she had frequently done before;
    And her spectacles lay on her aproned knees.

The piper he piped on the hill-top high,
    (*Butter and eggs and a pound of cheese*)
Till the cow said: 'I die,' and the goose asked: 'Why?'
    And the dog said nothing, but searched for fleas.

The farmer he strode through the square farmyard;
    (*Butter and eggs and a pound of cheese*)
His last brew of ale was a trifle hard—
    The connection of which with the plot one sees.

The farmer's daughter hath frank blue eyes;
    (*Butter and eggs and a pound of cheese*)
She hears the rooks caw in the windy skies,
    As she sits at her lattice and shells her peas.

The farmer's daughter hath ripe red lips;
    (*Butter and eggs and a pound of cheese*)
If you try to approach her, away she skips
    Over tables and chairs with apparent ease.

The farmer's daughter hath soft brown hair;
    (*Butter and eggs and a pound of cheese*)
And I met with a ballad, I can't say where,
    Which wholly consisted of lines like these.

Part II

She sat, with her hands 'neath her dimpled cheeks,
  (*Butter and eggs and a pound of cheese*)
And spake not a word. While a lady speaks
  There is hope, but she didn't even sneeze.

She sat, with her hands 'neath her crimson cheeks,
  (*Butter and eggs and a pound of cheese*)
She gave up mending her father's breeks,
  And let the cat roll in her new chemise.

She sat, with her hands 'neath her burning cheeks,
  (*Butter and eggs and a pound of cheese*)
And gazed at the piper for thirteen weeks;
  Then she followed him out o'er the misty leas.

Her sheep followed her, as their tails did them.
  (*Butter and eggs and a pound of cheese*)
And this song is considered a perfect gem,
  And as to the meaning, it's what you please.

                                    C. S. CALVERLEY

This is generally taken to be a parody of Morris, but Calverley had in mind other balladeers of the period as well. In the first instance he was spurred into action by a poem by his contemporary Jean Ingelow:

> *The martin flew to the finch's nest—*
> *Feathers and moss and a wisp of hay . . .*

BRET HARTE · 1836–1902

THE HEATHEN PASS-EE

[*after 'Plain Language from Truthful James', also known as*
'The Heathen Chinee']

Which I wish to remark,
  And my language is plain,
That for plots that are dark
  And not always in vain,
The Heathen Pass-ee is peculiar,
  And the same I would rise to explain.

I would also premise
   That the term of Pass-ee
Most fitly applies,
   As you probably see,
To one whose vocation is passing
   The 'ordinary B.A. degree.'

Tom Crib was his name,
   And I shall not deny
In regard to the same
   What that name might imply,
That his face it was trustful and childlike,
   And he had the most innocent eye.

Upon April the First
   The Little-Go fell,
And that was the worst
   Of the gentleman's sell,
For he fooled the Examining Body
   In a way I'm reluctant to tell.

The candidates came
   And Tom Crib soon appeared;
It was Euclid, the same
   Was 'the subject he feared';
But he smiled as he sat by the table
   With a smile that was wary and weird.

Yet he did what he could, .
   And the papers he showed
Were remarkably good,
   And his countenance glowed
With pride when I met him soon after
   As he walked down the Trumpington Road.

We did not find him out,
   Which I bitterly grieve,
For I've not the least doubt
   That he'd placed up his sleeve
Mr Todbunker's excellent Euclid,
   The same with intent to deceive.

But I shall not forget
   How the next day or two

A stiff paper was set
    By Examiner U——
On Euripides' tragedy, Bacchae,
    A subject Tom 'partially knew.'

But the knowledge displayed
    By that Heathen Pass-ee,
And the answers he made
    Were quite frightful to see,
For he rapidly floored the whole paper
    By about twenty minutes to three.

Then I looked up at U——
    And he gazed upon me,
I observed, 'This won't do';
    He replied, 'Goodness me!
We are fooled by this artful young person.'
    And he sent for that Heathen Pass-ee.

The scene that ensued
    Was disgraceful to view,
For the floor it was strewed
    With a tolerable few
Of the 'tips' that Tom Crib had been hiding
    For the 'subject he partially knew.'

On the cuff of his shirt
    He had managed to get
What we hoped had been dirt,
    But which proved, I regret,
To be notes on the rise of the Drama,
    A question invariably set.

In his various coats
    We proceeded to seek,
Where we found sundry notes
    And—with sorrow I speak—
One of Bohn's publications, so useful
    To the student of Latin or Greek.

In the crown of his cap
    Were the Furies and Fates,
And a delicate map
    Of the Dorian States,

And we found in his palms, which were hollow,
  What are frequent in palms—that is, dates;

Which is why I remark,
  And my language is plain,
That for plots that are dark
  And not always in vain,
The Heathen Pass-ee is familiar,
  Which the same I am free to maintain.

A. C. HILTON

Little-Go] *Nineteenth-century Oxford and Cambridge slang for the first examination for a BA degree.*

ALGERNON CHARLES SWINBURNE · 1837–1909

OCTOPUS

Strange beauty, eight limbed and eight handed,
  Whence camest to dazzle our eyes?
With thy bosom bespangled and banded
  With the hues of the seas and the skies;
Is thy home European or Asian,
  O mystical monster marine?
Part molluscous and partly crustacean,
      Betwixt and between.

Wast thou born to the sound of sea trumpets?
  Hast thou eaten and drunk to excess
Of the sponges—thy muffins and crumpets,
  Of the seaweed—thy mustard and cress?
Wast thou nurtured in caverns of coral,
  Remote from reproof or restraint?
Art thou innocent, art thou immoral,
      Sinburnian or Saint?

Lithe limbs curling free as a creeper
  That creeps in a desolate place,
To enrol and envelop the sleeper
  In a silent and stealthy embrace;
Cruel beak craning forward to bite us,
  Our juices to drain and to drink,

Or to whelm us in waves of Cocytus,
    Indelible ink!

Oh breast that 'twere rapture to writhe on!
    Oh arms 'twere delicious to feel
Clinging close with the crush of the Python
    When she maketh her murderous meal!

In thy eight-fold embraces enfolden
    Let our empty existence escape,
Give us death that is glorious and golden,
    Crushed all out of shape!

Ah thy red lips, lascivious and luscious,
    With death in their amorous kiss!
Cling round us and clasp us, and crush us,
    With bitings of agonised bliss;
We are sick with the poison of pleasure,
    Dispose us the potion of pain;
Ope thy mouth to its uttermost measure,
    And bite us again!

                      A. C. HILTON

NEPHELIDIA

[*a self-parody: 'nephelidia' is a Greek or quasi-Greek word meaning 'mistiness'*]

From the depth of the dreamy decline of the dawn through a notable
    nimbus of nebulous moon-shine,
    Pallid and pink as the palm of the flag-flower that flickers with fear
        of the flies as they float,
Are they looks of our lovers that lustrously lean from a marvel of
    mystic miraculous moon-shine,
    These that we feel in the blood of our blushes that thicken and
        threaten with throbs through the throat?
Thicken and thrill as a theatre thronged at appeal of an actor's
    appalled agitation,
    Fainter with fear of the fires of the future than pale with the
        promise of pride in the past;
Flushed with the famishing fullness of fever that reddens with radiance
    of rathe recreation,
    Gaunt as the ghastliest of glimpses that gleam through the gloom
        of the gloaming when ghosts go aghast?

Nay, for the nick of the tick of the time is a tremulous touch on the
    temples of terror,
  Strained as the sinews yet strenuous with strife of the dead who is
    dumb as the dust-heaps of death:
Surely no soul is it, sweet as the spasm of erotic emotional exquisite
    error,
  Bathed in the balms of beatified bliss, beatific itself by beatitude's
    breath.
Surely no spirit or sense of a soul that was soft to the spirit and soul of
    our senses
  Sweetens the stress of suspiring suspicion that sobs in the
    semblance and sound of a sigh;
Only this oracle opens Olympian, in mystical moods and triangular
    tenses—
  'Life is the lust of a lamp for the light that is dark till the dawn of the
    day when we die.'
Mild is the mirk and monotonous music of memory, melodiously
    mute as it may be,
  While the hope in the heart of a hero is bruised by the breach of
    men's rapiers, resigned to the rod;
Made meek as a mother whose bosom-beats bound with the
    bliss-bringing bulk of a balm-breathing baby,
  As they grope through the graveyard of creeds, under skies growing
    green at a groan for the grimness of God.
Blank is the book of his bounty beholden of old, and its binding is
    blacker than bluer:
  Out of blue into black is the scheme of the skies, and their dews are
    the wine of the bloodshed of things;
Till the darkling desire of delight shall be free as a fawn that is freed
    from the fangs that pursue her,
  Till the heart-beats of hell shall be hushed by a hymn from the hunt
    that has harried the kennel of kings.

ALGERNON CHARLES SWINBURNE

HENRY KENDALL · 1839–1882

BELL-BIRDS

*Henry Kendall was born in a small town in New South Wales. His 'Bell-Birds' is
one of the best-known nineteenth-century Australian poems:*

Welcome as waters unkissed by the summers
Are the voices of ring-birds to thirsty far-comers.
When fiery December sets foot in the forest,
And the need of the wayfarer presses the sorest,
Pent in the ridges for ever and ever
The bell-birds direct him to spring and to river,
With ring and with ripple, like runnels whose torrents
Are toned by the pebbles and leaves in the currents . . .

The story comes out
In dribbles and drabbles
Of longing to be
Near fluvial babbles,

Or dabbling in dingles
Or haunts that are herbal
While bell-birds compete
With creeks that are verbal

And ripple and runnel
To rhymes that are killing
But can't drown the bell-birds'
Incredible shrilling,

While glimpses of pebbles
And visions of gurgles
Uplift the sad poet
As he bibbles and burbles

Of running and ringing
(But can't resist waffle)
As his song of the bell-birds
Grows more and more awffle!

GWEN MELVAINE

THOMAS HARDY · 1840–1928

A LUNCHEON

Note accompanying the original private printing of the poem: 'In the summer
of 1923, when the Prince of Wales'—the future Duke of Windsor—'was about

to make his annual visit to the Duchy of Cornwall, someone at Court suggested to
him that he should, on his way, visit Mr Thomas Hardy. The Prince agreed to do
so, and in due course lunched with Mr and Mrs Hardy.'

Lift latch, step in, be welcome, Sir,
Albeit to see you I'm unglad
And your face is fraught with a deathly shyness
Bleaching what pink it may have had.
Come in, come in, Your Royal Highness.

Beautiful weather?—Sir, that's true,
Though the farmers are casting rueful looks
At tilth's and pasture's dearth of spryness.—
Yes, Sir, I've written several books.—
A little more chicken, Your Royal Highness?

Lift latch, step out, your car is there,
To bear you hence from this antient vale.
We are both of us aged by our strange brief nighness,
But each of us lives to tell the tale.
Farewell, farewell, Your Royal Highness.

MAX BEERBOHM

STOUTHEART ON THE SOUTHERN RAILWAY

[*after the poem 'Midnight on the Great Western'*]

What are you doing, oh high-souled lad,
    Writing a book about me?
And peering so closely at good and bad,
    That one thing you do not see:
A shadow which falls on your writing-pad;
It is not of a sort to make men glad.
    It were better should such unbe.

No: though you look up, but you do not chance
    To see in the railway-train,
Amid pale trackfarers with listless glance,
    One who enghosts him plain.
You throw him not even a look askance,
And your mind toils on, in a seeming trance,
    To unearth some hap or twain.

No: the wistful hand you do not mark,
   Laid weightless upon your sleeve;
To a phasmal breath you give no hark—
   To a disembodied heave,
That at memories wakened of bliss or cark
Goes sighing across the gritty dark
   In an iterate semi-breve.

No: you don't see the one the night-time brings
   To thuswise hover above
Your pages of quizzings and questionings
   Undertaken (say you) for love,
No: you don't see the shadow the lamp downflings.
But I've come to make sure there are just a few things
   You still are unwotful of.

                            HENRY REED

HENRY JAMES · 1843–1916

THE MOTE IN THE MIDDLE DISTANCE

It was with the sense of a, for him, very memorable something that he peered now into the immediate future, and tried, not without compunction, to take that period up where he had, prospectively, left it. But just where the deuce *had* he left it? The consciousness of dubiety was, for our friend, not, this morning, quite yet clean-cut enough to outline the figures on what she had called his 'horizon,' between which and himself the twilight was indeed of a quality somewhat intimidating. He had run up, in the course of time, against a good number of 'teasers'; and the function of teasing them back—of, as it were, giving them, every now and then, 'what for'—was in him so much a habit that he would have been at a loss had there been, on the face of it, nothing to lose. Oh, he always had offered rewards, of course—had ever so liberally pasted the windows of his soul with staring appeals, minute descriptions, promises that knew no bounds. But the actual recovery of the article—the business of drawing and crossing the cheque, blotched though this were with tears of joy—had blankly appeared to him rather in the light of a sacrilege, casting, he sometimes felt, a palpable chill on the fervour of the next quest. It was just this fervour that was threatened as, raising himself on his elbow, he stared at the foot of his bed. That his eyes refused to rest there for more than the fraction of an instant, may be taken—*was*, even then, taken by Keith Tantalus—as a hint of his recollection that after all the phenomenon wasn't to be singular. Thus the exact repetition, at the foot of Eva's bed, of the shape pendulous at the foot of *his* was hardly enough to account for the fixity with which he envisaged it, and for which he was to find, some years later, a motive in the (as it turned out) hardly generous fear that Eva had already made the great investigation 'on her own.' Her very regular breathing presently reassured him that, if she *had* peeped into 'her' stocking, she must have done so in sleep. Whether he should wake her now, or wait for their nurse to wake them both in due course, was a problem presently solved by a new development. It was plain that his sister was now watching him between her eyelashes. He had half expected that. She really was—he had often told her that she really was—magnificent; and her magnificence was never more obvious than in the pause that elapsed before she all of a sudden remarked, 'They so very indubitably *are*, you know!'

It occurred to him as befitting Eva's remoteness, which was a part of Eva's magnificence, that her voice emerged somewhat muffled by the bed-clothes. She was ever, indeed, the most telephonic of her sex. In talking to Eva you always had, as it were, your lips to the receiver. If you didn't try to meet her fine eyes, it was that you simply couldn't hope to: there were too many dark, too many buzzing and bewildering and all frankly not negotiable leagues in between. Snatches of other voices seemed often to intertrude themselves in the parley; and your loyal effort not to overhear these was complicated by your fear of missing what Eva might be twitter-ing. 'Oh, you certainly haven't, my dear, the trick of propinquity!' was a thrust she had once parried by saying that, in that case, *he* hadn't—to which his unspoken rejoinder that she had caught her tone from the peevish young women at the Central seemed to him (if not perhaps in the last, certainly in the last but one, analysis) to lack finality. With Eva, he had found, it was always safest to 'ring off.' It was with a certain sense of his rashness in the matter, therefore, that he now, with an air of feverishly 'holding the line,' said, 'Oh, as to that!'

Had *she*, he presently asked himself, 'rung off'? It was characteristic of our friend—was indeed 'him all over'—that his fear of what she was going to say was as nothing to his fear of what she might be going to leave unsaid. He had, in his converse with her, been never so conscious as now of the intervening leagues; they had never so insistently beaten the drum of his ear; and he caught himself in the act of awfully computing, with a certain statistical passion, the distance between Rome and Boston. He has never been able to decide which of these points he was psychically the nearer to at the moment when Eva, replying, 'Well, one does, anyhow, leave a margin for the pretext, you know!' made him, for the first time in his life, wonder whether she were not more magnificent than even he had ever given her credit for being. Perhaps it was to test this theory, or perhaps merely to gain time, that he now raised himself to his knees, and, leaning with outstretched arm towards the foot of his bed, made as though to touch the stocking which Santa Claus had, overnight, left dangling there. His posture, as he stared obliquely at Eva, with a sort of beaming defiance, recalled to him something seen in an 'illustration.' This reminiscence, how-ever—if such it was, save in the scarred, the poor dear old woebegone and so very beguilingly *not* refractive mirror of the moment—took a peculiar twist from Eva's behaviour. She had, with startling suddenness, sat bolt upright, and looked to him as if she were overhearing some tragedy at the other end of the wire, where, in the nature of things, she was unable to arrest it. The gaze she fixed on her extravagant kinsman was of a kind to make him wonder how he contrived to remain, as he beautifully did, rigid. His prop was possibly the reflection that flashed on him that, if *she* abounded in attenuations, well, hang it all, so did *he*! It was simply a dif-ference of plane. Readjust the 'values,' as painters say, and there you were! He was to feel that he was only too crudely 'there' when, leaning further forward, he laid a chubby forefinger on the stocking, causing that recep-tacle to rock ponderously to and fro. This effect was more expected than the tears which started to Eva's eyes and the intensity with which 'Don't you,' she exclaimed, 'see?'

'The mote in the middle distance?' he asked. 'Did you ever, my dear, know me to see anything else? I tell you it blocks out everything. It's a cathedral, it's a herd of elephants, it's the whole habitable globe. Oh, it's, believe me, of an obsessiveness!' But his sense of the one thing it *didn't* block out from his purview enabled him to launch at Eva a speculation as to just how far Santa Claus had, for the particular occasion, gone. The gauge, for both of them, of this seasonable distance seemed almost blatantly suspended in the silhouettes of the two stockings. Over and above the basis of (presum-ably) sweetmeats in the toes and heels, certain extrusions stood for a very plenary fulfilment of desire. And since Eva *had* set her heart on a doll of ample proportions and practicable eyelids—*had* asked that most admirable of her sex, their mother, for it with not less directness than he himself had put into his demand for a sword and helmet—her coyness now struck Keith as lying near to, at indeed a hardly measurable distance from, the border line of his patience. If she didn't *want* the doll, why the deuce had she made such a point of getting it? He was perhaps on the verge of putting this question to her, when, waving her hand to include both stockings, she said, 'Of course, my dear, you *do* see. There they are, and you know I know you know we wouldn't, either of us, dip a finger into them.' With a vibrancy of tone that seemed to bring her voice quite close to him, 'One doesn't,' she added, 'violate the shrine—pick the pearl from the shell!'

Even had the answering question 'Doesn't one just?' which for an instant hovered on the tip of his tongue, been uttered, it could not have obscured for

Keith the change which her magnificence had wrought in him. Something, perhaps, of the bigotry of the convert was already discernible in the way that, averting his eyes, he said, 'One doesn't even peer.' As to whether, in the years that have elapsed since he said this, either of our friends (now adult) has, in fact, 'peered,' is a question which, whenever I call at the house, I am tempted to put to one or other of them. But any regret I may feel in my invariable failure to 'come up to the scratch' of yielding to this temptation is balanced, for me, by my impression—my sometimes all but throned and anointed certainty—that the answer, if vouchsafed, would be in the negative.

MAX BEERBOHM (from A Christmas Garland)

ARTHUR O'SHAUGHNESSY · 1844–1881

ODE

*[after O'Shaughnessy's 'Ode'—'We are the music makers | We are the
dreamers of dreams . . .']*

> We are the masturbators,
> We are the dreamers of dreams,
> Spending in secretive places,
> Our totally purposeless streams;
> And one with a mind at leisure
> Can roger an ancient Queen
> And make from a moment's pleasure
> A map on the damascene.

OLIVER ST JOHN GOGARTY

damascene] *a fine, richly figured fabric.*

GERARD MANLEY HOPKINS · 1844–1889

BREAKFAST WITH GERARD MANLEY HOPKINS

'Delicious heart-of-the-corn, fresh-from-the-oven
flakes are sparkled and spangled with sugar for a
can't-be-resisted flavour.'—*Legend on a packet of
breakfast cereal*

Serious over my cereals I broke one breakfast my fast
    With something-to-read-searching retinas retained by print on a
       packet;
Sprung rhythm sprang, and I found (the mind fact-mining at last)
    An influence Father-Hopkins-fathered on the copy-writing racket.

Parenthesis-proud, bracket-bold, happiest with hyphens,
    The writers stagger intoxicated by terms, adjective-unsteadied—
Describing in graceless phrases fizzling like soda siphons
    All things, crisp, crunchy, malted, tangy, sugared and shredded.

Far too, yes, too early we are urged to be purged, to savour
    Salt, malt and phosphates in English twisted and torn,
As, sparkled and spangled with sugar for a can't-be-resisted flavour,
    Come fresh-from-the-oven flakes direct from the heart of the corn.

ANTHONY BRODE

EDMUND GOSSE · 1849–1928

A RECOLLECTION

'And let us strew
Twain wreaths of holly and of yew.'

WALLER

One out of many Christmas Days abides with peculiar vividness in my
memory. In setting down, however clumsily, some slight record of it, I feel
that I shall be discharging a duty not only to the two disparately illustrious
men who made it so very memorable, but also to all young students of
English and Scandinavian literature. My use of the first person singular,
delightful though that pronoun is in the works of the truly gifted, jars
unspeakably on me; but reasons of space baulk my sober desire to call
myself merely the present writer, or the infatuated go-between, or the
cowed and imponderable young person who was in attendance.

    In the third week of December, 1878, taking the opportunity of a brief
and undeserved vacation, I went to Venice. On the morning after my
arrival, in answer to a most kind and cordial summons, I presented myself
at the Palazzo Rezzonico. Intense as was the impression he always made
even in London, I think that those of us who met Robert Browning only
in the stress and roar of that metropolis can hardly have gauged the fullness of his potentialities for impressing. Venice, 'so weak, so quiet,' as Mr
Ruskin had called her, was indeed the ideal setting for one to whom neither

of those epithets could by any possibility have been deemed applicable. The steamboats that now wake the echoes of the canals had not yet been imported; but the vitality of the imported poet was in some measure a preparation for them. It did not, however, find me quite prepared for itself, and I am afraid that some minutes must have elapsed before I could, as it were, find my foot in the torrent of his geniality and high spirits and give him news of his friends in London.

He was at that time engaged in revising the proof-sheets of 'Dramatic Idylls,' and after luncheon, to which he very kindly bade me remain, he read aloud certain selected passages. The yellow haze of a wintry Venetian sunshine poured in through the vast windows of his *salone*, making an aureole around his silvered head. I would give much to live that hour over again. But it was vouchsafed in days before the Browning Society came and made everything so simple for us all. I am afraid that after a few minutes I sat enraptured by the sound rather than by the sense of the lines. I find, in the notes I made of the occasion, that I figured myself as plunging through some enchanted thicket on the back of an inspired bull.

That evening, as I was strolling in Piazza San Marco, my thoughts of Browning were all of a sudden scattered by the vision of a small, thick-set man seated at one of the tables in the Café Florian. This was—and my heart leapt like a young trout when I saw that it could be none other than—Henrik Ibsen. Whether joy or fear was the predominant emotion in me, I should be hard put to it to say. It had been my privilege to correspond extensively with the great Scandinavian, and to be frequently received by him, some years earlier than the date of which I write, in Rome. In that city haunted by the shades of so many Emperors and Popes I had felt comparatively at ease even in Ibsen's presence. But seated here in the homelier decay of Venice, closely buttoned in his black surcoat and crowned with his uncompromising top-hat, with the lights of the Piazza flashing back wanly from his gold-rimmed spectacles, and his lips tight-shut like some steel trap into which our poor humanity had just fallen, he seemed to constitute a menace under which the boldest might well quail. Nevertheless, I took my courage in both hands, and laid it as a kind of votive offering on the little table before him.

My reward was in the surprising amiability that he then and afterwards displayed. My travelling had indeed been doubly blessed, for, whilst my subsequent afternoons were spent in Browning's presence, my evenings fell with regularity into the charge of Ibsen. One of these evenings is for me 'prouder, more laurel'd than the rest' as having been the occasion when he read to me the MS of a play which he had just completed. He was staying at the Hôtel Danieli, an edifice famous for having been, rather more than forty years previously, the socket in which the flame of an historic *grande passion* had finally sunk and guttered out with no inconsiderable accompaniment of smoke and odour. It was there, in an upper room, that

I now made acquaintance with a couple very different from George Sand and Alfred de Musset, though destined to become hardly less famous than they. I refer to Torvald and Nora Helmer. My host read to me with the utmost vivacity, standing in the middle of the apartment; and I remember that in the scene where Nora Helmer dances the tarantella her creator instinctively executed a few illustrative steps.

During those days I felt very much as might a minnow swimming to and fro between Leviathan on the one hand and Behemoth on the other—a minnow tremulously pleased, but ever wistful for some means of bringing his two enormous acquaintances together. On the afternoon of December 24th I confided to Browning my aspiration. He had never heard of this brother poet and dramatist, whose fame indeed was at that time still mainly Boreal; but he cried out with the greatest heartiness, 'Capital! Bring him round with you at one o'clock to-morrow for turkey and plum-pudding!'

I betook myself straight to the Hôtel Danieli, hoping against hope that Ibsen's sole answer would not be a comminatory grunt and an instant rupture of all future relations with myself. At first he was indeed resolute not to go. He had never heard of this Herr Browning. (It was one of the strengths of his strange, crustacean genius that he never had heard of anybody.) I took it on myself to say that Herr Browning would send his private gondola, propelled by his two gondoliers, to conduct Herr Ibsen to the scene of the festivity. I think it was this prospect that made him gradually unbend, for he had already acquired that taste for pomp and circumstance which was so notable a characteristic of his later years. I hastened back to the Palazzo Rezzonico before he could change his mind. I need hardly say that Browning instantly consented to send the gondola. So large and lovable was his nature that, had he owned a thousand of those conveyances, he would not have hesitated to send out the whole fleet in honour of any friend of any friend of his.

Next day, as I followed Ibsen down the Danielian water-steps into the expectant gondola, my emotion was such that I was tempted to snatch from him his neatly-furled umbrella and spread it out over his head, like the umbrella beneath which the Doges of days gone by had made their appearances in public. It was perhaps a pity that I repressed this impulse. Ibsen seemed to be already regretting that he had unbent. I could not help thinking, as we floated along the Riva Schiavoni, that he looked like some particularly ruthless member of the Council of Ten. I did, however, try faintly to attune him in some sort to the spirit of our host and of the day of the year. I adumbrated Browning's outlook on life, translating into Norwegian, I well remember, the words 'God's in his Heaven, all's right with the world.' In fact I cannot charge myself with not having done what I could. I can only lament that it was not enough.

When we marched into the *salone*, Browning was seated at the piano, playing (I think) a Toccata of Galuppi's. On seeing us, he brought his hands

down with a great crash on the keyboard, seemed to reach us in one astonishing bound across the marble floor, and clapped Ibsen loudly on either
shoulder, wishing him 'the Merriest of Merry Christmases.'

Ibsen, under this sudden impact, stood firm as a rock, and it flitted through
my brain that here at last was solved the old problem of what would happen
if an irresistible force met an immoveable mass. But it was obvious that the
rock was not rejoicing in the moment of victory. I was tartly asked whether
I had not explained to Herr Browning that his guest did not understand
English. I hastily rectified my omission, and thenceforth our host spoke in
Italian. Ibsen, though he understood that language fairly well, was averse
to speaking it. Such remarks as he made in the course of the meal to which
we presently sat down were made in Norwegian and translated by myself.

Browning, while he was carving the turkey, asked Ibsen whether he had
visited any of the Venetian theatres. Ibsen's reply was that he never visited
theatres. Browning laughed his great laugh, and cried, 'That's right! We
poets who write plays must give the theatres as wide a berth as possible.
We aren't wanted there!' 'How so?' asked Ibsen. Browning looked a little
puzzled, and I had to explain that in northern Europe Herr Ibsen's plays
were frequently performed. At this I seemed to see on Browning's face a
slight shadow—so swift and transient a shadow as might be cast by a swallow flying across a sunlit garden. An instant, and it was gone. I was glad,
however, to be able to soften my statement by adding that Herr Ibsen had
in his recent plays abandoned the use of verse.

The trouble was that in Browning's company he seemed practically to
have abandoned the use of prose too. When, moreover, he did speak, it
was always in a sense contrary to that of our host. The Risorgimento was
a theme always very near to the great heart of Browning, and on this occasion he hymned it with more than his usual animation and resource (if
indeed that were possible). He descanted especially on the vast increase
that had accrued to the sum of human happiness in Italy since the success
of that remarkable movement. When Ibsen rapped out the conviction that
what Italy needed was to be invaded and conquered once and for all by
Austria, I feared that an explosion was inevitable. But hardly had my translation of the inauspicious sentiment been uttered when the plum-pudding
was borne into the room, flaming on its dish. I clapped my hands wildly at
sight of it, in the English fashion, and was intensely relieved when the yet
more resonant applause of Robert Browning followed mine. Disaster had
been averted by a crowning mercy. But I am afraid that Ibsen thought us
both quite mad.

The next topic that was started, harmless though it seemed at first,
was fraught with yet graver peril. The world of scholarship was at that
time agitated by the recent discovery of what might or might not prove to
be a fragment of Sappho. Browning proclaimed his unshakable belief in

the authenticity of these verses. To my surprise, Ibsen, whom I had been unprepared to regard as a classical scholar, said positively that they had not been written by Sappho. Browning challenged him to give a reason. A literal translation of the reply would have been 'Because no woman ever was capable of writing a fragment of good poetry.' Imagination reels at the effect this would have had on the recipient of 'Sonnets from the Portuguese.' The agonised interpreter, throwing honour to the winds, babbled some wholly fallacious version of the words. Again the situation had been saved; but it was of the kind that does not even in furthest retrospect lose its power to freeze the heart and constrict the diaphragm.

I was fain to thank heaven when, immediately after the termination of the meal, Ibsen rose, bowed to his host, and bade me express his thanks for the entertainment. Out on the Grand Canal, in the gondola which had again been placed at our disposal, his passion for 'documents' that might bear on his work was quickly manifested. He asked me whether Herr Browning had ever married. Receiving an emphatically affirmative reply, he inquired whether Fru Browning had been happy. Loth though I was to cast a blight on his interest in the matter, I conveyed to him with all possible directness the impression that Elizabeth Barrett had assuredly been one of those wives who do *not* dance tarantellas nor slam front-doors. He did not, to the best of my recollection, make further mention of Browning, either then or afterwards. Browning himself, however, thanked me warmly, next day, for having introduced my friend to him. 'A capital fellow!' he exclaimed, and then, for a moment, seemed as though he were about to qualify this estimate, but ended by merely repeating, 'A capital fellow!'

Ibsen remained in Venice some weeks after my return to London. He was, it may be conjectured, bent on a specially close study of the Bride of the Adriatic because her marriage had been not altogether a happy one. But there appears to be no evidence whatsoever that he went again, either of his own accord, or by invitation, to the Palazzo Rezzonico.

MAX BEERBOHM (from *A Christmas Garland*)

Browning and Ibsen (whose work he introduced into England) were both heroes of Gosse. This is the only record of their having met.

OSCAR WILDE · 1854–1900

from THE GREEN CARNATION

Published in September 1894, only six months or so before the trial that led to Wilde's imprisonment, The Green Carnation *is a satirical* roman-à-clef *that sailed too close to the wind. The character of Esme Amaranth was unmistakably based on Wilde, that of Lord Reggie could only have been taken for a portrait of Lord Alfred Douglas, and the author drops some by no means obscure hints about the two men's private lives. As soon as the legal proceedings against Wilde began, the book was withdrawn from circulation.*

'Are you really going to bed, Lady Locke? Eleven! I had no idea it was so early. I am going to sit up all night with Reggie, saying mad scarlet things, such as George Meredith loves, and waking the night with silver silences. Good-night. Come, Reggie, let us go to the smoking-room, since we are left alone. I will be brilliant for you as I have never been brilliant for my publishers. I will talk to you as no character in my plays has ever talked. Come! The young Endymion stirs in his dreams, and the pale-souled Selene watches him from her pearly car. The shadows on the lawns are violet, and the stars wash the spaces of the sky with primrose and with crimson. The night is old yet. Let me be brilliant, dear boy, or I feel that I shall weep for sheer wittiness, and die, as so many have died, with all my epigrams still in me.'

ROBERT HICHENS

A. E. HOUSMAN · 1859–1936

'WHAT, STILL ALIVE AT TWENTY-TWO . . .'

What, still alive at twenty-two,
A clean upstanding chap like you?
Sure, if your throat 'tis hard to slit,
Slit your girl's, and swing for it.

Like enough, you won't be glad,
When they come to hang you, lad:
But bacon's not the only thing
That's cured by hanging from a string.

So, when the spilt ink of the night
Spreads o'er the blotting pad of light,
Lads whose job is still to do
Shall whet their knives, and think of you.

HUGH KINGSMILL

ARTHUR CONAN DOYLE · 1859–1930

THE ADVENTURE OF THE TWO COLLABORATORS

The following 'adventure' commemorates the collaboration of Conan Doyle and J. M. Barrie on a comic opera. It was produced, but proved a complete flop.

In bringing to a close the adventures of my friend Sherlock Holmes I am perforce reminded that he never, save on the occasion which, as you will now hear, brought his singular career to an end, consented to act in any mystery which was concerned with persons who made a livelihood by their pen. 'I am not particular about the people I mix among for business purposes,' he would say, 'but at literary characters I draw the line.'

We were in our rooms in Baker Street one evening. I was (I remember) by the centre table writing out 'The Adventure of the Man without a Cork Leg' (which had so puzzled the Royal Society and all the other scientific bodies of Europe), and Holmes was amusing himself with a little revolver practice. It was his custom of a summer evening to fire round my head, just shaving my face, until he had made a photograph of me on the opposite wall, and it is a slight proof of his skill that many of these portraits in pistol shots are considered admirable likenesses.

I happened to look out of the window, and perceiving two gentlemen advancing rapidly along Baker Street asked him who they were. He immediately lit his pipe, and, twisting himself on a chair into the figure 8, replied:

'They are two collaborators in comic opera, and their play has not been a triumph.'

I sprang from my chair to the ceiling in amazement, and he then explained:

'My dear Watson, they are obviously men who follow some low calling. That much even you should be able to read in their faces. Those little pieces of blue paper which they fling angrily from them are Durrant's Press Notices. Of these they have obviously hundreds about their person (see how their pockets bulge). They would not dance on them if they were pleasant reading.'

I again sprang to the ceiling (which is much dented), and shouted: 'Amazing! but they may be mere authors.'

'No,' said Holmes, 'for mere authors only get one press notice a week. Only criminals, dramatists and actors get them by the hundred.'

'Then they may be actors.'

'No, actors would come in a carriage.'

'Can you tell me anything else about them?'

'A great deal. From the mud on the boots of the tall one I perceive that he comes from South Norwood. The other is as obviously a Scotch author.'

'How can you tell that?'

'He is carrying in his pocket a book called (I clearly see) "Auld Licht Something." Would any one but the author be likely to carry about a book with such a title?'

I had to confess that this was improbable.

It was now evident that the two men (if such they can be called) were seeking our lodgings. I have said (often) that my friend Holmes seldom gave way to emotion of any kind, but he now turned livid with passion. Presently this gave place to a strange look of triumph.

'Watson,' he said, 'that big fellow has for years taken the credit for my most remarkable doings, but at last I have him—at last!'

Up I went to the ceiling, and when I returned the strangers were in the room.

'I perceive, gentlemen,' said Mr Sherlock Holmes, 'that you are at present afflicted by an extraordinary novelty.'

The handsomer of our visitors asked in amazement how he knew this, but the big one only scowled.

'You forget that you wear a ring on your fourth finger,' replied Mr Holmes calmly.

I was about to jump to the ceiling when the big brute interposed.

'That Tommy-rot is all very well for the public, Holmes,' said he, 'but you can drop it before me. And, Watson, if you go up to the ceiling again I shall make you stay there.'

Here I observed a curious phenomenon. My friend Sherlock Holmes *shrank*. He became small before my eyes. I looked longingly at the ceiling, but dared not.

'Let us cut the first four pages,' said the big man, 'and proceed to business. I want to know why ——'

'Allow me,' said Mr Holmes, with some of his old courage. 'You want to know why the public does not go to your opera.'

'Exactly,' said the other ironically, 'as you perceive by my shirt stud.' He added more gravely, 'And as you can only find out in one way I must insist on your witnessing an entire performance of the piece.'

It was an anxious moment for me. I shuddered, for I knew that if Holmes went I should have to go with him. But my friend had a heart of gold. 'Never,' he cried fiercely, 'I will do anything for you save that.'

'Your continued existence depends on it,' said the big man menacingly.

'I would rather melt into air,' replied Holmes, proudly taking another chair. 'But I can tell you why the public don't go to your piece without sitting the thing out myself.'

'Why?'

'Because,' replied Holmes calmly, 'they prefer to stay away.'

A dead silence followed that extraordinary remark. For a moment the two intruders gazed with awe upon the man who had unravelled their mystery so wonderfully. Then drawing their knives ——

Holmes grew less and less, until nothing was left save a ring of smoke which slowly circled to the ceiling.

The last words of great men are often noteworthy. These were the last words of Sherlock Holmes: 'Fool, fool! I have kept you in luxury for years. By my help you have ridden extensively in cabs, where no author was ever seen before. *Henceforth you will ride in buses!*'

The brute sunk into a chair aghast.

The other author did not turn a hair.

J. M. BARRIE

"Auld Licht Something"] *a reference to Barrie's book* Auld Licht Idylls.

HOW WATSON LEARNED THE TRICK

Watson had been watching his companion intently ever since he had sat down to the breakfast table. Holmes happened to look up and catch his eye.

'Well, Watson, what are you thinking about?' he asked.

'About you.'

'Me?'

'Yes, Holmes, I was thinking how superficial are those tricks of yours, and how wonderful it is that the public should continue to show interest in them.'

'I quite agree,' said Holmes. 'In fact, I have a recollection that I have myself made a similar remark.'

'Your methods,' said Watson severely, 'are really easily acquired.'

'No doubt,' Holmes answered with a smile. 'Perhaps you will yourself give an example of this method of reasoning.'

'With pleasure,' said Watson. 'I am able to say that you were greatly preoccupied when you got up this morning.'

'Excellent!' said Holmes. 'How could you possibly know that?'

'Because you are usually a very tidy man and yet you have forgotten to shave.'

'Dear me! How very clever!' said Holmes. 'I had no idea, Watson, that you were so apt a pupil. Has your eagle eye detected anything more?'

'Yes, Holmes. You have a client named Barlow, and you have not been successful in his case.'

'Dear me, how could you know that?'

'I saw the name outside his envelope. When you opened it you gave a groan and thrust it into your pocket with a frown on your face.'

'Admirable! You are indeed observant. Any other point?'

'I fear, Holmes, that you have taken to financial speculation.'

'How *could* you tell that, Watson?'

'You opened the paper, turned to the financial page, and gave a loud exclamation of interest.'

'Well, that is very clever of you, Watson. Any more?'

'Yes, Holmes, you have put on your black coat, instead of your dressing gown, which proves that you are expecting some important visitor at once.'

'Anything more?'

'I have no doubt that I could find other points, Holmes, but I only give you these few, in order to show you that there are other people in the world who can be as clever as you.'

'And some not so clever,' said Holmes. 'I admit that they are few, but I am afraid, my dear Watson, that I must count you among them.'

'What do you mean, Holmes?'

'Well, my dear fellow, I fear your deductions have not been so happy as I should have wished.'

'You mean that I was mistaken.'

'Just a little that way, I fear. Let us take the points in their order: I did not shave because I have sent my razor to be sharpened. I put on my coat

because I have, worse luck, an early meeting with my dentist. His name is
Barlow, and the letter was to confirm the appointment. The cricket page
is beside the financial one, and I turned to it to find if Surrey was holding
its own against Kent. But go on, Watson, go on! It's a very superficial trick,
and no doubt you will soon acquire it.'

ARTHUR CONAN DOYLE

*This self-parody was handwritten by Conan Doyle in 1922 for Queen Mary's Dolls'
House, in a miniature book (later sumptuously bound) measuring an inch and a
half high, an inch and a quarter wide, and half an inch thick.*

HENRY NEWBOLT · 1862–1938

THE LITTLE COMMODORE

It was eight bells in the forenoon and hammocks running sleek
    (*It's a fair sea flowing from the West*),
When the little Commodore came a-sailing up the Creek
    (*Heave Ho! I think you'll know the rest*).
Thunder in the halyards and horses leaping high,
Blake and Drake and Nelson are listenin' where they lie,
Four and twenty blackbirds a-bakin' in a pie,
    And the *Pegasus* came waltzing from the West.

Now the little Commodore sat steady on his keel
    (*It's a fair sea flowing from the West*),
A heart as stout as concrete reinforced with steel
    (*Heave Ho! I think you'll know the rest*).
Swinging are the scuppers, hark, the rudder snores,
Plugging at the Frenchmen, downing 'em by scores.
Porto Rico, Vera Cruz, and also the Azores,
    And the *Pegasus* came waltzing from the West.

So three cheers more for the little Commodore
    (*It's a fair sea flowing from the West*).
I tell you so again as I've told you so before
    (*Heigh Ho! I think you know the rest*).
Aged is the Motherland, old but she is young
(Easy with the tackle there—don't release the bung),
And I sang a song like all the songs that I have ever sung
    When the *Pegasus* came sailing from the West.

J. C. SQUIRE

THE OLD LAND DOG

Old General Artichoke lay bloated on his bed,
  Just like the Fighting Téméraire.
Twelve responsive daughters were gathered round his head
  And each of them was ten foot square.

Old General Artichoke he didn't want to die:
He never understood the truth and that perhaps was why
It wouldn't be correct to say he always told a lie.
  Womenfolk of England, oh beware!

'Fetch me down my rifle—it is hanging in the hall'
  Just like the Fighting Téméraire;
'Lydia, get my cartridge cases, twenty-four in all',
  And each of them is ten foot square.

'I'll tell you all in detail, girls, my every campaign
In Tuscany, Bolivia, Baluchistan and Spain;
And when I've finished telling you, I'll tell you all again;'
  Womenfolk of England, oh beware!

Old General Artichoke he's over eighty-two,
  Just like the Fighting Téméraire.
His daughters all make rush mats when they've nothing
      else to do,
  And each of them is ten foot square.

Now all ye pension'd army men from Tunbridge Wells to Perth,
Here's to General Artichoke, the purplest man on earth!
Give three loud cheers for Cheltenham, the city of his birth.
  Womenfolk of England, oh beware!

                                        JOHN BETJEMAN

W. B. YEATS · 1865–1939

'OR ONE MIGHT WRITE IT SO': YEATS

One of a group of parodies which are used to vary the narrative in I Crossed the
Minch *(1938), an account of a visit to the Hebrides.*

One day I came to the village of Sorisdale. I remember that I did not know where I was walking as my mind at that time was much occupied with religious and other problems. In Sorisdale I met an old man who looked like George Mair but without Mair's vulgar insouciance and he told me some old legends dating from before the Norse Invasion. He spoke in Gaelic with which I was not acquainted, and owing perhaps to this or to some other reason I only partly understood him. I have often wondered since whether he was not pulling my leg. He told me that the sea lay down beyond the village and when I raised my eyes I saw that this was so. Presently an old woman came out from a white-washed house, and when she had looked at me for some time went back into the house and shut the door. I have no doubt that she thought I was one of the other-dwellers and that her shutting of the door was an instance of that atavism so common among Celtic peoples. It was not surprising that she was afraid of me, for at that time I had not been able to have my hair cut as there was no photographer on the island, and my eyes, as is common with persons on the verge of a trance, were enlarged like the eyes of a *revenant*. I felt, as I looked at the shut door, that if I had more courage or a greater conviction of my importance, I would knock at the door and ask the old woman some questions, but instead of doing this I turned round to walk back to my hotel, or rather, for all our actions are accomplished on two planes at once, to regain that equilibrium of spirit which human contacts disturb. I have often wondered since, when waking from sleep in the Reading Room of the British Museum, whether that old woman was really all that she seemed, or whether, when she shut the door, she did not retire into a more elemental chamber than the living room of her cottage. Such a question cannot be definitely answered though I have no doubt, since talking it over with an old man in Merrion Square who had once had tea with Parnell, that such a removal from the material plane to the psychic is as easily accomplished as the changing of gears on a car. The universe has seemed to me at moments like a series of Chinese boxes which we undo from the inside outwards. This was also the conception of the yogis and can be found in a modern guise in the poems of Lady Flora Barsac. When I stayed in her house in Hampshire, she showed me a poem which she had written with a wild goose quill and it seemed to me to be more profound, more exquisite, than the other poems of our century.

LOUIS MACNEICE

Mair] *G. H. Mair, English journalist and public official; married to the celebrated Irish actress Molly Allgood ('Maire O'Neill').*

Lady Flora Barsac] *A fictitious character. She is almost certainly meant to suggest Lady Dorothy Wellesley, to whom Yeats had allotted no fewer than fifteen pages in his* Oxford Book of Modern Verse *(1936).*

THE IRISH TEAM

After 'Beautiful Lofty Things', a celebration of Yeats's father and some of the poet's friends which begins by invoking 'O'Leary's noble head' and concludes with the lines

> . . . Maud Gonne at Howth station waiting a train
> Pallas Athene in that straight back and arrogant head:
> All the Olympians; a thing never known again.

Lowly, degraded things: *Guinness* with no head;
Yeats's Father at O'Donoghue's, shouting his usual joke:
'This Land of Saints' (ignored by the usual crowd)
'—Of plastered Saints'; his flies greatly undone.
Maud Gonne in need of help, lungeing between the tables,
Her great grey skirt hoiked up, abused by all;
Augusta Gregory huddling from scorpions under a
                                     Formica table,
And scaring the scorpions; *Lionel Johnson* challenging
                                     God:
'I told Him that nightly from six to eleven I perch on this
                                     barstool—
Haha!'—and over he goes; and *Yeats* in the corner,
                                    combing the heads
And the tables for bits of potato to turn into slabs of
                                    marble
In poems where his friends are made to look better than
                                    everyone else's,
Calls them 'Olympians'. (All's changed, etc.)

                                     MICK IMLAH

RUDYARD KIPLING · 1865–1936

P.C. X, 36

> Then it's collar 'im tight,
>   In the name o' the Lawd!
> 'Ustle 'im, shake 'im till 'e's sick,
>   Wot, 'e *would*, would 'e? Well,
>   Then yer've got ter give 'im 'Ell,
> An' it's trunch, trunch, truncheon does the trick.
>   POLICE STATION DITTIES

I had spent Christmas Eve at the Club, listening to a grand pow-wow between certain of the choicer sons of Adam. Then Slushby had cut in. Slushby is one who writes to newspapers and is theirs obediently 'HUMANITARIAN.' When Slushby cuts in, men remember they have to be up early next morning.

Sharp round a corner on the way home, I collided with something firmer than the regulation pillar-box. I righted myself after the recoil and saw some stars that were very pretty indeed. Then I perceived the nature of the obstruction.

'Evening, Judlip,' I said sweetly, when I had collected my hat from the gutter. 'Have I broken the law, Judlip? If so, I'll go quiet.'

'Time yer was in bed,' grunted X, 36. 'Yer Ma'll be lookin' out for yer.'

This from the friend of my bosom! It hurt. Many were the night-beats I had been privileged to walk with Judlip, imbibing curious lore that made glad the civilian heart of me. Seven whole 8×5 inch note-books had I pitmanised to the brim with Judlip. And now to be repulsed as one of the uninitiated! It hurt horrid.

There is a thing called Dignity. Small boys sometimes stand on it. Then they have to be kicked. Then they get down, weeping. I don't stand on Dignity.

'What's wrong, Judlip?' I asked, more sweetly than ever. 'Drawn a blank to-night?'

'Yuss. Drawn a blank blank blank. 'Aven't 'ad so much as a kick at a lorst dorg. Christmas Eve ain't wot it was.' I felt for my note-book. 'Lawd! I remembers the time when the drunks and disorderlies down this street was as thick as flies on a fly-paper. One just picked 'em orf with one's finger and thumb. A bloomin' battew, that's wot it wos.'

'The night's yet young, Judlip,' I insinuated, with a jerk of my thumb at the flaring windows of the 'Rat and Blood Hound.' At that moment the saloon-door swung open, emitting a man and woman who walked with linked arms and exceeding great care.

Judlip eyed them longingly as they tacked up the street. Then he sighed. Now, when Judlip sighs the sound is like unto that which issues from the vent of a Crosby boiler when the cog-gauges are at $260°$ F.

'Come, Judlip!' I said. 'Possess your soul in patience. You'll soon find some one to make an example of. Meanwhile'—I threw back my head and smacked my lips—'the usual, Judlip?'

In another minute I emerged through the swing-door, bearing a furtive glass of that same 'usual,' and nipped down the mews where my friend was wont to await these little tokens of esteem.

'To the Majesty of the Law, Judlip!'

When he had honoured the toast, I scooted back with the glass, leaving him wiping the beads off his beard-bristles. He was in his philosophic mood when I rejoined him at the corner.

'Wot am I?' he said, as we paced along. 'A bloomin' cypher. Wot's the sarjint? 'E's got the Inspector over 'im. Over above the Inspector there's the Sooprintendent. Over above 'im's the old red-tape-masticatin' Yard. Over above that there's the 'Ome Sec. Wot's 'e? A cypher, like me. Why?' Judlip looked up at the stars. 'Over above 'im's We Dunno Wot. Somethin' wot issues its horders an' regulations an' divisional injunctions, inscrootable like, but p'remptory; an' we 'as ter see as 'ow they're carried out, not arskin' no questions, but each man goin' about 'is dooty.'

'"'Is dooty,"' said I, looking up from my note-book. 'Yes, I've got that.'

'Life ain't a bean-feast. It's a 'arsh reality. An' them as makes it a bean-feast 'as got to be 'arshly dealt with accordin'. That's wot the Force is put 'ere for from Above. Not as 'ow we ain't fallible. We makes our mistakes. An' when we makes 'em we sticks to 'em. For the honour o' the Force. Which same is the jool Britannia wears on 'er bosom as a charm against hanarchy. That's wot the brarsted old Beaks don't understand. Yer remember Smithers of our Div.?'

I remembered Smithers—well. As fine, up-standing, square-toed, bullet-headed, clean-living a son of a gun as ever perjured himself in the box. There was nothing of the softy about Smithers. I took off my billicock to Smithers' memory.

'Sacrificed to public opinion? Yuss,' said Judlip, pausing at a front door and flashing his 45 c.p. down the slot of a two-grade Yale. 'Sacrificed to a parcel of screamin' old women wot ort ter 'ave gorn down on their knees an' thanked Gawd for such a protector. 'E'll be out in another 'alf year. Wot'll 'e do then, pore devil? Go a bust on 'is conduc' money an' throw in 'is lot with them same hexperts wot 'ad a 'oly terror of 'im.' Then Judlip swore gently.

'What should you do, O Great One, if ever it were your duty to apprehend him?'

'Do? Why, yer blessed innocent, yer don't think I'd shirk a fair clean cop? Same time, I don't say as 'ow I wouldn't 'andle 'im tender like, for sake o' wot 'e wos. Likewise cos 'e'd be a stiff customer to tackle. Likewise 'cos——'

He had broken off, and was peering fixedly upwards at an angle of 85° across the moonlit street. ' 'Ullo!' he said in a hoarse whisper.

Striking an average between the direction of his eyes—for Judlip, when on the job, has a soul-stirring squint—I perceived some one in the act of emerging from a chimney-pot.

Judlip's voice clove the silence. 'Wot are yer doin' hup there?'

The person addressed came to the edge of the parapet. I saw then that he had a hoary white beard, a red ulster with the hood up, and what looked like a sack over his shoulder. He said something or other in a voice like a concertina that has been left out in the rain.

'I dessay,' answered my friend. 'Just you come down, an' we'll see about that.'

The old man nodded and smiled. Then—as I hope to be saved—he came floating gently down through the moonlight, with the sack over his shoulder and a young fir-tree clasped to his chest. He alighted in a friendly manner on the curb beside us.

Judlip was the first to recover himself. Out went his right arm, and the airman was slung round by the scruff of the neck, spilling his sack in the road. I made a bee-line for his shoulder-blades. Burglar or no burglar, he was the best airman out, and I was muchly desirous to know the precise nature of the apparatus under his ulster. A back-hander from Judlip's left caused me to hop quickly aside. The prisoner was squealing and whimpering. He didn't like the feel of Judlip's knuckles at his cervical vertebrae.

'Wot was yer doin' hup there?' asked Judlip tightening the grip.

'I'm S-Santa Claus, Sir. P-please, Sir, let me g-go.'

'Hold him,' I shouted. 'He's a German!'

'It's my dooty ter caution yer that wotever yer say now may be used in hevidence against yer, yer old sinner. Pick up that there sack, an' come along o' me.'

The captive snivelled something about peace on earth, good will toward men.

'Yuss,' said Judlip. 'That's in the Noo Testament, ain't it? The Noo Testament contains some uncommon nice readin' for old gents an' young ladies. But it ain't included in the librery o' the Force. We confine ourselves to the Old Testament—O.T., 'ot. An' 'ot you'll get it. Hup with that sack, an' quick march!'

I have seen worse attempts at a neck-wrench, but it was just not slippery enough for Judlip. And the kick that Judlip then let fly was a thing of beauty and a joy for ever.

'Frog's-march him!' I shrieked, dancing. 'For the love of Heaven, frog's-march him!'

Trotting by Judlip's side to the Station, I reckoned it out that if Slushby had not been at the Club I should not have been here to see. Which shows that even Slushbys are put into this world for a purpose.

MAX BEERBOHM (from A Christmas Garland)

AMERICAN POPULAR FICTION · c.1900

from OUR TALES OF SENTIMENT

from 'Sundry Hearts'

When presented to the object of his devotion the earl could not suppress his sentiments. The Lady Gwendolin saw them as plainly as if they had been branded upon his brow. Her agitation was comparable to his. All the pent-up emotion of her deep, womanly nature surged to her countenance and paralyzed her so that she was unable to offer her hand. She consequently contented herself with a graceful inclination of the head. The earl was excessively disappointed. Turning upon his heel he bowed and walked away.

Gwendolin retired to the conservatory and uttered a deep-drawn sigh, then, returning to the ballroom, flung herself into the waltz with an assumed ectasy that elicited wide comment.

from 'Lance and Lute'

The faint booming of the distant cannon grew more and more deafening; the thunder of the charging cavalry reverberated o'er the field of battle: the enemies were evidently making a stand.

Plympton arrived at the scene of action just as the commanding general ordered an advance along the entire front. Spurring his steed to the centre of the line he rang out his voice in accents of defiance and was promoted for gallantry.

Bertram, who was an eye-witness, immediately withdrew his objection to the marriage. This took place shortly afterward and was attended with the happiest results.

from 'A Belle of Castile'

Josephina had progressed but a brief distance into the garden when some inner sense proclaimed that she was followed: the crunching of a gentleman's heel upon the gravel was indisputable. Partially terrified, she sought concealment in the shrubbery that bordered the path on the one side and the other. It passed by her there in the moonlight, that dreadful sound, yet no one visible! It went on and on, growing fainter and fainter, like herself, and was lost to hearing. Then she remembered the tradition of the Invisible Knight and her heart smote her for the absence of faith with which she had so often greeted it.

'I am fitly punished,' she conceded, 'for my sceptical attitude. Henceforth, so far as the constitution of my mind will permit, I will be more hospitable to the convictions of the simple.'

How she adhered to this expiational resolution we shall behold.

from 'A Study in Dissection'

Captain Gerard introspected. He spread his heart, as it were, upon the dissecting-table of conscience and examined it from several points of view. It is a familiar act—we call it analysis of motive. When he had concluded he knew why he had accepted the invitation of the countess to dinner. He knew why he had insulted the count. Equally obvious were his reasons for

mentioning to Iphigeneia the holy bonds of matrimony. In all his conduct
since his last introspection but one act baffled him: why, alas, had he spoken
to Iphigeneia of the bar-semester in his crest?

As he pondered this inexplicable problem a footfall fell upon his ear and
he shuddered as if the hand of death had stepped in.

It was the countess!

AMBROSE BIERCE

HILAIRE BELLOC · 1870–1953

FOOTNOTE TO BELLOC'S 'TARENTELLA'

Do you remember an inn, Miranda? It lost its licence of course—
Total neglect of the elementary rules of hygiene, not to mention
Wine contaminated with tar, and constant complaints
From the neighbours about the noise.
One visit of the Inspector
From the Spanish Tourist Board was quite enough.
Nevermore, Miranda, nevermore.

JOHN HEATH-STUBBS

W. H. DAVIES · 1871–1940

MR W. H. DAVIES SNARES NATURE

In every daisy in the field
Full thirty morals are concealed,
And though but one of them be mine,
And I forget the twenty-nine,
Yet am I better off by far
Than rich men and their butlers are,
Who ever have of morals none,
While happy I at least have one.

SAMUEL HOFFENSTEIN

BERTRAND RUSSELL · 1872–1970

EARLY DAYS AT CAMBRIDGE

[*after* Portraits from Memory]

One of the advantages of living in Great Court Trinity, I seem to recall, was the fact that one could always pop across any time of day or night and trap the then young and somewhat beautiful G. E. Moore into a logical falsehood by means of a cunning semantic subterfuge. I recall one occasion with particular vividness. I had popped across and knocked upon his door. 'Come in,' he said. I decided to wait awhile in order to test the ethical consistency of his proposition. 'Come in,' he said once again. 'Very well,' I replied, 'if that is in fact truly what you desire.' I opened the door accordingly and went in. Moore was seated by the fire with a basket upon his knee. 'Moore,' I said, 'have you any apples in that basket?' 'No,' he replied and smiled seraphically, as was his wont. I decided to try a different logical tack. 'Moore,' I said, 'have you then *some* apples in that basket?' 'No,' he replied again, leaving me in a logical cleft stick from which I had but one way out. 'Moore,' I said, 'have you then *apples* in that basket?' 'Yes,' he replied, and from that day forth we remained the very closest of friends.

from *Beyond the Fringe* (a revue by
ALAN BENNETT, PETER COOK, JONATHAN
MILLER, and DUDLEY MOORE)

G. K. CHESTERTON · 1874–1936

WHEN I LEAPT OVER TOWER BRIDGE

When I leapt over Tower Bridge
There were three that watched below,
A bald man and a hairy man,
And a man like Ikey Mo.

When I leapt over London Bridge
They quailed to see my tears,
As terrible as a shaken sword
And many shining spears.

But when I leapt over Blackfriars
The pigeons on St Paul's

    Grew ghastly white as they saw the sight
    Like an awful sun that falls;

    And all along from Ludgate
      To the wonder of Charing Cross,
    The devil flew through a host of hearts—
      A messenger of loss;

    With a rumour of ghostly things that pass
      With a thunderous pennon of pain,
    To a land where the sky is as red as the grass
    And the sun as green as the rain.

J. C. SQUIRE

SOME DAMNABLE ERRORS ABOUT CHRISTMAS

That it is human to err is admitted by even the most positive of our thinkers. Here we have the great difference between latter-day thought and the thought of the past. If Euclid were alive to-day (and I daresay he is) he would not say, 'The angles at the base of an isosceles triangle are equal to one another.' He would say, 'To me (a very frail and fallible being, remember) it does somehow seem that these two angles have a mysterious and awful equality to one another.' The dislike of schoolboys for Euclid is unreasonable in many ways; but fundamentally it is entirely reasonable. Fundamentally it is the revolt from a man who was either fallible and therefore (in pretending to infallibility) an impostor, or infallible and therefore not human.

Now, since it is human to err, it is always in reference to those things which arouse in us the most human of all our emotions—I mean the emotion of love—that we conceive the deepest of our errors. Suppose we met Euclid on Westminster Bridge, and he took us aside and confessed to us that whilst he regarded parallelograms and rhomboids with an indifference bordering on contempt, for isosceles triangles he cherished a wild romantic devotion. Suppose he asked us to accompany him to the nearest music-shop, and there purchased a guitar in order that he might worthily sing to us the radiant beauty and the radiant goodness of isosceles triangles. As men we should, I hope, respect his enthusiasm, and encourage his enthusiasm, and catch his enthusiasm. But as seekers after truth we should be compelled to regard with a dark suspicion, and to check with the most anxious care, every fact that he told us about isosceles triangles. For adoration involves a glorious obliquity of vision. It involves more than that. We do not say of Love that he is short-sighted. We do not say of Love that he is myopic.

We do not say of Love that he is astigmatic. We say quite simply, Love is blind. We might go further and say, Love is deaf. That would be a profound and obvious truth. We might go further still and say, Love is dumb. But that would be a profound and obvious lie. For love is always an extra-ordinarily fluent talker. Love is a wind-bag, filled with a gusty wind from Heaven.

It is always about the thing that we love most that we talk most. About this thing, therefore, our errors are something more than our deepest errors: they are our most frequent errors. That is why for nearly two thousand years mankind has been more glaringly wrong on the subject of Christmas than on any other subject. If mankind had hated Christmas, he would have understood it from the first. What would have happened then, it is impossible to say. For that which is hated, and therefore is persecuted, and therefore grows brave, lives on for ever, whilst that which is under-stood dies in the moment of our understanding of it—dies, as it were, in our awful grasp. Between the horns of this eternal dilemma shivers all the mystery of the jolly visible world, and of that still jollier world which is invisible. And it is because Mr Shaw and the writers of his school cannot, with all their splendid sincerity and acumen, perceive that he and they and all of us are impaled on those horns as certainly as the sausages I ate for breakfast this morning had been impaled on the cook's toasting-fork—it is for this reason, I say, that Mr Shaw and his friends seem to me to miss the basic principle that lies at the root of all things human and divine. By the way, not all things that are divine are human. But all things that are human are divine. But to return to Christmas.

I select at random two of the more obvious fallacies that obtain. One is that Christmas should be observed as a time of jubilation. This is (I admit) quite a recent idea. It never entered into the tousled heads of the shepherds by night, when the light of the angel of the Lord shone about them and they arose and went to do homage to the Child. It never entered into the heads of the Three Wise Men. They did not bring their gifts as a joke, but as an awful oblation. It never entered into the heads of the saints and scholars, the poets and painters, of the Middle Ages. Looking back across the years, they saw in that dark and ungarnished manger only a shrinking woman, a brood-ing man, and a child born to sorrow. The philomaths of the eighteenth century, looking back, saw nothing at all. It is not the least of the glories of the Victorian Era that it rediscovered Christmas. It is not the least of the mistakes of the Victorian Era that it supposed Christmas to be a feast.

The splendour of the saying, 'I have piped unto you, and you have not danced; I have wept with you, and you have not mourned' lies in the fact that it might have been uttered with equal truth by any man who had ever piped or wept. There is in the human race some dark spirit of recal-citrance, always pulling us in the direction contrary to that in which we are reasonably expected to go. At a funeral, the slightest thing, not in the least ridiculous at any other time, will convulse us with internal laughter. At a wedding, we hover mysteriously on the brink of tears. So it is with the modern Christmas. I find myself in agreement with the cynics in so far that I admit that Christmas, as now observed, tends to create melancholy. But the reason for this lies solely in our own misconception. Christmas is essentially a *dies irae*. If the cynics will only make up their minds to treat it as such, even the saddest and most atrabilious of them will acknowledge that he has had a rollicking day.

This brings me to the second fallacy. I refer to the belief that 'Christmas comes but once a year.' Perhaps it does, according to the calendar—a quaint and interesting compilation, but of little or no practical value to anybody. It is not the calendar, but the Spirit of Man that regulates the recurrence of feasts and fasts. Spiritually, Christmas Day recurs exactly seven times a week. When we have frankly acknowledged this, and acted on this, we shall begin to realise the Day's mystical and terrific beauty. For it is only every-day things that reveal themselves to us in all their wonder and their splendour. A man who happens one day to be knocked down by a motor-bus merely utters a curse and instructs his solicitor; but a man who has been knocked down by a motor-bus every day of the year will have begun to feel that he is taking part in an august and soul-cleansing ritual. He will await the diurnal stroke of fate with the same lowly and pious joy as animated the Hindoos awaiting Juggernaut. His bruises will be decorations, worn with the modest pride of the veteran. He will cry aloud, in the words of the late W. E. Henley, 'My head is bloody but unbowed.' He will add, 'My ribs are broken but unbent.'

I look for the time when we shall wish one another a Merry Christmas every morning; when roast turkey and plum-pudding shall be the staple of our daily dinner, and the holly shall never be taken down from the walls, and every one will always be kissing every one else under the mistletoe. And what is right as regards Christmas is right as regards all other so-called anniversaries. The time will come when we shall dance round the Maypole every morning before breakfast—a meal at which hot-cross buns will be a standing dish—and shall make April fools of one another every day before noon. The profound significance of All Fools' Day—the glorious lesson that we are all fools—is too apt at present to be lost. Nor is justice done to the sublime symbolism of Shrove Tuesday—the day on which all sins are shriven. Every day pancakes shall be eaten either before or after the plum-pudding. They shall be eaten slowly and sacramentally. They shall be fried over fires tended and kept for ever bright by Vestals. They shall be tossed to the stars.

I shall return to the subject of Christmas next week.

MAX BEERBOHM (from *A Christmas Garland*)

ROBERT FROST · 1874–1963

MR FROST GOES SOUTH TO BOSTON

[*the opening lines echo those of Frost's poem 'Birches'*]

When I see buildings in a town together,
Stretching all around to touch the sky,
I like to know that they come down again
And so I go around the block to see,
And, sure enough, there is the downward side.
I say to myself these buildings never quite
Arrived at heaven although they went that way.
That's the way with buildings and with people.
The same applies to colts and cats and chickens
And cattle of all breeds and dogs and horses.
I think the buildings Boston has are high
Enough. I like to ride the elevator
Up to the top and then back I come again.
Now, don't get me wrong. I wouldn't want
A ticket to New York to ride up higher.
These buildings come as close to heaven now
As I myself would ever want to go.

FIRMAN HOUGHTON

GERTRUDE STEIN · 1874–1946

BATTOLOGY

[*a review of Gertrude Stein's* Composition as Explanation *(1927)*]

There is oddly not nearly so much difficulty about reading the beginning
of a book by Gertrude Stein like this book of hers called Composition as
Explanation (Hogarth Essays) as there is in reading it later on when it gets
nearer the end. It is all written like this with no punctuation of course but
it does sound as if it meant something. Every now and then a word or two
is written twice over twice over but of course that may be the printer. It is
a little confusing to be told that people are the composing of the composition that at the time they are living is the composition of the time in which
they are living, but probably it all works out somehow. She goes on like
this for about thirty pages and then she says now that is all. But it isn't it

isn't it isn't. It's only about half. She starts putting in headlines after that to symbolically no doubt make her meaning clearer, but it isn't clearer. It is ever so much not clearer. SITWELL EDITH SITWELL.

She says that quite suddenly in capitals as if it were a line of Onward Christian Soldiers. And in this part of the book all the parts of speech get mixed up anyhow as if she had been taking a lesson in typewriting. The quick brown fox jumps over the lazy dog lazy dog lazy fox the quick jumps jumps brown. There is only one sentence in this part which is English, it says toasted susie is my ice-cream, and that is not sense, is it? So awfully not sense. I suppose she must either think it looks pretty or think it sounds pretty when you read it but it doesn't it doesn't either it really doesn't.

Then every now and then she gives you a series of sentences which look like a spelling lesson or testing a new nib. Or sometimes it might be a French exercise. I make fun of him of her. I make fun of them. They make fun of them of this. They make fun of him of her. That sort of thing. I don't make fun of her. She makes fun of herself.

I don't understand why she says it is not usually her habit to mention anything. She is always mentioning things and leaving it at that. Weeks and weeks able and weeks. I can see she is mentioning something. But why does she mention it so often? They make them they make them they make them they make them they make them they make them they make them at once. It is very easy to type-write that sentence. But it would be easier still to write they make them repeat seven times at once. And it would save paper. She wastes paper. Baskets and paper, paper and baskets.

Now and then she seems to be telephoning. Eight eight and eight, eight eight and eight. Eight eight and eight and eight. She ought to have said eight double eight. They must address with tenderness. Yes but the girl at the exchange wouldn't address with tenderness. I think she must do it by taking hashish. Has she has his hashish? Hashish and haberdashers. Dash her hashish.

RONALD KNOX

JOHN BUCHAN · 1875–1940

from FORTY YEARS ON

[*a play within a play*]

LEITHEN: You've got some first-class Holbeins.
HANNAY: Ned.
LEITHEN: Yes?
HANNAY: I asked you here for a purpose.

LEITHEN: Yes.

HANNAY: Do you remember the last time I saw you?

LEITHEN: Intimately. It was at a little thing called Mons.

HANNAY: Since then I seem to have lost your spoor.

LEITHEN: I came through the war more or less intact. I lost an arm here, an ear there, but I was all right, a damn sight better off than a few million other poor devils anyway. Then I got back home and there were these Weary Willies and Tired Tims in their hand-woven ties, writing gibberish they called poetry saying we'd all been wasting our time. I couldn't see it myself. If we'd done nothing by 1918 at least we'd saved the follow-on.

SANDY CLANROYDEN: Ned. Did you ever hear of a man called George Ampersand?

LEITHEN: Bostonian philanthropist and friend of kings! Who hasn't?

SANDY: I had some talk with Mr Baldwin this morning. I never saw a man more worried.

HANNAY: Of late, Ned, there have been a succession of small disasters, oh trifling in themselves . . . a Foreign Secretary's sudden attack of dysentery at the funeral of George V, an American ambassador found strangled in his own gym-slip, and in Sudetenland, most mysterious of all, a Laughing Leper who destroys whole villages with his infectious giggles.

SANDY: The tide is flowing fast against monarchy in Europe. Scarcely a week passes but a throne falls. Mr Baldwin thinks it may be our turn next.

LEITHEN: Who is behind it all this time?

HANNAY: Who? That poses something of a problem. To the good people of the neighbourhood he is a white-haired old man with a nervous habit of moving his lips as he talks. To the members of a not unfamiliar London club he is our second most successful theologian. But the world knows him as . . . George Ampersand.

LEITHEN: Ampersand. Good God.

HANNAY (handing him snapshots): He is surrounded by some of the worst villains in Europe. Irma, his wife. Nature played a cruel trick upon her by giving her a waxed moustache. Sandro, his valet. A cripple of the worst sort, and consumptive into the bargain.

LEITHEN: Is he sane?

SANDY: Sane? He is brilliantly sane. The second sanest in Europe. But like all sane men he has at one time or another crossed that thin bridge that separates lunacy from insanity. And this last week the pace has quickened. Else explain why a highly respected Archbishop of Canterbury, an international hairdresser and a very famous king all decide to take simultaneous holidays on the Black Sea.

HANNAY: Take a look at this snapshot. It's of a simultaneous holiday on
the Black Sea.

LEITHEN: But that's . . .

HANNAY: Exactly. A young man not entirely unconnected with the English
throne.

LEITHEN: Who is she?

SANDY: She's beautiful, isn't she. An American. Women are queer cattle at
the best of times but she's like no other woman I've ever known. She has
all the slim grace of a boy and all the delicacy of a young colt.

LEITHEN: It's a rare combination. Who's this?

HANNAY: Completely Unscrupulos, the Greek shipping magnate.

LEITHEN: He's got himself into a pretty rum set. And yet he looks happy.

HANNAY: That's what Mr Baldwin doesn't like about it. During the past few
months certain reports have been appearing in what for want of a better
word the Americans call their newspapers.

LEITHEN: About her?

HANNAY: Yes.

LEITHEN: And him?

HANNAY: Yes.

LEITHEN: But . . . I don't understand . . . where lies the difficulty? If he
loves her . . .

HANNAY: I don't think you understand. She is what we in the Church of
England called a divorced woman.

LEITHEN: God! It's filthy!

HANNAY: A divorced woman on the throne of the house of Windsor would
be a pretty big feather in the cap of that bunch of rootless intellectuals,
alien Jews and international pederasts who call themselves the Labour
Party.

LEITHEN: Your talk is like a fierce cordial.

SANDY: As yet the British public knows nothing. Mr Baldwin is relying on
us to see they remain in that blissful state.

LEITHEN: I like the keen thrust of your mind, but where does friend
Ampersand fit into all this?

HANNAY: That is what I want you to find out. Sandy will accompany you
disguised as a waiter. That should at least secure you the entrée. But be
careful. And on no account let His Majesty know that you are meddling
in this affair. A sport called Shakespeare summed it up: There's a divinity
that doth hedge a King, Rough hew it how you will.

ALAN BENNETT

LYTTON STRACHEY · 1880–1932

A PORTRAIT OF LYTTON STRACHEY, IN HIS OWN MANNER

Crouching under the ilex tree in his chaise longue, remote, aloof, self-occupied, and mysteriously contented, lay the venerable biographer. Muffled in a sealskin coat (for although it was July he felt the cold) he knitted with elongated fingers a coatee for his favourite cat, Tiberius. He was in his 99th year. He did not know it was his last day on earth.

A constable called for a subscription for the local sports. 'Trop tard, trop tard; mes jeux sont finis.' He gazed at the distant downs; he did not mind—not mind in the very least the thought that this was probably his last summer; after all, summers were now infinitely cold and dismal. One might as well be a mole. He did not care that he was no longer thought the greatest biographer, or that the Countess no longer—or did she? Had he been a woman he would not have shone as a writer, but as a dissipated mistress of infinite intrigues.

But lying on the grass was a loose button, a particularly revolting specimen; it was intolerable, an unspeakable catastrophe. He stooped from his chaise longue to pick it up, murmuring to his cat 'Mais quelle horreur!' for once stooped too far—and passed away for ever.

'CARRINGTON' (DORA CARRINGTON)

Carrington's parody was written only six months before his actual death. It was submitted (under the pseudonym 'Mopsa') as an entry for a competition set by a magazine in July 1931, and won first prize. Strachey telegraphed his congratulations; she replied, 'Darling Lytton, My most venerable Biographer, knitter of coatees, most dissipated of masters, do you know your wire gave me more pleasure than anything in the world?'

Michael Holroyd has described the parody as 'composed with the loving malice of someone who was moved at times by a furtive wish to escape'. Carrington had been under Strachey's spell for many years; she committed suicide shortly after he died.

JAMES JOYCE · 1882–1941

PLEASUREBUBBLE HUBBYHOUSE

[*a critical account of* Finnegans Wake]

Cobblears, I queek, con naught con all. This is a misbegoblin effart from swive of wive to brickfist type and four pines ninetofive in any buddy's monure. Where's your woollen tears, I asp yo, to be token by're lurke-wake root sex-hundread pagan laing (in your Fibre papalbag) back to Head Case Engineering, wench we came. (No anchor was the stern reply.)

Finagles Waste, bejamers joist, cannondrum in excresis, insproats a crumplicadent nexicon of dumpstincts within yr fightful reportwire. He sews seemseeds in the earshell (moultigreyed). Echo homo, littlesurs! Yet in the upperroof of our puerole Humptyhead, alass, wee stans a ghost. All tug Heather now, Here Comes Excess! (Nutting degrees like digress, my old donski use to shay, God press his iddle-gotten saul.) Well a big fat darty booker it is to be Shaw, and I wouldn't have the spiers to be waterlogging all the arks and chunderment of openprism reduxdiceased betwee these greeny backs, so geld me Hobson. Suffixit touche, o gintill redrum, it's oh, allerline schoolerschrift filluphaben in a therasputin donghell incarnabine. (Otis lifteywater I must dyke for it, Father, plash me for I have skimmed. Or shuteye see, flush me, Farber, for I am skint? Hamsters on a boastcart, please.)

I'll not abound to say you won't fine yourself tungling over the odd tibs and bogs that hueffer to the kyries mine pleasurebubble sensehavens of interlarkin dizzypin. Not at Hall, the very tort of it is anaspirin for Deloittes of me. Old Joys is low-undo-himself. (And don't wee all.) Notwithshandy he guts no eyes with ewers drooling. And why should he, Gott safes the Mark, we cannot all be Hainault Hobcecils scrimbling lists of the midevil sainsburys, we'd all go roust the twins.

But, you interplate (those of you in whom the shap of egremont is heather rising, gold blast you sirs, would you heave the price of a Riles-Royals about yez?) this is no rumtomb teararts billyphant from the Dully Bullygraft! This is Highly Charged Engrishe or I'm a touchmum! How ripe you are, penine interlexapples, I bough to your supearier fudgement. But are you shaun, are you dolgelly convicted we are dwelling with a Wort of Ark and not a Pickforth's vain of finto seems belunging to a literarty hen's teeth diva? Hom? You mistumblestand the jeskin? Swerve you right, you anchor! (Part my fringe.)

In the embolism comes it doubt to this: Filigrees Whelk, bejams juice is a bleeding grant for pores, a hubbyhouse for the aldebarans of the acadome, och it's an obsolate condgeree of your hockmugrandiose christable prankhearse, and all the finn in it is in the parting together (on Joisus' path) and biggerole in the pollen-asonder by ourshelf, misteral stingers that we bee. Sore knackers to Sham and Shawn! Annie Luvya Liverpool a la long term! Abbasso profungus in arsepick! Flaherty-o for the Missus! (The remarque is out of plays. I withdrawl it entimely with sunblest apollogrease.)

Now *Boatrace of the Hearties as a Ying Yang*, on the upperham, I meal your *Potroast of the Hartebeeste as a York Ham*, ah yer *Prostitute of the Alldust as our Yom Mahon*, well that's a dufferin Cathal O'Fish altargodder. Innis?

RUSSELL DAVIES

VIRGINIA WOOLF · 1882–1941

CLAFOUTIS GRANDMÈRE À LA VIRGINIA WOOLF

[*from* Kafka's Soup: A Complete History of Literature in 17 Recipes.
*Clafoutis Grandmère is a dish from the Limousin region of France, consisting of
black cherries covered with thick pancake batter*]

500g cherries
3 eggs
150g flour
150g sugar
10g yeast, prepared in warm water if necessary
100g butter
1 cup of milk

She placed the cherries in a buttered dish and looked out of the window.
The children were racing across the lawn, Nicholas already between the
clumps of red-hot pokers, turning to wait for the others. Looking back at
the cherries, that would not be pitted, red polka dots on white, so bright
and jolly, their little core of hardness invisible, in pity she thought of
Mrs Sorley, that poor woman with no husband and so many mouths to
feed, Mrs Sorley who knew the hard core but not the softness; and she
placed the dish of cherries to one side.

Gently she melted the butter, transparent and smooth, oleaginous and
clear, clarified and golden, and mixed it with the sugar in a large bowl.
Should she have made something traditionally English? (Involuntarily, piles
of cake rose before her eyes.) Of course the recipe was French, from her
grandmother. English cooking was an abomination: it was boiling cab-
bages in water until they were liquid; it was roasting meat until it was
shrivelled; it was cutting out the flavours with a blunt knife.

She added an egg, pausing to look up at the jacmanna, its colour so
vivid against the whitewashed wall. Would it not be wonderful if Nicholas
became a great artist, all life stretching before him, a blank canvas, bright
coloured shapes gradually becoming clearer? There would be lovers, triumphs, the colours darkening, work, loneliness, struggle. She wished he
could stay as he was now, they were so happy; the sky was so clear, they
would never be as happy again. With great serenity she added an egg, for
was she not descended from that very noble, French house whose female
progeny brought their arts and energy, their sense of colour and shape, wit
and poise to the sluggish English? She added an egg, whose yellow sphere,
falling into the domed bowl, broke and poured, like Vesuvius erupting into
the mixture, like the sun setting into a butter sea. Its broken shell left two

uneven domes on the counter, and all the poverty and all the suffering of Mrs Sorley had turned to that, she thought.

When the flour came it was a delight, a touch left on her cheek as she brushed aside a wisp of hair, as if her beauty bored her and she wanted to be like other people, insignificant, sitting in a widow's house with her pen and paper, writing notes, understanding the poverty, revealing the social problem (she folded the flour into the mixture). She was so commanding (not tyrannical, not domineering; she should not have minded what people said), she was like an arrow set on a target. She would have liked to build a hospital, but how? For now, this clafoutis for Mrs Sorley and her children (she added the yeast, prepared in warm water). The yeast would cause the mixture to rise up into the air like a column of energy, nurtured by the heat of the oven, until the arid kitchen knife of the male, cutting mercilessly, plunged itself into the dome, leaving it flat and exhausted.

Little by little she added the milk, stopping only when the mixture was fluid and even, smooth and homogenous, lumpless and liquid, pausing to recall her notes on the iniquity of the English dairy system. She looked up: what demon possessed him, her youngest, playing on the lawn, demons and angels? Why should it change, why could they not stay as they were, never ageing? (She poured the mixture over the cherries in the dish.) The dome was now become a circle, the cherries surrounded by the yeasty mixture that would cradle and cushion them, the yeasty mixture that surrounded them all, the house, the lawn, the asphodels, that devil Nicholas running past the window, and she put it in a hot oven. In thirty minutes it would be ready.

MARK CRICK

This scene is partly inspired by the dinner in To the Lighthouse *in which Mrs Ramsay (whose grandmother was French) serves a triumphant* bœuf en daube.

A. A. MILNE · 1882–1956

WHEN WE WERE VERY SILLY

John Percy
Said to his nursy,
    'Nursy,' he said, said he,
'Tell father
I'd much rather
    He didn't write books about me.'

'Lawkamercy!'
Shouted nursy,
    'John Percy,' said she,
'If dad stopped it,
If dad dropped it,
    We shouldn't have honey for tea!'
            'BEACHCOMBER' (J. B. MORTON)

HAPPINESS

[after the poem of that name]

John had
Great Big
Waterproof
Boots on;
John had a
Great Big
Waterproof
Hat;
John had a
Great Big
Waterproof
Mackintosh—
Let's face it,
John had a thing about Waterproof.
                    ANON.

CHRISTOPHER ROBIN GOES COUGHETY COUGH

Christopher Robin is drawing his pension;
    He lives in a villa in Spain;
He suffers from chronic bronchitis and tension,
    And never goes out in the rain.

He never wears wellies; he has to eat jellies,
    He peers through a pair of bifocals;
He talks quite a lot to a bear that he's got
    Who is known as El Pu to the locals.

Christopher Robin goes coughety coughety
    Coughety coughety cough;

All sorts and conditions of Spanish physicians
   Have seen him and written him off.

But drowsily still in his house in Seville
   He dreams of the Forest, and Anne,
Who waits in the buttercups—deep in the buttercups—
   Down by the stream—for her man.

PAUL GRIFFIN

WILLIAM CARLOS WILLIAMS · 1883–1963

VARIATIONS ON A THEME BY WILLIAM CARLOS WILLIAMS

[after 'This Is Just to Say'—'I have eaten | the plums | that were in | the icebox . . .']

1

I chopped down the house that you had been
   saving to live in next summer.
I am sorry, but it was morning, and I had nothing
   to do
and its wooden beams were so inviting.

2

We laughed at the hollyhocks together
and then sprayed them with lye.
Forgive me, I simply do not know what I am doing.

3

I gave away the money that you had been saving
   to live on for the next ten years.
The man who asked for it was shabby
And the firm March wind on the porch was so
   juicy and cold.

4

Last evening we went dancing and I broke your leg.
Forgive me. I was clumsy, and
I wanted you here in the wards, where I am a doctor.

KENNETH KOCH

D. H. LAWRENCE · 1885–1930

'OR ONE MIGHT WRITE IT SO': LAWRENCE

One of a group of parodies which are used to vary the narrative in I Crossed the Minch *(1938), an account of a visit to the Hebrides.*

She walked slowly along the road from Barvas to Ness. There were no trees, so she could not observe the sexual shapes of their vegetation, but the sun shining upon the moors assured her that all was not lost. The peewits kept crying, crying, as they chivvied each other with an interminable vivacity. The life of the peewits was a life which was not hers but it was a life akin to hers, a succession of white-hot pinpricks on the dark lining of her senses. Suddenly she saw two crofters engaged in peat-cutting. One of them stood in the ditch and cut the peats with deft strokes of an instrument, the other man received the peats and piled them up in a wall as if they were sandbags. The crofters did not look at her but she knew that they sensed her presence. Though their backs were towards her she knew that they knew she was there. They knew it not with their minds but deep down somewhere in the darkness below the diaphragm. A great joy filled her that the crofters should know she was there even though they turned their backs to her. The soft fresh cakes of peat, fleshly as the thighs of a mulatto woman, called to her like notes of music. As the first crofter cut each peat from the earth it was like a note on the piano. And as the second crofter took the peat-cake from him, took it from its dark bed amid the tacit womb-wisdom of the earth, and placed it on the top of the pile in the hungry glare of the sun, it was like another note on the piano but a note higher up the scale and sustained with a fiercer intensity. Then as she looked at the crofters she felt afraid. She felt afraid that they might suddenly turn and look at her not with their diaphragms but with the intolerable male questioning of their eyes. The crofters were part of the landscape but she was something alien to the landscape. She knew that she was something alien, her flesh contained an alloy, she was something newer and inferior. If the crofters turned and looked at her, it would be as if the whole long sea of the peat moors were to turn round and challenge her presence and tell her she had no right to be there. Ah, but she had a right, she thought, reassured by the crying of the peewits. The shadows of the peewits chivvied each other on the road. They chivvied each other, the peewits, they turned in their tracks in the air, then they came down again low—low and low as if to whisper a message in her ear. She knew in her blood the burden of the message of the peewits and a new self sprang up in her. Not the self which she had brought with her from Glasgow but a new self and yet an older than any of the selves which she had known. A great joy rang through her blood like massed bands and she thought 'I am as old as the crofters. I am only twenty-two in years but I am old with the wisdom of the earth. I am old like the peat which has lain beneath the surface for centuries. I am only waiting like the peat for someone to bring me to the surface, with kind ferocious hands to cut me in blocks and lay me in a pile in the sun.' She began to feel a terrible assurance, an assurance that nothing would stop her, that she would always now get what she wanted, infused with the wisdom of the earth, with the quickness and fullness of the earth that cannot be exhausted. She took the little ordnance map from her pocket and smelled it gently. There was no need to open it or look at it. She knew where she was going. With proud female steps she walked towards Ness like a swallow flying north in the spring.

Louis MacNeice

Marianne Moore · 1887–1972

MISS MOORE AT ASSEMBLY

Based Finically upon an Item in the New York Times *describing Marianne Moore's Lecture Appearance before the students of a Brooklyn High School*

> A 'chattering, gum-snapping audience'
>   held rapt by poetess, hat
>   tricorn, 'gigantic white orchid
>   fluttering at her shoulder'—that
>   suffices, in mid-
> century, to tax one's fittingness's sense.
>
> But why? . . . Birds heard Francis. Who else could come
>   to Eastern District High School
>   ('slum,' 'bubble-gum-snapping') and stand—
>   tobacco-eschewer but Bol-
>   lingen Prize-winner—and
> say, 'I've always wanted to play a snare drum'?

John Updike

EDITH SITWELL · 1887–1964

A THIN FAÇADE FOR EDITH SITWELL

When
Dr
Edith (Hon. D. Litt. [Leeds], Hon. D. Litt. [Durham])
Descends in Mayfair from her brougham
Tall as a chimney stack,
Her
    straight
          back
Encased in a pelisse as black
As cloven Lucifer's silk sack,
She
Enters a bluestockinged club
And, through the Grub Street antics
Of best-selling Corybantes
Who
From castles and from hovels
Meet to contemplate their novels,
Elicits sudden hushes
'Mongst the pudding-colored plushes.
Her hat is a black wheel,
With six spokes of tempered steel,
From her swan's neck hang medallions
Brought from Tenerife in galleons,
And her fingers are afire
With cut amethyst, sapphire,
When
At ease with duke and Cockney,
A transmigratory Procne,
She folds her flutt'ring wing and tail
And perches on the Chippendale.

Yet in that grace marmoreal,
Mantilla'd and Escorial,
Deep
As the sea
On which sails the slant Chinee
She
Sounds the mad note of Ophelia,

The sad organ of Cecilia,
The song of Dian as, a-hunting,
She outraced the brute and grunting
Dryads of the lewd and moody wood.
Up to no good!
She orders Martinis
And quick as Houdinis
The waiters in gaiters return in a trice.
They know as well as we
It
  —was
      she
Who took a verse a-dying
And with her sweet bazooka
Sent its fusty fragments flying.
Encircled by critics
Benign and mephitic,
By poets long dead and *nouveaux*,
She blesses, caresses, and what she dismisses
She kills with the dart of a *mot*.
So.

At lunch as the bards nip
Mutton and parsnip,
The homage like *fromage*
Comes in with the fruit.
'Ah, laureate lady,'
Says one as he reaches
Toward apples and peaches,
'Once cottoned and bent to,
Your tones *quattrocento*,
Who then could descend to
The deserts of prose?'
      'You are sweet,' says she
      (Purring and stirring the oolong),
'To admit you've been smitten
      By these bits that I've written.'
    'Not at all,' says he,
'For the charm, don't you see,
Is a matter, *à fond*, of English *esprit*:
When
Bertie and Harry,
Dirty and hairy,

Loaf by the docks of the gull-splattered sea
In Plymouth and Harwich and Dover,
Who's to oppose their sordid repose,
Who's to amuse them but you?'
        'Lunch is over!' says she.

JOHN MALCOLM BRINNIN

T. S. ELIOT · 1888–1965

WASTE LAND LIMERICKS

I

In April one seldom feels cheerful;
Dry stones, sun and dust make me fearful;
Clairvoyantes distress me,
Commuters depress me—
Met Stetson and gave him an earful.

II

She sat on a mighty fine chair,
Sparks flew as she tidied her hair;
She asks many questions,
I make few suggestions—
Bad as Albert and Lil—what a pair!

III

The Thames runs, bones rattle, rats creep;
Tiresias fancies a peep—
A typist is laid,
A record is played—
Wei la la. After this it gets deep.

IV

A Phoenician called Phlebas forgot
About birds and his business—the lot,
Which is no surprise,
Since he'd met his demise
And been left in the ocean to rot.

V

No water. Dry rocks and dry throats,
Then thunder, a shower of quotes
From the Sanskrit and Dante.
Da. Damyata. Shantih.
I hope you'll make sense of the notes.

WENDY COPE

CHARD WHITLOW

(Mr Eliot's Sunday Evening Postscript)

As we get older we do not get any younger.
Seasons return, and today I am fifty-five,
And this time last year I was fifty-four,
And this time next year I shall be sixty-two.
And I cannot say I should care (to speak for myself)
To see my time over again—if you can call it time,
Fidgeting uneasily under a draughty stair,
Or counting sleepless nights in the crowded Tube.

There are certain precautions—though none of them very reliable—
Against the blast from bombs, or the flying splinter,
But not against the blast from Heaven, *vento dei venti*,
The wind within a wind, unable to speak for wind;
And the frigid burnings of purgatory will not be touched
By any emollient
                    I think you find this put,
Far better than I could ever hope to express it,
In the words of Kharma: 'It is, we believe,
Idle to hope that the simple stirrup-pump
Can extinguish hell.'
                    Oh, listeners,
And you especially who have switched off the wireless,
And sit in Stoke or Basingstoke, listening appreciatively to the silence
(Which is also the silence of hell), pray not for yourselves but your souls.

And pray for me also under the draughty stair.
As we get older we do not get any younger.

And pray for Kharma under the holy mountain.

HENRY REED

One of the finest parodies of Eliot is a Yiddish version of 'The Love Song of J. Alfred Prufrock', 'Der shir hashirim fun Mendl Pumshtok'—'The Song of Songs of Mendl Pumshtok'. ('Shir ha-Shirim' is the Hebrew name of the biblical Song of Songs.)

'Pumshtok' was written in 1937 by Saul Bellow, who was 21 at the time, and his fellow-Chicagoan, the future novelist Isaac Rosenfeld, who was only 19. The greater part of it was the work of Rosenfeld.

Eliot's poem opens, unforgettably,

> Let us go then, you and I,
> When the evening is spread out against the sky
> Like a patient etherised upon a table . . .

The Rosenfeld and Bellow version has an unmistakable Yiddish lilt from its very first word, and it plunges us straight into Jewish lore:

> Nu-zhe, kum-zhe, ikh un du
> Ven der ovnt shteyt uf kegn dem himl
> Vi a leymener goylm af tishebov . . .

('Nu, let us go, you and I, when the evening stands against the sky, like a clay golem on Tisha be-Av . . .' A golem, in medieval Jewish legend, was a creature made of clay and brought to life by magic; Tisha be-Av is the fast day commemorating the destruction of the Temple.)

The streets through which Prufrock then invites us 'follow like a tedious argument | Of insidious intent'. The streets where Pumshtok asks us to accompany him twist themselves 'Vi di bord bay dem rov', 'Like a rabbi's beard'.

Much of the subsequent detail of the parody is comic and downmarket. Prufrock's 'I grow old . . . I grow old . . .' is transformed into 'Ikh ver alt, ikh ver alt | Un der pupik vert mir kalt' ('I grow old, I grow old | And my navel grows cold'). 'Do I dare to eat a peach?' becomes 'Meg ikh oyfesen a floym?' ('May I eat a prune?').

There is a serious point to all this. Rosenfeld and Bellow were hitting out at the notion that they were the products of an inferior culture—that the commanding heights of English literature would be for ever closed to them. And although their parody testifies to Eliot's power as a poet, they were plainly thinking of the unpleasant passages about Jews in his work as well.

RAYMOND CHANDLER · 1888–1959

LAMB WITH DILL SAUCE À LA RAYMOND CHANDLER

[*from* Kafka's Soup: A Complete History of Literature in 17 Recipes]

1 kg lean leg of lamb, cut into large chunks
1 onion, sliced
1 carrot, cut into sticks
1 tablespoon crushed dill seeds, or 3–4 sprigs fresh dill
1 bay leaf
12 peppercorns
½ teaspoon salt
850ml chicken stock
50g butter
1 tablespoon plain flour
1 egg yolk
3 tablespoons cream
2 teaspoons lemon juice

I sipped on my whisky sour, ground out my cigarette on the chopping board and watched a bug trying to crawl out of the basin. I needed a table at Maxim's, a hundred bucks and a gorgeous blonde; what I had was a leg of lamb and no clues. I took hold of the joint. It felt cold and damp, like a coroner's handshake. I took out a knife and cut the lamb into pieces. Feeling the blade in my hand I sliced an onion, and before I knew what I was doing a carrot lay in pieces on the slab. None of them moved. I threw the lot into a pan with a bunch of dill stalks, a bay leaf, a handful of peppercorns and a pinch of salt. They had it coming to them, so I covered them with chicken stock and turned up the heat. I wanted them to boil slowly, just about as slowly as anything can boil. An hour and a half and a half-pint of bourbon later they weren't so tough and neither was I. I separated the meat from the vegetables and covered it to keep it moist. The knife was still in my hand but I couldn't hear any sirens.

In this town the grease always rises to the top, so I strained the juice and skimmed off the fat. I added more water and put it back on the heat. It was time to deal with the butter and flour, so I mixed them together into a paste and added it to the stock. There wasn't a whisk, so using my blackjack I beat out any lumps until the paste was smooth. It started to boil, so I let it simmer for two minutes.

I roughed up the egg yolk and cream and mixed in some of the hot sauce before putting the lot back into the pan. I put the squeeze on a lemon and it soon juiced. It was easy. It was much too easy, but I knew if I let the sauce boil the yolk was gonna scramble.

By now I was ready to pour the sauce over the meat and serve, but I wasn't hungry. The blonde hadn't showed. She was smarter than I thought. I went outside to poison myself, with cigarettes and whisky.

MARK CRICK

AGATHA CHRISTIE · 1890–1976

from THE ACT OF ROGER MURGATROYD

The Act of Roger Murgatroyd (2006) is the first of three novels featuring a celebrated author of detective stories called Evadne Mount, who is at once very unlike Agatha Christie and curiously reminiscent of her. The two subsequent volumes in the trilogy are A Mysterious Affair of Style *(2007) and the more convoluted* And Then There Was No One *(2008).*

Roger Murgatroyd, which takes place over Christmas in the mid-1930s, is set in a manor house on the edge of Dartmoor, the home of Colonel ffolkes and his wife. The ffolkeses have invited a number of guests for the holidays; they also have to put up with an obnoxious gatecrasher, until he is murdered under baffling circumstances.

The house is snowbound, and the telephone lines are down, but fortunately a retired Scotland Yard Chief-Inspector is living in an isolated cottage a few miles away. Two guests battle their way through the snow and bring him back to the house, where he takes temporary charge of the case. First, accompanied by the Colonel and one or two others, he goes up to take a look at the attic where the body was discovered, and is still lying. Then he returns to the drawing room, where Mrs ffolkes and the remaining guests are assembled, along with Chitty the butler.

Downstairs in the drawing-room the ffolkeses' house-guests were looking more dishevelled than ever. Stale cigarette smoke hung in the air, two of the womenfolk, Mary ffolkes and Cynthia Wattis, the Vicar's wife, had nodded off, faded fashion magazines lying half-browsed on their laps, and even Chitty, who prided himself that his employers had never once had occasion to see him other than unbowed and upright, was starting to flag.

When the Colonel entered, however, followed by the rest of the small investigative party, they all wearily roused themselves, the women adjusting their hair, the men re-knotting the cords of their dressing-gowns, and waited expectantly to hear what the man from Scotland Yard had to say.

It was, however, Roger ffolkes who spoke first. Turning to the Chief-Inspector, he asked:

'Perhaps now you'd like me to introduce my guests?'

'Certainly,' said Trubshawe. 'Be my guest. Or rather, be my host, what?'

'Ha, very neat, yes,' said the Colonel with a half-hearted smile. 'Oh, and I trust you'll excuse our varying states of undress. We've all been caught a bit off-guard, you know.'

'Please, please . . . In my profession, ladies, gentlemen, I'm quite used to it. I remember once arresting a villain while he was taking his bath. Can you believe it, even though I'd begun to read him his rights—"You aren't obliged to say anything, but anything you do say, etc., etc."—he continued to sit there calmly soaping himself!

'When I protested, you know what his answer was, the cheeky blighter? "You do want me to come clean, don't you, Mr Trubshawe?" '

There was more mild laughter at this witticism. But since no one was really in the mood for jocular wordplay, the Colonel at once proceeded to the round of presentations.

'Well now, Trubshawe—cigarettes on the table beside you, by the way, so please do help yourself.'

'Thanks, but I'll stick to this if you don't mind,' answered the Chief-Inspector, waving his still-unlit pipe in the air.

'As you wish,' said the Colonel. 'Now, let's see. On the sofa near the fireplace, over there, that's Clem Wattis, our Vicar, and his wife, Cynthia. Next to Cynthia is Cora Rutherford, the well-known actress, who I'm sure needs no introduction, as they say. Then there's Madge Rolfe, the wife of Dr Rolfe, who's the gentleman standing to her left.'

'Colonel,' interrupted Trubshawe, 'Rolfe and I *have* met. You forget, it was he who drove over to my cottage with young Duckworth.'

'Ah, yes, yes, yes, course it was. Foolish of me. Frightful thing, old age. Now who else haven't you been introduced to yet? Oh yes, my wife Mary.'

'How d'you do, Mrs ffolkes?'

'How d'you do, Inspector Trubshawe?'

'Snap!' said the policeman, and they both smiled, as one does.

'And, of course, Chitty, my butler.'

'Chitty.'

'Sir.'

'As for my daughter Selina,' the Colonel went on, 'I'm afraid . . .'

'Yes?'

'She really was awfully attached to Gentry, so his murder has come as a tremendous shock to her. She's gone up to her room to rest. Naturally, if you insist on her being here, I can always—'

'That won't be necessary for the moment. Later—when she's better able to tell me what she knows. I think, too, it might be wise if your butler is excused.'

On hearing these words, Chitty gave the policeman a respectful nod and may even have said something equally respectful, except that, if he did, he said it so butlerishly *sotto voce* the Chief-Inspector was unlikely to have heard what it was. Then, without waiting to be requested to do so by the Colonel, he left the room.

After watching him go, Trubshawe turned to face the whole company.

'Well now, ladies and gentlemen,' he said, 'as you don't need to be told, this is a most terrible and mysterious crime you've got yourselves entangled in. I literally couldn't believe my ears when I was first told what had happened but, having been up to the attic and seen for myself, I have to believe them now. In effect, the murderer contrived to get in, kill Raymond Gentry, then get out again, apparently without opening either a door or a window. I don't mind admitting I'm dumbfounded.

'What I require, though, is for one of you to fill me in on the events that led up to the murder itself. Coming over here in the car, Dr Rolfe and Mr Duckworth did give me a sketchy account, but, what with stopping and starting and getting out to push and getting back in again, well—you'll excuse me, gents, I'm sure you understand what I'm saying—but what I need now is a more coherent version, one with a beginning, a middle and an end in that order. Would any of you,' he said, glancing at everybody in turn, 'care to volunteer? Just one, mind.'

There was a moment's silence, then Mary ffolkes began to say:

'Well, it does seem to me that . . .'

'Yes, Mrs ffolkes?'

'I was going to suggest Evie. She's the writer Evadne Mount, you know. And, well, it *is* her job to tell stories—indeed, just this sort of a story. So I thought . . .'

'Uh huh,' murmured Trubshawe, his fingers drumming a restless tattoo on the mantelpiece. 'Ye-es, I suppose she would be the obvious choice.'

You could see, however, that he was less than ecstatic at the prospect of even temporarily surrendering the reins to his redoubtable rival in matters of criminality.

Evadne Mount could see it too.

'Now look, Trubshawe,' she said pettishly, 'I'll be happy to oblige but, if you'd rather it weren't me, then all you have to do is say so. I don't easily take offence, you know,' she added with less conviction.

'Oh, but you're wrong, Miss Mount,' he tactfully replied. 'I'd be pleased, very pleased, if you were to give me a rundown of what occurred here yesterday. All I'd say—but I'm sure I really don't need to—is, well, just stick to the facts. Keep your imagination for your whodunits.'

'Now that *is* a remark I might be offended by,' said the novelist, 'if I were so minded. But because it's you, Trubshawe, and I've already taken a shine to you, I'm going to pretend I didn't hear it. So, yes, I'd be happy to give you an account of everything leading up to Gentry's murder. When would you like it?'

'No time like the present.'

Stepping away from the fireside, Trubshawe indicated that place on the sofa next to where the Reverend Wattis was seated.

'Mind if I park myself here? Beside you?'

'Not at all,' answered the Vicar, shifting sideways to make room for the detective's generous frame.

'Now,' said the Chief-Inspector to Evadne Mount, 'if you would . . .'

GILBERT ADAIR

COLE PORTER · 1891–1964

YOU'RE THE TOP

[a revised version]

You're the top!
You're Miss Pinkham's tonic.
You're the top!
You're a high colonic.
You're the burning heat of a bridal suite in use,
You're the breasts of Venus,
You're King Kong's penis,
You're self-abuse.
You're an arch
In the Rome collection.
You're the starch
In a groom's erection.
I'm a eunuch who
Has just been through an op,
But if, Baby, I'm the bottom
You're the top.

ANON.

The authorship of this 'underground' version of one of Porter's most famous songs is in dispute. It has often been assumed to be by Porter himself, but it has also frequently been attributed to Irving Berlin. (The two composers were friends.)

from 'LET'S DO IT'

[*a revised version*]

Our leading writers in swarms do it,
Somerset and all the Maughams do it,
Let's do it, let's fall in love.
The Brontës felt that they must do it,
Mrs Humphry Ward could just do it,
Let's do it, let's fall in love.
Anouilh and Sartre—God knows why—do it,
As a sort of a curse
Eliot and Fry do it,
But they do it in verse.
Some mystics, as a routine do it,
Even Evelyn Waugh and Graham Greene do it,
Let's do it, let's fall in love.

NOËL COWARD

The fifth line of this verse has sometimes been sung with 'Ernest Hemingway'
substituted for 'Mrs Humphry Ward'.

EDNA ST VINCENT MILLAY · 1892–1950

MISS MILLAY SAYS SOMETHING TOO

I want to drown in good-salt water,
I want my body to bump the pier;
Neptune is calling his wayward daughter,
Crying, 'Edna, come over here!'

I hate the town and I hate the people;
I hate the dryness of floor and pave;
The spar of a ship is my tall church-steeple;
My soul is wet as the wettest wave.

I'm seven-eighths salt and I want to roister
Deep in the brine with the submarine;
I speak the speech of the whale and oyster;
I know the ways of the wild sardine.

I'm tired of standing still and staring
Across the sea with my heels in dust:
I want to live like the sober herring,
And die as pickled when die I must.

SAMUEL HOFFENSTEIN

ALDOUS HUXLEY · 1894–1963

from 'TOLD IN GATH'

Inspired by Aldous Huxley's early novels in general. The title, 'Told in Gath', points a finger at Eyeless in Gaza, *published in 1936, but the spirit of the piece is rather closer to that of such works of the 1920s as* Crome Yellow *and* Antic Hay.

> *'Vulgarity is the garlic in the salad of charm.'*
>
> ST BUMPUS

It was to be a long week-end, thought Giles Pentateuch apprehensively, as the menial staggered up the turret stairs with his luggage—staggered all the more consciously for the knowledge that he was under observation, just as, back in Lexham Gardens, his own tyrannical Amy would snort and groan outside the door to show how steep the back-stairs were, before entering with his simple vegetarian breakfast of stink-wort and boiled pond-weed. A long week-end; but a week-end at Groyne! And he realized, with his instinct for merciless analysis that amounted almost to torture, that in spite, yes, above all, in spite of the apprehension, because of it even, he would enjoy all the more saying afterwards, to his friend Luke Snarthes perhaps, or to little Reggie Ringworm, 'Yes, I was at Groyne last week-end,' or 'Yes, I was there when the whole thing started, down at Groyne.'

The menial had paused and was regarding him. To tip or not to tip? How many times had he not been paralysed by that problem? To tip was to give in, yes, selfishly to give in to his hatred of human contacts, to contribute half a crown as hush-money, to obtain 'protection,' protection from other people, so that for a little he could go on with the luxury of being Giles Pentateuch, 'scatologist and eschatologist,' as he dubbed himself. Whereas not to tip . . .

For a moment he hesitated. What would Luke Snarthes have done? Stayed at home, with that splayed ascetic face of his, or consulted his guru, Chandra Nandra? No—no tip! The menial slunk away. He looked round the room. It was comfortable, he had to admit; a few small Longhis round the walls, a Lupanar by Guido Guidi, and over the bed an outsize Stuprum Sabinarum, by Rubens—civilized people, his hosts, evidently.

He glanced at the books on the little table—the *Odes of Horace, Rome* 23 B.C., apparently a first edition, the *Elegancies of Meursius* (Rochester's copy), *The Piccadilly Ambulator, The Sufferings of Saint Rose of Lima, Nostradamus* (the Lérins Press), *Swedenborg, The Old Man's Gita.* 'And cultivated,' he murmured, 'too.' The bathroom, with its sun-lamp and Plombières apparatus, was such as might be found in any sensible therapeutic home. He went down to tea considerably refreshed by his lavage.

The butler announced that Lady Rhomboid was 'serving' on the small west lawn, and he made his way over the secular turf with genuine pleasure. For Minnie Rhomboid was a remarkable woman.

'How splendid of you to come,' she croaked, for she had lost her voice in the old suffragette days. 'You know my daughter, Ursula Groyne.'

'Only too well,' laughed Giles, for they had been what his set at Balliol used to call 'lovers.'

'And Mrs. Amp, of course?'

'Of course!'

'And Mary Pippin?'

'Decidedly,' he grimaced.

'And the men,' she went on. 'Giles Pentateuch—this is Luke Snarthes and Reggie Ringworm and Mr Encolpius and Roland Narthex. Pentateuch writes—let me see?—like a boot, isn't it?' (Her voice was a husky roar.) 'Yes, a boot with a mission! Oh, but I forgot'—and she laughed delightedly—'you're all writers!'

'Encantado, I'm sure!' responded Giles. 'But we've all met before. I see you have the whole Almanach de Golgotha in fact,' he added.

Mary Pippin, whose arm had been eaten away by termites in Tehuantepec, was pouring out with her free hand. 'Orange Pekoe or *Chandu*, Giles?' she burbled in her delicious little voice. 'Like a carrier pigeon's,' he thought.

'*Chandu*, please.' And she filled him a pipe of the consoling poppy, so that in a short while he was smoking away like all the others.

'Yes, yes,' continued Mr Encolpius, in his oily voice which rose and fell beneath the gently moving tip of his nose, 'Man axalotl here below but I ask very little. Some fragments of Pamphylides, a Choctaw blood-mask, the prose of Scaliger the Elder, a painting by Fuseli, an occasional visit to the all-in wrestling, or to my meretrix; a cook who can produce a passable "poulet à la Khmer," a Pong vase. Simple tastes, you will agree, and it is my simple habit to indulge them!'

Giles regarded him with fascination. That nose, it was, yes, it was definitely a proboscis. . . .

'But how can you, how can you?' It was Ursula Groyne. 'How *can* you when there are two million unemployed, when Russia has reintroduced anti-abortionary legislation, when Iceland has banned *Time and Tide*, when the Sedition Bill hangs over us all like a rubber truncheon?'

Mary Pippin cooed delightedly; this was intellectual life with a vengeance—definitely haybrow—only it was so difficult to know who was right. Giles, at that moment, found her infinitely desirable.

'Yes, and worse than that.' It was Luke Snarthes, whose strained voice emerged from his tortured face like a cobra from the snake-charmer's basket. 'Oh, decidedly, appallingly worse. The natives of Ceylon take the slender Loris and hold it over the fire till its eyes pop, to release the magic juices. Indicible things are done to geese that you may eat your runions with a sauce of *foie gras*. Caviare is ripped from the living sturgeon, karakul fur torn from the baby lamb inside its mother. The creaking plates of the live dismembered lobster scream to you from the *Homard Newburg*, the oyster winces under the lemon. How would *you* like, Mr Encolpius, to be torn from your bed, embarrelled, prised open with a knife, seasoned with a few drips of vitriol, shall we say, and sprayed with a tabasco as strong as mustard-gas to give you flavour; then to be swallowed alive and handed over to a giant's digestive juices?'

'I shouldn't like it at all!' said Mr Encolpius, 'just as I shouldn't, for that matter, like living at the bottom of the sea and changing my sex every three years. Not that it might not'—and he twitched his nose at Mary Pippin—'have its compensations.'

'S-s-s-s-s-s-s-s-s-s-s-s-s-s-s-s-s-s-s-s-s-suppose,' said Reggie Ringworm, who stammered, etc., 'vat ve thilly oythter is weally weady and villing to be ab-s-s-s-s-orbed, I mean ab-th-th-th-th-th-thorbed, by our fwend, vat vat is in f-f-f-fact exactly ve end for which it has been cweated. Vat th-then?'

'What are we to think then,' snarled Snarthes savagely, 'of the Person or Purpose who created creatures for such an end? Awful!' And he took out his notebook and wrote rapidly, 'The end justifies the means! But the end *is* the means! And how rarely, how confoundedly rarely, can we even say the end justifies the end! Like Oxenstierna, like Ximenes, like Waldorf, we must be men of means'—he closed the book with a snap—'men of golden means.'

'I know what you mean,' cried Mary Pippin from her dovecot. 'That if Cleopatra's nose had been half an inch longer Menelaus would never have run away with her!'

Luke's face softened, and he spread out his splayed fingers almost tenderly. 'And I don't mind wagering, if we can believe Diodorus Siculus, that, the nose unaltered, she bore a remarkable likeness, Mary, to you!'

'Ah, but can we believe old Siculus?' The other nose quested speculative. 'Any more than we can believe old Paterculus, old Appian, Arrian, Ossian, and Orrian? Now a Bolivar Corona or a nicely chambered glass of sparkling Douro—even a pretty tea-gown by Madame Groult, I opine'—and he bowed to Mary—'these convince me. They have a way with one. Oh, yes, a way, decidedly! And just because they have that way it is necessary for me to combine them, how often, how distressingly often, with my lamentable visits to the Ring at Blackfriars, or to my meretrix in Holland Park. Why is it that we needs must see the highest though we loathe it? That happy in my mud—my hedonistic, radio-active, but never-the-less quite genuine nostalgic *boue*, I should be reminded of the stars, of you, Miss Pippin, and of Cleopatra?' And he snuffled serio-comically, 'Why can't you let Hell alone?'

A gong rang discreetly. The butler removed the pipes and Mrs Amp and Roland Narthex, who were still in a state of kif, while the others went away to dress . . .

Cyril Connolly

Ernest Hemingway · 1899–1961

ACROSS THE STREET AND INTO THE GRILL

[*written shortly after the publication of Hemingway's least esteemed novel,* Across the River and into the Trees]

This is my last and best and true and only meal, thought Mr Perley as he descended at noon and swung east on the beat-up sidewalk of Forty-fifth Street. Just ahead of him was the girl from the reception desk. I am a little fleshed up around the crook of the elbow, thought Perley, but I commute good.

He quickened his step to overtake her and felt the pain again. What a stinking trade it is, he thought. But after what I've done to other assistant treasurers, I can't hate anybody. Sixteen deads, and I don't know how many possibles.

The girl was near enough now so he could smell her fresh receptiveness, and the lint in her hair. Her skin was light blue, like the sides of horses.

'I love you,' he said, 'and we are going to lunch together for the first and only time, and I love you very much.'

'Hello, Mr Perley,' she said, overtaken. 'Let's not think of anything.'

A pair of fantails flew over from the sad old Guaranty Trust Company, their wings set for a landing. A lovely double, thought Perley, as he pulled. 'Shall we go to the Hotel Biltmore, on Vanderbilt Avenue, which is merely a feeder lane for the great streets, or shall we go to Schrafft's, where my old friend Botticelli is captain of girls and where they have the mayonnaise in fiascos?'

'Let's go to Schrafft's,' said the girl, low. 'But first I must phone Mummy.'
She stepped into a public booth and dialled true and well, using her finger.
Then she telephoned.

As they walked on, she smelled good. She smells good, thought Perley.
But that's all right, I add good. And when we get to Schrafft's, I'll order
from the menu, which I like very much indeed.

They entered the restaurant. The wind was still west, ruffling the edges
of the cookies. In the elevator, Perley took the controls. 'I'll run it,' he said
to the operator. 'I checked out long ago.' He stopped true at the third floor,
and they stepped off into the men's grill.

'Good morning, my Assistant Treasurer,' said Botticelli, coming forward
with a fiasco in each hand. He nodded at the girl, who he knew was from
the West Seventies and whom he desired.

'Can you drink the water here?' asked Perley. He had the fur trapper's
eye and took in the room at a glance, noting that there was one empty table
and three pretty waitresses.

Botticelli led the way to the table in the corner, where Perley's flanks
would be covered.

'Alexanders,' said Perley. 'Eighty-six to one. The way Chris mixes them.
Is this table all right, Daughter?'

Botticelli disappeared and returned soon, carrying the old Indian
blanket.

'That's the same blanket, isn't it?' asked Perley.

'Yes. To keep the wind off,' said the Captain, smiling from the backs of
his eyes. 'It's still west. It should bring the ducks in tomorrow, the chef
thinks.'

Mr Perley and the girl from the reception desk crawled down under the
table and pulled the Indian blanket over them so it was solid and good and
covered them right. The girl put her hand on his wallet. It was cracked and
old and held his commutation book. 'We are having fun, aren't we?' she
asked.

'Yes, Sister,' he said.

'I have here the soft-shelled crabs, my Assistant Treasurer,' said Botticelli.
'And another fiasco of the 1926. This one is cold.'

'Dee the soft-shelled crabs,' said Perley from under the blanket. He put
his arm around the receptionist good.

'Do you think we should have a green pokeweed salad?' she asked. 'Or
shall we not think of anything for a while?'

'We shall not think of anything for a while, and Botticelli would bring
the pokeweed if there was any,' said Perley. 'It isn't the season.' Then he
spoke to the Captain. 'Botticelli, do you remember when we took all the
mailing envelopes from the stockroom, spit on the flaps, and then drank
rubber cement till the foot soldiers arrived?'

'I remember, my Assistant Treasurer,' said the Captain. It was a little joke they had.

'He used to mimeograph pretty good,' said Perley to the girl. 'But that was another war. Do I bore you, Mother?'

'Please keep telling me about your business experiences, but not the rough parts.' She touched his hand where the knuckles were scarred and stained by so many old mimeographings. 'Are both your flanks covered, my dearest?' she asked, plucking at the blanket. They felt the Alexanders in their eyeballs. Eighty-six to one.

'Schrafft's is a good place and we're having fun and I love you,' Perley said. He took another swallow of the 1926, and it was a good and careful swallow. 'The stockroom men were very brave,' he said, 'but it is a position where it is extremely difficult to stay alive. Just outside that room there is a little bare-assed highboy and it is in the way of the stuff that is being brought up. The hell with it. When you make a breakthrough, Daughter, first you clean out the baskets and the half-wits, and all the time they have the fire escapes taped. They also shell you with old production orders, many of them approved by the general manager in charge of sales. I am boring you and I will not at this time discuss the general manager in charge of sales as we are unquestionably being listened to by that waitress over there who is setting out the decoys.'

'I am going to give you my piano,' the girl said, 'so that when you look at it you can think of me. It will be something between us.'

'Call up and have them bring the piano to the restaurant,' said Perley. 'Another fiasco, Botticelli!'

They drank the sauce. When the piano came, it wouldn't play. The keys were stuck good. 'Never mind, we'll leave it here, Cousin,' said Perley.

They came out from under the blanket and Perley tipped their waitress exactly fifteen per cent minus withholding. They left the piano in the restaurant, and when they went down the elevator and out and turned in to the old, hard, beat-up pavement of Fifth Avenue and headed south toward Forty-fifth Street, where the pigeons were, the air was as clean as your grandfather's howitzer. The wind was still west.

I commute good, thought Perley, looking at his watch. And he felt the old pain of going back to Scarsdale again.

E. B. WHITE

GRAHAM GREENE · 1904–1991

In August 1965 a week-end competition in the New Statesman *invited readers to submit an extract from the life of a public figure by a namesake—from Angus Wilson writing about Harold Wilson, for example. One of the winners was Sebastian Eleigh, who offered a passage from a biography of Hugh Carleton Greene (Director General of the BBC) by his brother Graham:*

Hugh lost his faith the day I hit him on the head with a croquet mallet, and years later at his desk in Broadcasting House, arranging some series of talks by atheists, he would feel his mind darkened by the shadow of the falling mallet as by the wing of a great bird.

I was twelve that summer and already conscious of God moving among the weeds between the raspberry canes. Hugh was six.

The nursery maid of the day (our mother changed them with the frequency of young girls in a Gran Bassa brothel) crunched by on the gravel, her thighs sleek as a cat's. But it was in one of her plump calves that Hugh sank his teeth, through the acrid black stocking to the succulent flesh.

I swung the mallet. Was it a foretaste of adult jealousy? I had known her for a week as an instrument of pleasure. Or was it that, as the blood spurted, I had some vague presentiment of my brother's future, the godless and orgiastic roads he was to follow, the too brilliant ascent, the sudden fall exactly fifty years later under the goads of the Puritans, the seedy and mysterious end.

It subsequently turned out that 'Sebastian Eleigh' was in fact none other than Hugh Greene. And meanwhile Graham, writing as 'Malcolm Collins', had also won a prize. He too—pretending to be someone imitating himself—had submitted an extract from a biography of his brother:

I begin this biography therefore in the year 1920—on one of those long summer days at Berkhamsted, among the empty buildings of a school out-of-term, when my green gauge O clockwork train burst through a cordon of lead soldiers (in the uniforms of the South African war) and broke the siege of my headquarters. 'I am betrayed by my own men,' Hugh said, and climbed sadly the long stairway, past silent dormitories, to the room we both shared.

Graham Greene had twice before submitted parodies of himself to New Statesman *competitions under assumed names, once in 1948 and once in 1961. The second of them, a passage from a supposed verse autobiography, he later turned into prose and incorporated in his memoir* A Sort of Life.

In 1980 he also tried his hand at a competition in the Spectator, *for 'an extract from an imaginary novel by Graham Greene'. (This time he used the name 'Colin Bates'.) His entry was not one of the five which the magazine chose to print, but he had the consolation of being able to use it some years later as the opening of his novella* The Captain and the Enemy.

NANCY MITFORD · 1904–1973

THE PURSUIT OF FAME

'His grace doesn't half sound in a wax this morning, ducks.'

And certainly the fairly big house, that in France would have been called a private hotel, in Kensington Gardens resounded with roars of rage from Uncle Hambrose's study downstairs.

'Bet he's had another bad review,' sighed Popsy, who was having her ears scrubbed and attempting to read *La Madone des Sleepings* at the same time. 'He'll be gunning for me any moment now, I suppose.'

The explosion of a blunderbuss pistol—a relic of Uncle Hambrose's service in the Artists' Rifles (Home Guard Section)—proved her to possess prophecy in addition to her other gifts.

'Come down at once, Popsy, you dreary little witch!'

'Oh dear, I better dash,' and disregarding Nannie's 'Put on a clean pinny first,' Popsy headed for the staircase.

Uncle Hambrose—a name which had been in the family for generations, the H silent as in *heraldique*—motioned her grimly through the door of his study with the smoking antique. Over the mantel- or rather *chimney*-piece hung the dried heads of four critics who had reviewed adversely his *Anatomy of Snobbery*, and the framed copy of *Burke's Peerage* with which he had battered them to death.

'Rotten press, Uncle?'

'*Press!*' said Uncle Hambrose disgustedly. 'An expression, I presume, you've picked up from that correspondence course of yours—what? Damned if I know where all this modern Non-U education is leading to, I'm sure.'

'The Book Society Choice, I hope, Uncle Hambrose.'

'And the best-seller lists, eh? Well, one thing about you, you certainly know what you want, even if you do write about "the gift of the gab" and people "unburdening" themselves and "flats" "decorated in the most expensive kind of modern taste". Comes of reading too many fashion magazines, I suppose. Still, if you want to sell thirty thousand copies you can't have too much of that kind of tripe, alas!'

'That's what I thought, Uncle.'

'Now, this novel of yours—shocking stuff, but it's got points already—what the deuce made you call it *Love à la Française*? Nothing about Frogs in it.'

'Good selling-title, Uncle. Besides——'

'*Title!*' interrupted Uncle Hambrose scornfully. 'Only book-sellers and travellers and sewers—I mean reviewers—talk about *titles*. It's a trade-term, fit only for the use of tradesmen! *I* have a *title*—books have names. Is that plain?'

'Yes, Uncle. But I was going to tell you about this Frenchman. The hero of my novel. He comes in half-way through, sweeps poor blissful Belinda off her feet, and sets her up in a fl—an *appartement* in the Bois. She becomes a sort of *tartine de haute classe*, you see, with mounds of swish Paris frocks and simply ravishing hats with flowers all over them and high cork-soled shoes, and——'

'But what about the Frog himself? Has he got a title?'

'His *name*, Uncle, is Jean-Marie-Dagobert de la Haultcouture-Clichy.'

'I mean, does he belong to the *noblesse*? *Les gens de la haute, quoi!*'

'He's a *Marquis*, descent as long as your arm, coming straight down from Charlemagne. Of course, I *could* make him a *Duc* if you think it'd have more snob-appeal . . .'

'Rubbish! *I'm* a duke, and where did it ever get me? Called a snob by some puling highbrow, that's what, and all because I had a coronet stamped on the cover of my book! No, Popsy, you take my tip and play safe. Make him a Prince—a Prince of the Blood! You can't go far wrong then.'

'Oh, Uncle Hambrose, what a spiffing idea! Why, that'd make Belinda almost a—a King's Mistress, wouldn't it?' said Popsy, enchanted at this prospect. Already new scenes were taking shape in her mind: a dinner-party at some great French House, perhaps even a Ball: the door opening on 'a kaleidoscope of glitter', women—all beauties, of course—'sparkling with jewels', moving on 'warm waves of scent . . .'

'Plenty of clichés, that's the ticket,' Uncle Hambrose was saying, as though he'd read her thoughts. ' 'Course, they teach you all that at the correspondence school, I dare say, but still, in handling the scenes in *la Société* you can't have too many. Now this Jean-Thing, what's he look like, eh? Tall, dark and elegant, I'll be bound. And what's he say when he first meets this girl?'

' "*Vous avez failli me faire attendre*," Uncle. You see, he's frightfully over-bearing, really madly rude—at least he would be for an Englishman, but French aristocrats haven't any manners except when they're with people of their own *genre*, and that's just what makes Belinda such a sitter for him . . .'

'Yes, yes, the Rochester touch. Never fails with the female reading public, never has, never will. Don't forget to have him say that opening sentence is a quotation from an ancestor of his—gives the clue to his royal descent right away. Play the French stuff as blatantly *snob* as you like, everyone'll lap it up. *But*—and here's a word of warning, my girl—go easy on the English side. Naturally the English characters must all have titles too, and you must get that information over in the first few pages, but *do it gently*. Let the reader find it out almost for herself. Casual understatement. Modesty. Bit of quiet patriotic blah about the beautiful country-side here and there——'

'And then, once we're in France, I can really go to town?'

Uncle Hambrose shuddered. '*London*, my dear—not *"town"*. Really, these bourgeois expressions aren't suitable for a gentlewoman. Where was I now? Oh, yes. Encourage all the conventional ideas about the French— that Frenchwomen, especially of the upper *ton*, are chic and have "perfect taste", that the French are "practical" and have love-affairs—"discreetly", of course—all over the shop after marriage, that French handwriting is unreadable and French *cuisine* always delicious—you know the sort of muck, I don't doubt.'

'I do indeed, Uncle. I'm giving darling Belinda a rival—Reine-Bécas-sine de la Tour Eiffel, she's called, married to a *Vicomte*—but Jean-Marie-Dagobert's wise old *cousine-germaine*, who's been a terrific hit with the *gentilhommes* in her day . . .'

'Yes, yes. Spare me the rest. I'm sure it all works out happily in the end. But a last bit of advice—don't keep your Frenchman from appearing until the middle. Bring him on straight away—in the first few lines, if possible. Then the female public'll be slayed—as you'd doubtless put it—from the word Go. And it's the gentlewomen—God bless 'em!—that we're really after, eh?'

'*Et comment*, Uncle Hambrose!'

'Oh, and make this Frog-Prince a general too. Never does any harm— remember Miss Du Maurier.'

'She's never absent from my thoughts, Uncle.'

'Excellent! Well that's all for now, you little stinker. Run along and play with your skunk.'

'Nightie-night, Uncle. And *noblesse* blooming well *oblige*.'

JULIAN MACLAREN-ROSS

ANTHONY POWELL · 1905–2000

LITTLE JACK HORNER

Horner had got himself established as far as possible from the centre of the room and I was suddenly made aware, as one often is by actions which are in themselves quite common-place, that he was about to do something which would give him enormous satisfaction. He had somehow acquired a large seasonal confection which he was beginning to attack with a degree of enthusiasm I had not seen him display since the midnight feasts we had enjoyed at school. Eschewing the normal recourse to eating utensils, he plunged his hand through the pastry and extracted an entire fruit, an achievement which was accompanied by a cry of self-congratulation and a beatific expression reminiscent of some of those on the faces one sees in the more popular of the Pre-Raphaelite portraits.

ALAN ALEXANDER

AN EXTRACT FROM THE DIARY OF ANTHONY POWELL

22nd January 1995: I received a telephone call from a Professor Wildenstein at Princeton University. He wanted to give me a large amount of money. This is the sort of thing the Americans do very well. He said that I was to be awarded some literary prize or other worth 50,000 dollars, and would I do him the honour, etc, of accepting it. Really the most awful bore, but I suppose one must humour these types. Reluctantly, I accept, wondering why he could just have posted it to me, without the need for 'acceptance'. Needless to say, he was delighted. I have noticed in the past that many Americans pronounce 'Dance' with a sharp 'a', rather than a long 'a'. Have others noticed this too, or is it my novelist's ear? I ask him to send the cheque, but, please, no accompanying letter, as these congratulatory missives can prove tedious to plough through.

Re-read the poems of W. B. Yeats. Very Irish.

CRAIG BROWN

JOHN BETJEMAN · 1906–1984

BETJEMAN, 1984

I saw him in the Airstrip Gardens
   (Fahrenheit at 451)
Feeding automative orchids
   With a little plastic bun,
While above his brickwork cranium
   Burned the trapped and troubled sun.

'Where is Piper? Where is Pontefract?
   (Devil take my boiling pate!)
Where is Pam? and where's Myfanwy?
   Don't remind me of the date!
Can it be that I am *really*
   Knocking on for 78?

'In my splendid State Apartment
   Underneath a secret lock
Finger now forbidden treasures
   (Pray for me St Enodoc!):
TV plate and concrete lamp-post
   And a single nylon sock.

'Take your ease, pale-haired admirer,
   As I, half the century saner,
Pour a vintage Mazawattee
   Through the Marks and Spencer strainer
In a *genuine* British Railways
   (Luton Made) cardboard container.

'Though they say my verse-compulsion
   Lacks an interstellar drive,
Reading Beverley and Daphne
   Keeps *my* sense of words alive.
Lord, but *how* much beauty was there
   Back in 1955!'

CHARLES CAUSLEY

CLIFFORD ODETS · 1906–1963

WAITING FOR SANTY

A Christmas Playlet

Scene: The sweatshop of S. Claus, a manufacturer of children's toys, on North Pole Street. Time: The night before Christmas.

At rise, seven gnomes, RANKIN, PANKEN, RIVKIN, RISKIN, RUSKIN, BRISKIN, *and* PRASKIN, *are discovered working furiously to fill orders piling up at stage right. The whir of lathes, the hum of motors, and the hiss of drying lacquer are so deafening that at times the dialogue cannot be heard, which is very vexing if you vex easily. (Note: The parts of* RANKIN, PANKEN, RIVKIN, RISKIN, RUSKIN, BRISKIN, *and* PRASKIN *are interchangeable, and may be secured directly from your dealer or the factory.)*

RISKIN (*filing a Meccano girder, bitterly*): A parasite, a leech, a bloodsucker— altogether a five-star nogoodnick! Starvation wages we get so he can ride around in a red team with reindeers!

RUSKIN (*jeering*): Hey, Karl Marx, whyn'tcha hire a hall?

RISKIN (*sneering*): Scab! Stool pigeon! Company spy! (*They tangle and rain blows on each other. While waiting for these to dry, each returns to his respective task.*)

BRISKIN (*sadly, to* PANKEN): All day long I'm painting 'Snow Queen' on these Flexible Flyers and my little Irving lays in a cold tenement with the gout.

PANKEN: You said before it was the mumps.

BRISKIN (*with a fatalistic shrug*): The mumps—the gout —go argue with City Hall.

PANKEN (*kindly, passing him a bowl*): Here, take a piece fruit.

BRISKIN (*chewing*): It ain't bad, for wax fruit.

PANKEN (*with pride*): I painted it myself.

BRISKIN (*rejecting the fruit*): Ptoo! Slave psychology!

RIVKIN (*suddenly, half to himself, half to the Party*): I got a belly full of stars, baby. You make me feel like I swallowed a Roman candle.

PRASKIN (*curiously*): What's wrong with the kid?

RISKIN: What's wrong with all of us? The system! Two years he and Claus's daughter's been making googoo eyes behind the old man's back.

PRASKIN: So what?

RISKIN (*scornfully*): So what? Economic determinism! What do you think the kid's name is—J. Pierpont Rivkin? He ain't even got for a bottle Dr Brown's Celery Tonic. I tell you, it's like gall in my mouth two young people shouldn't have a room where they could make great music.

RANKIN (*warningly*): Shhh! Here she comes now! (*Stella Claus enters, carrying a portable phonograph. She and* RIVKIN *embrace, place a record on the turntable, and begin a very slow waltz, unmindful that the phonograph is playing 'Cohen on the Telephone'.*)

STELLA (*dreamily*): Love me, sugar?

RIVKIN: I can't sleep, I can't eat, that's how I love you. You're a double malted with two scoops of whipped cream; you're the moon rising over Mosholu Parkway; you're a two weeks' vacation at Camp Nitgedaiget! I'd pull down the Chrysler Building to make a bobbie pin for your hair!

STELLA: I've got a stomach full of anguish. Oh, Rivvy, what'll we do?

PANKEN (*sympathetically*): Here, try a piece fruit.

RIVKIN (*fiercely*): Wax fruit—that's been my whole life! Imitations! Substitutes! Well, I'm through! Stella, to-night I'm telling your old man. He can't play mumblety-peg with two human beings! (*The tickle of sleigh bells is heard offstage, followed by a voice shouting, 'Whoa, Dasher! Whoa, Dancer!' A moment later* S. CLAUS *enters in a gust of mock snow. He is a pompous bourgeois of sixty-five who affects a white beard and a false air of benevolence. But to-night the ruddy colour is missing from his cheeks, his step falters, and he moves heavily. The gnomes hastily replace the marzipan they have been filching.*)

STELLA (*anxiously*): Papa! What did the specialist say to you?

CLAUS (*brokenly*): The biggest professor in the country . . . the best cardiac man that money could buy. . . . I tell you I was like a wild man.

STELLA: Pull yourself together, Sam!

CLAUS: It's no use. Adhesions, diabetes, sleeping sickness, decalcomania—oh, my God! I got to cut out climbing in chimneys, he says—me, Sanford Claus, the biggest toy concern in the world!

STELLA (*soothingly*): After all, it's only one man's opinion.

CLAUS: No, no, he cooked my goose. I'm like a broken uke after a Yosian picnic. Rivkin!

RIVKIN: Yes, Sam.

CLAUS: My boy, I had my eye on you for a long time. You and Stella thought you were too foxy for an old man, didn't you? Well, let bygones be bygones, Stella, do you love this gnome?

STELLA (*simply*): He's the whole stage show at the Music Hall, Papa; he's Toscanini conducting Beethoven's Fifth; he's——

CLAUS (*curtly*): Enough already. Take him. From now on he's a partner in the firm. (*As all exclaim,* CLAUS *holds up his hand for silence.*) And to-night he can take my route and make the deliveries. It's the least I could do for my own flesh and blood. (*As the happy couple kiss,* CLAUS *wipes away a suspicious moisture and turns to the other gnomes.*) Boys, do you know what day to-morrow is?

GNOMES (*crowding around expectantly*): Christmas!

CLAUS: Correct. When you look in your envelopes to-night, you'll find a little present from me—a forty per cent pay cut. And the first one who opens his trap—gets this. (*As he holds up a tear-gas bomb and beams at them, the gnomes utter cries of joy, join hands, and dance around him shouting exultantly. All except* RISKIN *and* BRISKIN, *that is, who exchange a quick glance and go underground.*)

Curtain

S. J. PERELMAN

Odets made his name with the political drama Waiting for Lefty.

W. H. AUDEN · 1907–1973

AUDENESQUE FOR AN INITIATION

[*after the untitled poem in Auden's* Poems *(1930) beginning* 'Get there if you can and see the land you once were proud to own . . .']

Don't forget the things we taught you by the broken
    water-wheel,
Don't forget the middle-classes fight much harder going
    downhill,

Don't forget that new proscriptions are being posted now and then,
Dr Johnson, Dr Leavis and the other Grand Old Men—

Although they've very often told us that they try to do their best,
Are they up to the Full Fruit Standard, would they pass the
    Spelling Test?

—Because we've got our eyes to keyholes, we know everything
    they've done,
Lecturing on minor poets. 'Literature is quite good fun.'

And if you should try to fool us, imitate them, do the same,
We'll refuse your dummy bullets, we've had time to take
    our aim.

We've been drinking stagnant water for some twenty years
    or more
While the politicians slowly planned a bigger reservoir.

But we've dammed a different river, the water-wheel is going again.
Now we've stopped designing sweaters and we've started in
     to train.

We've given up the Georgian poets, teaching dance bands how
     to croon,
Bicycling in coloured goggles underneath a pallid moon.

We've destroyed the rotting signposts, made holes in all the
     pleasure boats;
We'll pull down ancestral castles when we've time to swim the
     moats.

When we've practised we shall beat you with our Third or Fourth
     Fifteen,
In spite of Royalists on the touchline. 'Oh, well played, Sir!' 'Keep it
     clean!'

Our backs are fast as motor-cycles, all our forwards twenty-stone.
Each of them can score unaided, running strongly on his own.

Every minute scouts give signals, come reporting what they've seen.
'Captain Ferguson is putting.' 'Undermine the eighteenth green.'

Before next month we'll storm the clubhouse. Messages are coming
     through:
'Darwin, doing crossword puzzles, tries to find the missing clue.'

The *Times* Third Leaders are decoded, pigeon-holed for
     future use;
Tennyson has been convicted of incessant self-abuse.

We've been sending notes to Priestley, orange pips to J. C. Squire—
'Don't defend the trench you're holding.' 'Now the fat is in the fire.'

We've got control of all the railways and the perfume factories,
We're supercharged and have connection with the strongest
     batteries.

So if you feel like playing truant, remember that the game is up
Or you'll find that quite politely you've been sold a nasty pup.
                                     GAVIN EWART

First published in 1933, when Ewart was 17.

THE NIGHT TRAIN

[after 'Night Mail']

This is the Night Train crossing the Border
Air conditioning out of order

Windows sealed, atmosphere muggy
Outside breezy, inside fuggy

Seats for the rich, straps for the poor
Everyone else stuffed up by the door

'We apologise for the sudden halt
We'd like to remind you it's all Railtrack's fault'

This is the Night Train re-crossing the Border
Forward lever out of order

'Ladies and gentlemen, no cause for concern
In eight miles time, we'll attempt to turn

'Why not try a microwaved Pasty
Or our new Spongiburger, naughty but nasty'

Coffee for the rich, chips for the poor
With a sudden lurch, they're all over the floor

Hissing noisily, horribly crammed
Deary me! The sliding door's jammed

This is the Night Train, re-re-crossing the Border
Toilets temporarily out of order

Ladies are requested to cross their legs
Gentlemen advised to purchase pegs

'Customers are requested to remain at ease
If you still feel desperate, try crossing your knees'

Leaves are busy growing, dreaming of the day
They can fall on the line causing major delay

Cows staring at passengers all asleep
Think to themselves 'They're just like sheep'

This is the Night Train re-re-crossing the Border
Signals and points all out of order

'No time of arrival billed as yet—
So why not try our new filled baguette?'

Groans of defiance, sighs of despair
Hands clenched in anger or pulling out hair,

Passengers demanding information
On times of arrival at their destination
Executives bursting with curses and moans
Fishing in pockets for their mobile phones
Calls to the secretary: 'Cancel that meeting!'
Calls to the conference: 'Rearrange that seating!'
Calls to the PA: 'Reschedule my life!'
Calls to the colleagues and calls to the wife,
Calls to the Operator: 'I demand compensation!'
Calls to the mistress in a huff at the station.
Moans from the oldies ('Disgraceful, innit?')
Threats to the kiddies ('Stop that this minute!')
Abuse from hooligans, harrumphs from commuters
Tapping out grievances on personal computers:
'Never again . . . prepared to do battle . . .
Absolute outrage . . . herded like cattle'
At last! The Conductor, braving the squeeze
'When will we get there?' 'Don't ask! Tickets please!'

This is the Night Train, re-re-re-crossing the Border
Overhead lighting out of order

Arrival delayed until 15.22
So why not try our Pizza Vindaloo?

Or a tasty Masala, buy-two-get-one-free—
Or a piping hot beverage, spilt straight on your knee?

This is the Night Train, re-re-re-re-crossing the Border
Whoops! We're clean off the rails! Apologies in order!

Owing to derailment, we suggest you alight
And if you run fast, you'll be home Monday night.

CRAIG BROWN

IAN FLEMING · 1908–1964

from 'BOND STRIKES CAMP'

Shadows of fog were tailing him through the windows of his Chelsea
flat; the blonde had left a broken rosette of lipstick on the best Givan's
pillowcase—he would have to consult last night's book-matches to find
out where he had grabbed her. It was one bitch of a morning. And, of
course, it turned out to be the day! For there was always one breakfast
in the month when a very simple operation, the boiling of an egg so that
the yolk should remain properly soft and the white precisely hard, seemed
to defeat his devoted housekeeper, May. As he decapitated the fifth abort
on its Wedgwood launching-pad he was tempted to crown her with the
sixteen-inch pepper mill. Three minutes and fifty-five seconds later by his
stopwatch and the sixth egg came up with all systems go. As he was about
to press the thin finger of wholemeal toast into the prepared cavity the
telephone rang. It was probably the blonde: 'Don't tell me: it all comes
back—you're the new hat-check from "The Moment of Truth",' he snarled
into the receiver. But the voice which cut in was that of his secretary, Miss
Ponsonby. 'He wants you now, smart pants, so step on the Pogo.'
   Swearing pedantically, Bond pulled away from his uneaten egg and hur-
ried from the flat to the wheel of his souped-up Pierce Arrow, a Thirty-one
open tourer with two three-piece windscreens. A sulphurous black rain
was falling and he nearly took the seat off a Beatnik as he swerved into
Milner. It was that kind of a Christmas. Thirteen minutes later his lean
body streaked from the tonneau-cover like a conger from its hole and he
stood outside M.'s door with Lolita Ponsonby's great spaniel eyes gazing
up at him in dog-like devotion.
   'Sorry about the crossed line,' he told her. 'I'll sock you a lunch if they
don't need you at Crufts.' Then the green lights showed and he entered.
   'Sit down, 007.' That was Grade C welcome indicating the gale warning.
There had been several lately. But M. did not continue. He surveyed Bond
with a cold, glassy stare, cleared his throat and suddenly lowered his eyes.
His pipe rested unlit beside the tobacco in the familiar shell-cap. If such

a thing had been possible, Bond would have sworn he was embarrassed. When at length he spoke, the voice was dry and impersonal. 'There are many things I have asked you to do, Bond; they have not always been pleasant but they have been in the course of duty. Supposing I were to ask you to do something which I have no right to demand and which I can justify only by appealing to principles outside your service obligations. I refer to your patriotism. You are patriotic, Bond?'

'Don't know, sir, I never read the small print clauses.'

'Forgive the question, I'll put it another way. Do you think the end justifies the means?'

'I can attach no significance of any kind to such expressions.'

M. seemed to reflect. The mood of crisis deepened.

'Well, we must try again. If there were a particularly arduous task—a most distasteful task—and I called for a volunteer—who must have certain qualifications—and only one person had those qualifications—and I asked him to volunteer. What would you say?'

'I'd say stop beating about the bush, sir.'

'I'm afraid we haven't even started.'

'Sir?'

'Do you play chess, Bond?'

'My salary won't run to it.'

'But you are familiar with the game?'

'Tolerably.' As if aware that he was in the stronger position, Bond was edging towards insolence.

'It has, of course, been thoroughly modernised; all the adventure has been taken out of it; the opening gambits in which a piece used to be sacrificed for the sake of early development proved unsound and therefore abandoned. But it is so long since they have been tried that many players are unfamiliar with the pitfalls and it is sometimes possible to obtain an advantage by taking a risk. In our profession, if it be a profession, we keep a record of these forgotten traps. Ever heard of Mata Hari?'

'The beautiful spy?' Bond's voice held derision. The school prefect sulking before his housemaster.

'She was very successful. It was a long time ago.' M. still sounded meek and deprecating.

'I seem to remember reading the other day that a concealed microphone had replaced the *femme fatale*.'

'Precisely. So there is still a chance for the *femme fatale*.'

'I have yet to meet her.'

'You will. You are aware there is a Russian military mission visiting this country?'

Bond let that one go into the net.

'They have sent over among others an elderly general. He looks like a

general, he may well have been a general, he is certainly a very high ech-
elon in their K.G.B. Security is his speciality; rocketry, nerve gases, germ
warfare—all the usual hobbies.' M. paused. 'And one rather unusual one.'

Bond waited, like an old pike watching the bait come down.

'Yes. He likes to go to night clubs, get drunk, throw his money about and
bring people back to his hotel. All rather old-fashioned.'

'And not very unusual.'

'Ah.' M. looked embarrassed again. 'I'm just coming to that. We happen
to know quite a bit about this chap, General Count Apraxin. His family
were pretty well known under the old dispensation though his father was
one of the first to join the party; we think he may be a bit of a throw-
back. Not politically, of course. He's tough as they come. I needn't tell
you Section A make a study of the kind of greens the big shots go in for.
Sometimes we know more about what these people are like between the
sheets than they do themselves; it's a dirty business. Well, the General is
mad about drag.'

'Drag, sir?'

M. winced. 'I'm sorry about this part, Bond. He's "so"—"uno di quelli"—
"one of those"—a sodomite.'

Bond detected a glint of distaste in the cold blue eyes.

'In my young days,' M. went on, 'fellows like that shot themselves. Now
their names are up for every club. Particularly in London. Do you know
what sort of a reputation this city has abroad?' Bond waited. 'Well, it stinks.
These foreigners come here, drop notes of assignation into sentries' top-
boots, pin fivers on to guardsmen's bearskins. The Tins are livid.'

'And General Apraxin?' Bond decided to cut short the Wolfenden.

'One of the worst. I told you he likes drag. That's—er—men dressed up
as women.'

'Well, you tell me he's found the right place. But I don't quite see where
we come in.'

M. cleared his throat. 'There's just a possibility, mind, it's only a possibility, that even a top K.G.B. might be taken off guard—if he found the
company congenial—perhaps so congenial that it appealed to some secret
wish of his imagination—and if he talked at all (mind you, he is generally absolutely silent), well then anything he said might be of the greatest
value—anything—it might be a lead on what he's really here for. You will
be drawing a bow at a venture. You will be working in the dark.'

'Me, sir?'

M. rapped out the words like a command. '007, I want you to do this
thing. I want you to let our people rig you up as a moppet and send you to
a special sort of club and I want you to allow yourself to be approached by
General Apraxin and sit at his table and if he asks you back to his hotel I
want you to accompany him and any suggestion he makes I request you to

fall in with to the limit your conscience permits. And may your patriotism
be your conscience, as it is mine.'

It was a very odd speech for M. Bond studied his finger-nails. 'And if the
pace gets too hot?'

'Then you must pull out—but remember. T. E. Lawrence put up with
the final indignity. I knew him well, but knowing even that, I never dared
call him by his christian name.'

Bond reflected. It was clear that M. was deeply concerned. Besides, the
General might never turn up. 'I'll try anything once, sir.'

'Good man.' M. seemed to grow visibly younger.

'As long as I'm not expected to shake a powder into his drink and run
away with his wallet.'

'Oh, I don't think it will come to that. If you don't like the look of things,
just plead a headache; he'll be terrified of any publicity. It was all Section A
could do to slip him a card for this club.'

'What's its name?'

M. pursed his lips. 'The Kitchener. In Lower Belgrave Mews. Be there
about eleven o'clock and just sit around. We've signed you in as "Gerda".'

'And my—disguise?'

'We're sending you off to a specialist in that kind of thing—he thinks
you want it for some Christmas "do". Here's the address.'

'One more question, sir. I have no wish to weary you with details of my
private life but I can assure you I've never dressed up in "drag" as you call
it since I played Katisha in "The Mikado" at my prep. school. I shan't look
right, I shan't move right, I shan't talk right; I shall feel about as convincing
arsing about as a night-club hostess as Randolph Churchill.'

M. gazed at him blankly and again Bond noticed his expression of weariness, even of repulsion. 'Yes, 007, you will do all of those things and I am
afraid that is precisely what will get him.'

Bond turned angrily but M.'s face was already buried in his signals. This
man who had sent so many to their deaths was still alive and now the
dedicated bachelor who had never looked at a woman except to estimate
her security risk was packing him off with the same cold indifference into
a den of slimy creatures . . .

CYRIL CONNOLLY

STEPHEN SPENDER · 1909–1995

PARACHUTIST

[inspired by a number of poems by Stephen Spender, in particular 'Airman'—'He will watch the hawk with an indifferent eye . . .']

I shall never forget his blue eye,
Bright as a bird's but larger,
Imprinting on my own
Tear-wounded but merciless iris
The eternal letters
Of his blond incomprehension.

He came down lightly by the lilypool
Where a bird was washing,
But he did not frighten her:
A touselled boy from the skies
Petrol should not have signed
Shamefully to his surprised dishonour;
His uniform like an obscene shroud
Fretted his hands that should have held in peace
A girl's two kind ones in a public park,
Handled a boat or fashioned simple things,
Flutes, clogs, and little wooden bears,
Or in beer gardens by the ribboning Rhine
Mirthfully gestured under linden trees.

Now these once loving-kindly hands
Cherished, like an adder picked up on a walk,
A tommy gun, cold threat to love in steel:
Icarus he stands; his silken clouds of glory
Trailing behind him—a bird's broken wing—
Still trembling from his fallen angel's flight
Down the sky weeping death.

DYLAN THOMAS AND JOHN DAVENPORT

From The Death of the King's Canary, *a satirical novel about the appointment of a new Poet Laureate.*

LAWRENCE DURRELL · 1912–1990

VOLUPTIA

[*from the previously unpublished fifth volume of Durrell's* Alexandria Quartet]

In my mind, I was thinking. Alexandria, Queen of Cities, gathered round me as if it were a violet dusk. Mauve clouds like sheered seaweed filtered across the sky. Somewhere, over boxes of nougat, ambassadors wrangled. I scratched a love-bite on my shoulder and gazed down at my pallid body, clad in its tartan underdrawers, stretched out before me, a long, sad groan of fate. O, how lonely I felt. I called Ali, in my best Greek, to bring me a nectarine of Scythian *krash*. I was so subtracted I forgot he was deaf, and probably knew no Greek anyway. But he KNEW, even as I held up a finger which hung in the velvet air like a tendril of verbena.

Then Voluptia was there. She laid a hand over my ears, and whispered softly. I could not hear her. I gazed upon her dank lips, rubbed with old kisses, those obfuscating osculations suspended there, recalled on the instant she reappeared. That her words were endearments of love (L-O-V-E) I was sure. Then, with a brisk chattering snatch of laughter, she sat: as delicately as a mushroom on the green sward.

'Darley!' she whispered.

'Voluptia!' I murmured.

'Darley!' she said.

Then I noticed she had lost her nose! I stared spellbound at the hole like a fox's hide which lay gaping between her eyes. A long moment wound itself away; I knew she would tell me. 'I've had a tiresome day,' she began. Ali came in with my *krash*, and I signalled one for her in my second-best Greek. 'First,' she whispered, 'let us drink to . . . love!' 'Life!' I said.

She arranged herself into a pattern of Byzantine order, her clothes fighting for their colour with the grass. 'I lost an ear this morning,' she uttered at last. 'Hamid cut it off in pique. Then the left eye Memlik dashed out at lunchtime, because I wouldn't take him on Mountolive's spider-shoot.' But it was still the nose that took me by surprise. I looked at her, trying to fathom the labyrinths of her silence. What can I give you, I cogitated with myself, but sympathy? (As Pursewarden—the devil—wrote: TO ALL WHO SUFFER SHALL COME . . . SUFFERING.)

The heat popped and eddied in my eardrums; I watched lazily as a bead of sweat formed on the skin of my baggy, shapeless hand. 'Let us make love,' I outspake at last, 'even on a punt, even on Mareotis, which by now must be the colour of gunmetal, the texture of boiled offal. Now!' I feared that she would feel unwanted.

'No,' she responded, vivid in grass, 'I must tell you the story, and without obfuscation. There are three versions so far, as many as there are persons, and there might be more if we wait. If we have time to wait. You see, it is so cruel, not really knowing WHY!'

'Yes,' I muttered. My heart was drenched in brilliants of violet love. But before she could even begin her first explanation, there was the sound of footfalls, many footfalls. Scobie dashed in on us, his glass lips blubbering. Behind, the soft-footed Ali beat out his lighter yet fundamentally arrogant note. He stood protective as Scobie, disagreeably abnormal, spoke in a tottering voice.

'Sorry, Darley,' he said, avoiding looking directly at the nipples on my chest, 'but I've got to cart Voluptia off to chokey. She's been interfering down in the circumcision booths. There've been complaints.'

Voluptia, to give her credit, resisted.

'YA SCOBIE,' I yelled, 'are you sure you're not under the influence?' After a moment he nodded, closing his eyes. Then musingly he *loquitur*: 'Sometimes the mind strays further than life allows. It is easy to excuse, but one's duty is in the end to judge. Alas, our pitiless city demands . . .'

Voluptia rose. I glanced at her warningly. There was a terrible *mêlée*. I became another person, utterly different from the person I'm usually talking to. In the frantic struggle, Scobie sweated, and Voluptia had her foot pinned to the floor by a Bimbashi's dagger. I was aghast!

Then she had all her clothes pulled off. UNDERNEATH SHE WAS DRESSED AS A MAN! 'Voluptia!' Scobie cried out, his voice stark, nude. 'She eschews definition,' he finally said. Voluptia, wax pale, moaned on the note of a distant sirocco. Then she broke from Scobie's grip and her lips touched my ankle. She murmured, brokenly, half a dozen lines from Cavafy, their spirit untranslatable. Scobie watched and uttered: 'Sex speaks rapidly between unbridgeable cultures.' Then Scobie took her, not as a lawgiver takes a lawbreaker but as a dragoman leads a spirited horse. 'Allah be praised!' said Ali by dumb-sign as he left with his prisoner. Prisoner! (As Pursewarden writes: we are all prisoners.) I heard her go, soft-footed to the last.

'Another Scythian *krash*,' I signalled, my head askew on my shoulders. Mareotis grinned back at me under the puce moon. I felt almost sick. Alexandria! Her voice came again from below, swept up on the hot airs of the city. '*Chéri!*' she cried, and I could sense the vibration of those firm slanting breasts, 'We must all go back.'

Sweaty, my tartan undershorts clung coldly to my alabaster thighs. Again I was lonely. I wanted to press someone's elbow, but there was only Ali; and after some thought I simply pressed my own. Outside smugglers drove past in old cars; somewhere, over boxes of nougat, ambassadors still wrangled. A smell of decay, the smell that goes indeed with perfection,

came up from the city. Excited, my nostrils quivered. For then it came to
me, throbbingly out of the desert, over Mareotis, over minaret and palm,
through the circumcision booths, through the pierced cheeks of the demon
dancers, straight as a glinting arrow through the musk and maze of what
we think of as reality. As Pursewarden said: Love is a four-letter word! In
a feeling of exultation, I rubbed my hands together, thankful that, despite
the company I mixed with, I still had them to rub.

MALCOLM BRADBURY

R. S. THOMAS · 1913–2000

R. S. THOMAS AT ALTITUDE

The reason I am leaning over
At this pronounced angle is simply
That I am accustomed to standing
On Welsh hillsides
Staring out over escarpments stripped
And pitiless as my vision,
Where God says: Come
Back to the trodden manure
Of the chapel's warm temptation.
But I see the canker that awaits
The child, and say no.
I see the death that ends
Life, and say no.
Missing nothing, I say
No, no.
And God says: you can't
Say no to me, cully,
I'm omnipotent.
But I indicate the
Flying birds and the
Swimming fish and the trudging
Horse with my pointing
Finger and with customary
Economy of language, say
Nothing.
There is a stone in my mouth,
There is a storm in my
Flesh, there is a wind in

My bone.
Artificer of the knuckled, globed years
Is this your answer?
I've been up on this hill
Too long.

CLIVE JAMES

DYLAN THOMAS · 1914–1953

DYLAN THOMAS REWRITES *PRIDE AND PREJUDICE*

FIRST VOICE: It is night in the smug snug-as-a-bug-in-a-rug household of Mr and Mrs Dai Bennet and their simpering daughters—five breast-bobbing man-hungry tittivators, innocent as ice-cream, panting for balls and matrimony.

MRS BENNET: Our new neighbour, Mr Darcy, quite tickles my fancy.

MR BENNET: Don't let him turn Lizzy's head Darcy-versy.

ELIZABETH: I shall wed whom I please.

FIRST VOICE: And busy Lizzie retires to her room with visions of bridling up the aisle to 'I will' with half-a-dozen lovers. She dreams of coaches and pairs and being a fine lady; dressing for dinner in a silken gown and undressing afterwards for heaven knows what in the saucy haven of a double bed; swoons, seductions and *sal volatile*; tears, tantrums and tedium; the pettish petticoquettish world of the country-house marriage-go-round from which she and her whinnying sisterhood can never hope to escape.

STANLEY J. SHARPLESS

ROALD DAHL · 1916–1990

ADAM AND THE AWFUL APPLE

In the beginning was the word. It wasn't a big word. It was a little word but it was a bossy one. 'Don't'. 'Don't eat the apple.' That was what Mr Lord said to Adam and Eve when he let them into his garden. They could eat anything else they wanted—even snozzleberries or bits of the giant peach. But they mustn't eat the apple.

And they didn't. Until a snake—that looked like a wriggly liquorice boot-lace (only bright green)—came slithering up to them. 'Have a nibble of that apple', the snake hissed in a friendly-sounding way. 'It's fabulous—like a kind of terrific gob-stopper.' Eve couldn't resist and took a bite. So did Adam when she told him how delicious it was.

Then, suddenly, Mr Lord appeared. He stared at the round red apple. And the two white bite marks in it stared back at him like frightened ghost's eyes. 'I was saving that apple for your first day at school', he said, 'so you could give it to your teacher and put her in a good mood. Now you've ruined it. Get out of the garden.'

Clang, clang: the gates closed behind them. 'Oh dear,' said Eve, 'all this trouble over something like a gob-stopper.' 'Gob-stopper?' said the snake, slithering up again. 'Oh no. Sorry. What I meant to say was "It's like a kind of terrific god-stopper" '.

PETER KEMP

ROBERT LOWELL · 1917–1977

from ROBERT LOWELL'S NOTEBOOK

Notes for a Sonnet

Stalled before my metal shaving mirror
With a locked razor in my hand I think of Tantalus
Whose lake retreats below the fractured lower lip
Of my will. Splinter the groined eyeballs of our sin,
Ford Madox Ford: you on the Quaker golf-course
In Nantucket double-dealt your practised lies
Flattering the others and me we'd be great poets.
How wrong you were in their case. And now Nixon,
Nixon rolls in the harpoon ropes and smashes with his flukes
The frail gunwales of our beleaguered art. What
Else remains now but your England, Ford? There's not
Much Lowell-praise left in Mailer but could be Alvarez
Might still write that book. In the skunk-hour
My mind's not right. But there will be
Fifty-six new sonnets by tomorrow night.

Revised Notes for a Sonnet

On the steps of the Pentagon I tucked my skull
Well down between my knees, thinking of Cordell Hull
Cabot Lodge Van du Plessis Stuyvesant, our gardener,
Who'd stop me playing speedway in the red-and-rust
Model A Ford that got clapped out on Cape Cod

And wound up as a seed-shed. Oh my God, my God,
How this administration bleeds but will not die,
Hacking at the rib-cage of our art. You were wrong, R.P.
Blackmur. Some of the others had our insight, too:
Though I suppose I had endurance, toughness, faith,
Sensitivity, intelligence and talent. My mind's not right.
With groined, sinning eyeballs I write sonnets until dawn
Is published over London like a row of books by Faber—
Then shave myself with Uncle's full-dress sabre.

Notes for a Revised Sonnet

Slicing my head off shaving I think of Charles I
Bowing to the groined eyeball of Cromwell's sinning will.
Think too of Orpheus, whose disembodied head
Dumped by the Bacchants floated singing in the river,
His love for Eurydice surviving her dumb move
By many sonnets. Decapitation wouldn't slow me down
By more than a hundred lines a day. R.P. and F.M.F.
Play eighteen holes together in my troubled mind,
Ford faking his card, Blackmur explicating his,
And what is love? John Berryman, if you'd had what it took
We could have both blown England open. Now, alone,
With a plush new set-up to move into and shake down,
I snow-job Stephen Spender while the liquor flows like lava
In the parlour of the Marchioness of Dufferin and Ava.

CLIVE JAMES

MURIEL SPARK · 1918–2006

LAST THINGS

It has been widely noted that the recent fiction of Miss Muriel
Spark has been concerned with those two crucial enterprises,
fiction and death, and that somehow this has been making
her novels shorter and shorter. The following, then, is not an
excerpt from, but the entirety of, her newest, shortest, and
most deathly work, *The Nuns of Terminus*.

'I hope you are both keeping an extremely careful eye on the weather,' says
Sister Felicity, who is small and fat, with a shrewd mouth, 'It is perhaps the
commonest way available of procuring our downfall.'

'I can't think of any reason why it should be,' says Sister Mercy, who is famous for being stupid, and for getting the weaker lines of dialogue, and who will die, in distressing circumstances, rather closer to the beginning of this story than any of the others.

'Felicity is right, of course,' says Sister Georgina, still one of the novices, but taken up by Sister Felicity for her cunning: she is reputed to have worked for the Political Intelligence Department of a certain Foreign Office during the war, 'It is a question of sustaining an adequate level of probability. Even a simple change of barometric pressure can lead with unbroken logic to a chill, and a chill to bronchial pneumonia, which in turn can have fatal consequences without disturbing at all what people are pleased to think of as the normal order of things.'

'That is why Sister Georgina urged you to put on your thickest shoes,' says Sister Felicity, walking on with her quite long stride.

The three nuns, black like crows in the habit of their order, walk, on the grass, under the trees, up and down, round and round, in the private and unseen grounds of this rigorous convent, notable for its chastity, in an unnamed northern country. It is, for the moment, a nice day. The sun is shining in an apparently pleasant way on the grass, on the leaves of the trees, and the barometric pressure, while subject to sudden fluctuation in these parts, is recorded as steady and fair in the newspapers that will, on the following day, have so much to report, in long black columns of type, about these lawns, these trees, this famous and rigorous convent. Inside the cold stone buildings, just visible over the wall, the other nuns are even now performing the appropriate observances. The Prioress, in her white habit, is looking at her watch and noting, so that she will be able to report tomorrow, when it all comes out, the extent of Felicity's absence. But, at this moment, she is not alarmed. Felicity's absences are famous. She has been at this convent longer than any other nun, and her shrewd tongue and her authoritative manners have won her exceptional privileges, privileges now as ritualized, in their way, as the Vespers and the Complines, the duties and observances, that the reporters will record for their columns, the television crews film for their audiences, in the weeks of publicity that are to follow.

'The real torment,' says Sister Georgina, drawing Mercy away from a large puddle which has appeared before them in the path, 'is to know that there is a hand at work, yet not to know where and when it will choose to reveal itself.'

'I don't think I want anything more to do with this plot,' says Sister Mercy suddenly, putting her hands to her face, and bursting into tears. 'I'm not even sure there is a plot,' she cries, looking at the other two.

Sister Felicity stops abruptly, and looks at Mercy, appraising her with her judging brow. 'I'm sorry, my dear,' she says, 'I am afraid you have very little choice. It is the way of things to be necessary, when *we* wish them to be contingent. But this you know, from your faith. There is little any of us can do about it, except take every intelligent precaution. That is why Sister Georgina has brought a sunshade, as I, you see, have brought my umbrella. Of course,' she adds, 'the best thing of all is just not to be her type.'

A small white cloud appears in the blue sky above the trees in the convent garden.

'I think Felicity should notice this cloud,' says Georgina.

'I have already noticed it, my dear,' says Felicity, walking round and round, up and down.

'If one were to leave and go somewhere else under another name,' says Mercy.

'I very much doubt if that would work, except in the most exceptional circumstances,' says Felicity.

'But what circumstances?' cries Mercy.

'If, perhaps, one were being saved for something,' says Felicity, 'You must understand, Mercy, I have been in a novel before. I know what it's like. It is extremely uncomfortable, unless one manages to stay entirely peripheral to the main line of the action, and not to draw attention to oneself in any way. I have always thought,' she adds, drawing Sister Georgina from the vicinity of a large overhanging branch on an old tree, 'that the best way is to be a member of the servant classes, or to be asleep in another room most of the time.'

'It *has* been done,' says Sister Georgina, 'There have been some who have escaped. One was called Golly Mackintosh, who conducted herself with very sensible restraint, I thought, in remaining out of Italy entirely over the period when that English film-actress had such a bad time.'

'Which actress was that?' asks Mercy.

'Felicity will know her name,' says Georgina, 'She is stupendously well-read.'

'Annabel Christopher,' says Sister Felicity, 'There was also a sickly looking man in a plane and a hotel who was wise enough to confine himself to the minimum of conversation with Lise.'

'Who is Lise?' asks Sister Mercy.

'She is in another by the same hand,' says Sister Georgina, 'A woman of great linguistic abilities, but I'm afraid the effect of that sort of cleverness is only to get oneself noticed.'

'I think it would be unwise to say much in front of Mercy about what happened to Lise,' says Felicity, 'I fear they are much of a type. Am I mistaken, or is that cloud growing darker? I'm sure we'd be wise to return as quickly as we can to our offices.'

Under the trees, at the very end of the garden, the three nuns turn. 'I wish we could get ourselves into the hands of Mr Fowles,' says Sister

Mercy, as they walk back in their dark habits, 'He's much kinder, and allows his people an extraordinary freedom of choice.'

'We understand your feelings,' says Sister Georgina, 'but it's a very secular judgment. In any case, you'd find with him that what's sauce for the goose is sauce for the gander, if you understand me.'

'I think not,' says Mercy.

'One would almost certainly find oneself being rogered by one of his libidinous heroes,' says Felicity, 'At least our context here is not particularly Freudian.'

'It could be interesting,' says Mercy.

'I have never myself taken any pleasure in the sex part,' says Georgina, 'It is all right at the time, but not afterwards.'

'I think I could put up with it,' says Mercy, 'I expect one could enjoy it a great deal, if one was prepared to become famous at it.'

There is a sudden burst of lightning from the darkening cloud above the trees, causing Mercy to fall inert to the ground. The other two nuns, in their black habits, kneel beside her. In a moment they rise, their faces solemn. 'It was lucky she murmured something sensitive just before she passed on,' says Georgina, looking down on the recumbent body, which before the night will lie in the chapel of the convent, the composed and stupid face staring sightlessly up at the nuns who file by and, later, at the police inspector who finally orders the autopsy.

'I am afraid we were not paying sufficient attention,' says Felicity, 'We had dropped our guard.'

Georgina breathes hard, as if fighting off inevitable tears. 'It is not very kind of Miss Spark,' she says, 'And it is hardly as if Mercy were a full protagonist.'

'Come,' says Felicity, 'I think we should sit over there by the wall and be quiet for a while. If there were no dialogue, there could be nothing to incense her.'

The two nuns, in their black habits, walk to a corner of the garden that is treeless and, putting down the sunshade, putting down the umbrella, they seat themselves, backs against the wall, at a place that, in tomorrow's papers, will be marked with a stark X. They look across the bright trimmed green of the turf, beyond the crumpled black corpse, to the columns of trees, the once again blue sky. In the blue of the sky appears a white plume rather like a feather, the trail of an aeroplane that carries many travellers from homes to meetings, from holidays to homes, travellers who will read with surprise in their next day's journals of the events that unfolded, apparently without connection, below them.

'Even she could hardly want to push coincidence too far,' says Georgina, inspecting the plane with some anxiety. 'Surely her critics would begin to talk.'

Felicity, too, looks at the plane. 'I think you may be right to see a hand,' she says. 'And I am afraid the critics themselves are not entirely innocent in these matters.'

'I had not known there could be others,' says Georgina.

'You have not heard of a Professor Kermode?'

'I had not thought of him in this connection,' says Sister Georgina, 'I thought he was usually in America.'

'The Atlantic may be a substantial stretch of water, Georgina,' says Felicity, 'but it is not an outright barrier to intellectual intercourse. I think we should go in.'

But Sister Georgina is still looking at the plane, with its many travellers, and glimpsing, with a growing horror, the silvery piece of metal, a part of a wing perhaps, a piece of a wheel, that has detached itself from it and, twirling, changing in shape but not in direction, angles down through the air towards the treeless corner of the garden. She rises and runs, her gaze fixed in the air. The aeroplane part whistles in its descent and falls harmlessly into an adjoining field. Felicity rises, in her black habit, and runs to Georgina who, looking upward, has stumbled over a crocquet hoop, inadvertently left in the grass, and fallen to the ground. 'You were lucky, Georgina,' she says, 'You might well have been dead.' But a closer inspection reveals the truth; the fall has clearly been a heavy one, for Georgina, in fact, is.

For a moment Sister Felicity stands there, in her dark habit. She looks at the two crumpled bodies that lie in the grass, in spots which, tomorrow, will be staked around, and examined intently by many policemen. Then, in a sudden movement, she disappears behind an adjacent bush. 'She's caught me,' she shouts, in seven languages. There is a sound as of cloth ripping: a white coif flies above the bush and falls some distance away on the grass. A short while after a figure appears from behind the bush, in familiar street clothes, a dress of slightly more than miniskirt length. The shoes are perhaps heavy, and the blackness of the material of the dress duller than would suit most people's tastes. The figure rapidly crosses the grass of the convent garden, walking not towards the buildings but away from them, towards the high wall that shuts out the diurnal world beyond. And now the figure reaches this high stone wall, climbing it with agility and some speed. It gives a last glance to the garden that will be in so many newspapers, and then disappears from sight.

Later Felicity will do many things. She will fly to Africa, to Canada, to South America. She will hunt tiger in India, and take a small canoe down the Amazon river, through disease-infested waters and snake-inhabited swamps. She will climb precipitous mountains in the Tyrol, where sheer drops overlook green and church-filled valleys far below. She will die, in New York City, in the year 2024, at the age of ninety-eight, of benign old age. She will lie in bed at the last, and look up, and say: 'What did you want

of me? What have you been waiting for all this time?' But I don't feel that
it's my business to go around answering questions like that.

MALCOLM BRADBURY

IRIS MURDOCH · 1919–1999

A JAUNDICED VIEW

'Flavia says that Hugo tells her that Augustina is in love with Fred.'

Sir Alex Mountaubon stood with his wife Lavinia in one of the deeply
recessed mullion windows of the long gallery at Bishop's Breeches, looking out at the topiary peacocks on the terrace beyond. In front of them
the fountain, topped with statuary in which a naked Mars played joyously
with a willing Venus, gently coruscated, its tinkle audible through the open
windows. The scene before them was of order and peace. They could look
down the park at the mile-long drive of lindens, the colour of jaundice;
to one side, away from its necessary order, stood one dark and contingent
cedar tree. Beneath it their older daughter, Flavia, could be seen from the
window, sitting on a white wooden seat, in her unutterable otherness, her
pet marmoset on her shoulder, her cap of auburn hair shining like burnished gold on her head. Nearer to the house, in the rose-garden, their
younger daughter, seven-year-old Perdita, strange, mysterious and self-
absorbed as usual, was beheading a litter of puppies with unexpectedly
muscular and adult twists of her slender arm. Her cap of golden hair shone
like burnished auburn on her head.

Alex turned, catching sight of himself in the big, gilt, rather battered
cupid-encrusted mirror that soared over the mantel. Mortality was there
in the darkened eyes, but most of what he saw there, the solid, round face
of a man of principle, pleased him exceedingly. His book, a philosophical
study of Niceness, was almost complete; in its writing Lavinia, his second wife, had proved the perfect helpmeet and companion. No one lay
dying upstairs. He looked around at the familiar objects, the Titians and
Tintorettos, glowing in their serried ranks with jewelled beneficence, the
twined, golden forms of bodies twisted together suggesting a radiant
vision of another world. In cases stood the Sung cups, the Ting plates, the
Tang vases, the Ming statuettes, the Ching saucers; these last must, almost
certainly, go.

'Who says whom tells her that who is in love with whom?'

Lavinia, her arms full of lilies, did not turn. 'Flavia,' she said.

'And are they?'

'They think so. I don't think they quite know.'

'But at least we know. About us,' said Alex lovingly. He looked out of the window and saw Perdita staring strangely up at the house; and suddenly, involuntarily, he recalled again that experience of utter freedom he had known for the first time when he and Moira LeBenedictus had lain naked together in the Reading Room of the British Museum, after hours of course; he, as a senior civil servant, had been entitled to a key. Other moments came back: Moira walking through Harrods without her shoes, Moira on the night they had boxed together on the roof of St Paul's Cathedral, Moira threatening him in the Tottenham Hotspurs football ground at midnight with her whaler's harpoon.

Two miles away, in the bathroom at his house, Buttocks, Sir Hugo Occam laid down his razor. He walked through into the bedroom where Moira LeBenedictus lay. She was his good towards which he magnetically swung. She lay on the bed, gathering her hair together into a cap of black.

'Are we acting rightly?'

'I think we are,' she said.

'Oh, Moira.'

'Come, come, Hugo,' she said. From the alcove, Leo Chatteris, a spoiled priest, long in love with Moira, watched them in protective benediction. Could he surrender her? The pain was so much he knew it was right.

'Do we?' Lavinia had thrown down her lilies and now stood facing Alex. 'Alex,' she said with sudden passion, 'I have resigned from the presidency of the WI.' The words struck a sudden chill over him, and he knew that the shapeliness and order about him were about to be violated. 'I am in love with Fred.'

'You can't be,' said Alex, speaking without thought, absorbed in his own misery, 'Augustina is in love with Fred, Hugo is in love with Augustina, Flavia is in love with Hugo, Fred is in love with Flavia, Moira is in love with Fred, I am in love with Moira, and you are in love with me.'

'No, Fred . . . Hugo . . . Alex rather,' said Lavinia, her voice trembling, 'I'm afraid you have it *all the wrong way round*. I am in love with Fred, you are in love with me, Moira is in love with you, and you utterly missed out Leo, who is as unutterably particular as anyone else, and who is in love with Moira.'

'But how, why?' Alex murmured, his hands over his face.

'It's one of the wonders of the world.'

'All right,' he said, 'Here we go again. Will you call them, or shall I?'

'Do be careful of the Gainsboroughs,' said Alex to the men, 'And I do think the Renoirs ought to have a van to themselves, and not be put in with the fountain, which is liable to wet them irreparably.'

Already seven of the thirteen furniture vans had been filled, and were on their way to Buttocks, where Moira was awaiting him. Bishop's Breeches, descending through the female line, stayed with Lavinia, but most of its exquisite contents, including some singularly heavy statuary, belonged to Alex. He stood in the noble portico, feeling the familiar, loved house around him, so fit for free characters to live in, and knowing he must leave soon, for the last time. The heavy van lumbered away down the drive, beneath the yellow of the lindens, towards the North Lodge. He turned to go back into Bishop's Breeches, and then heard a strange splintering noise. He walked towards the drive, passed under the deep yellow lindens. A very dove-grey Rolls was parked at the side. 'I'm afraid there's been a rather nasty accident,' said Fred Tallin, getting out, 'Your first van ran into my first van. There's stuff spilled all over the road. We can't tell whose Titians are whose. As for the Sung and the Ting and the Tang and the Ming and the Ching, I'm afraid all that's gone bang. Awful business, this packing. How the deuce do you pack up a herd of deer? Lav all ready for me?'

'She's in her room, holding daffodils,' said Alex.

A flotilla of pantechnicons was turning in by the West Lodge and coming up the other avenue. 'I say, that's funny,' said Fred, resting his very white hand on the bonnet of the very dove-grey Rolls, 'Those vans aren't mine. Mine are from Harrod's.'

'They're not mine, either,' said Alex, 'You don't think Moira's got it all wrong? She did know I'm going to Buttocks, not her coming here to me?'

'It rather looks as if not,' said Fred, 'In any case, I thought Buttocks belonged to Hugo.'

'Moira told me it belonged to Leo, who had given it to her,' said Alex.

'Very funny girl, Moira,' said Fred, 'Did she ever show you her sarcophagus?'

A horn blared behind them, and they both turned. There, on the gravel in front of the house, stood another row of pantechnicons, which had evidently come in from the East Lodge, and drawn up unnoticed. 'I say,' said Fred.

'Now whose . . .?' began Alex, but his question was quickly answered. For now Flavia came running from her white seat by the cedar, the marmoset chattering after her.

'Have these to do with you?' he asked.

'Dear Hugo,' said Flavia. She put her arms behind her and suddenly released her hair, which fell across her shoulders and down her back like a shower of gold.

'Flavia,' said Alex. Then he stood spellbound. For the unused gate at the South Lodge had been swung open, and up the drive came another line of vans.

'We live in a realm of startling coincidences,' said Fred.

They stood and watched as they saw a figure, bounding with joy, running to meet the vans. It was Perdita, strange and mysterious, her puppies forgotten.

*

Sir Alex Mountaubon stood with his wife Lavinia in one of the deeply recessed mullion windows of the long gallery at Bishop's Breeches, looking down the mile-long drive of lindens to the tightly locked gates at the bottom. The trees, the colour of jaundice, stood in their necessary order; to one side, beneath the dark, contingent cedar tree, their daughter Flavia sat on the white wooden seat, unutterably particular, while in the rose-garden Perdita, still strange and mysterious, was twisting the neck of Flavia's marmoset. 'You know, Lavinia, I'm glad matters have reverted to normal,' said Alex, 'I know it's philosophically wrong, and I'm afraid we've done little for the plot. Am I wicked to say it?'

He leaned forward and, putting his arms round Lavinia, gently loosened her hair. His book on Niceness was now complete, and Lavinia was proving a perfect proof-reader. Lavinia turned her face and then, her arms full of roses, she smiled at him. 'No, it's marvellous,' she said, 'I love you, you love Moira, Moira loves Fred, Fred loves Flavia, Flavia loves Hugo . . .'

'You missed out Leo,' said Alex.

'To hell with Leo,' said Lavinia, 'I don't care how unutterably particular he is. There is one thing that worries me, though, Alex. Why is it that, when we sleep with all these people, they're all either titled or in the Civil Service?'

'I don't know. I suppose you might say it's a condition of our world,' said Alex, looking around the gallery. Only a few gaps on the wall among the Tintorettos revealed the ravages of the last days. 'However,' he said, as they both turned and looked out at the Mars and Venus sporting in stone on the fountain, and then, further beyond, the deep yellow light under the lindens, 'I do know this. Love is a strange, mysterious and wonderful revelation of others. But, for people in our station in life, it's really far too much of a bother.'

MALCOLM BRADBURY

RICHARD WILBUR · 1921–

RICHARD WILBUR'S FABERGÉ EGG FACTORY

If Occam's Razor gleams in Massachusetts
In time the Pitti Palace is unravelled:
An old moon re-arising as the new sets
To show the poet how much he has travelled.

Laforgue said missing trains was beautiful
But Wittgenstein said words should not seduce:

Small talk from him would at the best be dutiful—
And news of trains, from either man, no use.

Akhmatova finds echoes in Akhnaten.
The vocables they share *a fortiori*
Twin-yolk them in the self-same kindergarten
Though Alekhine might tell a different story.

All mentioned populate a limpid lyric
Where learning deftly intromits precision:
The shots are Parthian, the victories Pyrrhic,
Piccarda's ghost was not so pale a vision,

But still you must admit this boy's got class—
His riddles lead through vacuums to a space
Where skill leans on the parapet of farce
And sees Narcissus making up his face.

CLIVE JAMES

PHILIP LARKIN · 1922–1985

MR STRUGNELL

[*after 'Mr Bleaney'*]

'This was Mr Strugnell's room,' she'll say—
And look down at the lumpy, single bed.
'He stayed here up until he went away
And kept his bicycle out in that shed.

'He had a job in Norwood library—
He was a quiet sort who liked to read—
Dick Francis mostly, and some poetry—
He liked John Betjeman very much indeed

'But not Pam Ayres or even Patience Strong—
He'd change the subject if I mentioned them,
Or say, "It's time for me to run along—
Your taste's too highbrow for me, Mrs M."

'And up he'd go and listen to that jazz.
I don't mind telling you it was a bore—
Few things in this house have been tiresome as
The sound of his foot tapping on the floor.

'He didn't seem the sort for being free
With girls or going out and having fun.
He had a funny turn in 'sixty-three
And ran round shouting "Yippee! It's begun!"

'I don't know what he meant, but after that
He had a different look, much more relaxed.
Some nights he'd come in late, too tired to chat,
As if he had been somewhat overtaxed.

'And now he's gone. He said he found Tulse Hill
Too stimulating—wanted somewhere dull.
At last he's found a place that fits the bill—
Enjoying perfect boredom up in Hull.'

WENDY COPE

JACK KEROUAC · 1922–1969

ON THE SIDEWALK

(after reading, at long last, On the Road)

I was just thinking around in my sad backyard, looking at those little drab
careless starshaped clumps of crabgrass and beautiful chunks of some old
bicycle crying out without words of the American Noon and half a newspaper with an ad about a lotion for people with dry skins and dry souls,
when my mother opened our frantic banging screendoor and shouted,
'Gogi Himmelman's here.' She might have shouted the Archangel Gabriel
was here, or Captain Easy or Baron Charlus in Proust's great book: Gogi
Himmelman of the tattered old greenasgrass knickers and wild teeth and
the vastiest, most vortical, most insatiable wonder-filled eyes I have ever
known. 'Let's go, Lee,' he sang out, and I could see he looked sadder than
ever, his nose all rubbed raw by a cheap handkerchief and a dreary Bandaid
unravelling off his thumb. 'I know the WAY!' That was Gogi's inimitable
unintellectual method of putting it that he was on fire with the esoteric
paradoxical Tao and there was no holding him when he was in that mood.

I said, 'I'm going, Mom,' and she said, 'O.K.,' and when I looked back at her hesitant in the pearly mystical UnitedStateshome light I felt absolutely sad, thinking of all the times she had vacuumed the same carpets.

His scooter was out front, the selfsame, the nonpareil, with its paint scabbing off intricately and its scratchedon dirty words and its nuts and bolts chattering with fear, and I got my tricycle out of the garage, and he was off, his left foot kicking with that same insuperable energy or even better. I said, 'Hey wait,' and wondered if I could keep up and probably couldn't have if my beltbuckle hadn't got involved with his rear fender. This was IT. We scuttered down our drive and right over Mrs Cacciatore's rock garden with the tiny castles made out of plaster that always made me sad when I looked at them alone. With Gogi it was different; he just kept right on going, his foot kicking with that delirious thirtyrevolutionsasecond frenzy, right over the top of the biggest, a Blenheim six feet tall at the turrets; and suddenly I saw it the way he saw it, embracing everything with his unfluctuating generosity, imbecile saint of our fudging age, a mad desperado in our Twentieth Century Northern Hemisphere Nirvana deserts.

We rattled on down through her iris bed and broke into the wide shimmering pavement. 'Contemplate those holy hydrants,' he shouted back at me through the wind. 'Get a load of those petulant operable latches; catch the magic of those pickets standing up proud and sequential like the arguments in Immanuel Kant; boom, boom, bitty-boom BOOM!' and it was true.

'What happens when we're dead?' I asked.

'The infinite never-to-be-defiled subtlety of the late Big Sid Catlett on the hushed trap drums,' he continued, mad with his own dreams, imitating the whisks, 'Swish, swish, swishy-swish SWOOSH!'

The sun was breaking over the tops of Mr Linderman's privet hedge, little rows of leaves set in there delicate and justso like mints in a Howard Johnson's roadside eatery. Mitzi Leggett came out of the house, and Gogi stopped the scooter, and put his hands on her. 'The virginal starchblue fabric; printed with stylized kittens and puppies,' Gogi explained in his curiously beseechingly transcendent accents. 'The searing incredible *innocence!* Oh! Oh! Oh!' His eyes poured water down his face like broken blisters.

'Take me along,' Mitzi said openly to me, right with Gogi there and hearing every word, alive to every meaning, his nervous essence making his freckles tremble like a field of Iowa windblown nochaff barley.

'I want to,' I told her, and tried to, but I couldn't, not there. I didn't have the stomach for it. She pretended to care. She was a lovely beauty. I felt my spokes snap under me; Gogi was going again, his eyes tight-shut in ecstasy, his foot kicking so the hole in his shoesole showed every time, a tiny chronic rent in the iridescent miasmal veil that Intrinsic Mind tries to hide behind.

Wow! Dr Fairweather's house came up on the left, delicious stucco like piecrust in the type of joints that attract truckers, and then the place of the beautiful Mrs Mertz, with her *canny* deeprooted husband bringing up glorious heartbreaking tabourets and knickknacks from his workshop in the basement, a betooled woodshavingsmelling fantasy worthy of Bruegel or Hegel or a seagull. Vistas! Old Miss Hooper raced into her yard and made a grab for us, and Gogi Himmelman, the excruciating superbo, shifted to the other foot and laughed at her careworn face. Then the breathless agape green space of the Princeling mansion, with its rich calm and potted Tropic of Cancer plants. Then it was over.

Gogi and I went limp at the corner under a sign saying ELM STREET with irony because all the elms had been cut down so they wouldn't get the blight, sad stumps diminishing down the American perspective whisperingly.

'My spokes are gone,' I told him.

'Friend—ahem—*zip, zip*—parting a relative concept—Bergson's invaluable marvelchocked work—tch, tch.' He stood there, desperately wanting to do the right thing, yet always lacking with an indistinguishable grandeur that petty ability.

'Go,' I told him. He was already halfway back, a flurrying spark, to where Mitzi waited with irrepressible womanwarmth.

Well. In landsend despair I stood there stranded. Across the asphalt that was sufficiently semifluid to receive and embalm millions of star-sharp stones and bravely gay candywrappers a drugstore twinkled artificial enticement. But I was not allowed to cross the street. I stood on the gray curb thinking, They said I could cross it when I grew up, but what do they mean grown up? I'm thirty-nine now, and felt sad.

JOHN UPDIKE

ALLEN GINSBERG · 1926–1997

SQUEAL

[inspired or provoked by Howl]

I saw the best minds of my generation
Destroyed—Marvin
Who spat out poems; Potrzebie
Who coagulated a new bop literature in fifteen
Novels; Alvin
Who in his as yet unwritten autobiography
Gave Brooklyn an original *lex loci*.

They came from all over, from the pool room,
The bargain basement, the rod,
From Whitman, from Parkersburg, from Rimbaud
New Mexico, but mostly
They came from colleges, ejected
For drawing obscene diagrams of the Future.
They came here to L. A.,
Flexing their members, growing hair,
Planning immense unlimited poems,
More novels, more poems, more autobiographies.

It's love I'm talking about, you dirty bastards!
Love in the bushes, love in the freight car!
I saw them fornicating and being fornicated,
Saying to Hell with you!

America.
America is full of Babbitts.
America is run by money.

What was it Walt said? Go West!
But the important thing is the return ticket.
The road to publicity runs by Monterey.
I saw the best minds of my generation
Reading their poems to Vassar girls,
Being interviewed by *Mademoiselle*.
Having their publicity handled by professionals.
When can I go into an editorial office
And have my stuff published because I'm weird?
I could go on writing like this forever . . .

LOUIS SIMPSON

TED HUGHES · 1930–1998

A POLICEMAN'S LOT

The progress of any writer is marked by those moments
when he manages to outwit his own inner police
system.

TED HUGHES

Oh, once I was a policeman young and merry
(young and merry),
Controlling crowds and fighting petty crime
(petty crime),
But now I work on matters literary (litererry)
And I am growing old before my time ('fore my time).
No, the imagination of a writer (of a writer)
Is not the sort of beat a chap would choose
(chap would choose)
And they've assigned me a prolific blighter
('lific blighter)—
I'm patrolling the unconscious of Ted Hughes.

It's not the sort of beat a chap would choose
(chap would choose)—
Patrolling the unconscious of Ted Hughes.

All our leave was cancelled in the lambing season
(lambing season),
When bitter winter froze the drinking trough
(drinking trough),
For our commander stated, with good reason
(with good reason),
That that's the kind of thing that starts him off
(starts him off).
But anything with four legs causes trouble
(causes trouble)—
It's worse than organizing several zoos (several zoos),
Not to mention mythic creatures in the rubble
(in the rubble),
Patrolling the unconscious of Ted Hughes.

It's worse than organizing several zoos (several zoos),
Patrolling the unconscious of Ted Hughes.

Although it's disagreeable and stressful
                                (bull and stressful)
Attempting to avert poetic thought ('etic thought),
I could boast of times when I have been successful
                                (been successful)
And conspiring compound epithets were caught
                                ('thets were caught).
But the poetry statistics in this sector (in this sector)
Are enough to make a copper turn to booze
                                (turn to booze)
And I do not think I'll make it to inspector (to inspector)
Patrolling the unconsious of Ted Hughes.

It's enough to make a copper turn to booze
                                (turn to booze)—
Patrolling the unconscious of Ted Hughes.

after W. S. Gilbert
WENDY COPE

LINES ON THE QUEEN'S 60TH BIRTHDAY

        Wolf headed magpie
        Stalks black white
        Black over
        Flint cracked mangle
        Frost-shredded
        Field.

        Stoat watches.

        Bloodred nettle
        Sprouts acid
        Frond.

        Old Stoatie.

        Peewit shrieking
        Buzzard grey
        Feather drooping
        Death call.

        Old Stoatie listens.

Swollen river
Rushes down Blood
Gorge torrent filled
Roar of white-flecked
Molten snow.

Old Stoatie falls in.

Rotting stoat
Body carcass
Gleaming fish nibbled

Carrion of death
Sodden fur bulging
Eyes

Old Stoatie's
Rather had it.

Happy Birthday
Your Majesty.

ANON., *Private Eye*

Ted Hughes became Poet Laureate in 1984.

SYLVIA PLATH · 1932–1963

GODIVA

I wear a cobra's black bonnet,
A granite
Grin,

With an acetylene
Tongue
Behind the row of headstones.

Don't touch, Herr . . .
Just look.
Look. Look. Look.

A jacket of ashes,
Ragged umbrellas for hands,
The shadow of this lip a pit,

Just look at it.
Good God!
A mole in a spotlight of knives,

A puppet with no strings
Attached. Nothing.
Lady Godiva on a nag, nag, nag.

Suck this living doll's
Last tear if you will,
But beware

I eat in
Like Hiroshima ash.
I sizzle,

Herr Love, Herr Lucifer,
Your flash
In the pan.

D. C. BERRY

LEONARD COHEN · 1934–

THE EMPEROR'S NEW ALBUM

I want you but I don't deserve you
My soul is not healthy or clean
For a moose with undisciplined trousers
Is slightly less smart than it seems

But you'd like my friend, his name's Jesus
He's tall and he's handsome and cool
He's especially relaxed among lepers
He's the grooviest kid in the school

I awake from a dream that I'm sleeping
In the soft magazine of your hair

It's warm and it's dark and it's raining
And I'm coming to Scarborough Fair

There's a man on the TV who's standing
On a mountain of glasses and shoes
They've ambushed the train from Vienna
On the six and a half o'clock news

There are ten thousand Aryan women
In position and firing at will
I'll take the ones in the tower
And Jesus the fools on the hill

And we synchronise watches and guide books
And our weapons, false papers and charts
General Mills on deployment of symbols
General Boon on the breaking of hearts

Then I'll send in my troops in their millions
I've trained them to swim in the dark
Resistance is futile, we're poets,
And we'll touch your perfect bodies
With our shlong

La la la la la la la la
La la la la la la la
La la la la la la la la
La la la la la la la

JOHN CLARKE

THOMAS PYNCHON · 1937–

THE CRYING OF LOT 49

[*a digested version of the novel, which was published in 1966*]

Mrs Oedipa Maas came home from a Tupperware party to find that she had
been named executor, or she supposed executrix, of the estate of her former
lover, Pierce Inverarity, a California property mogul who once lost $2m in
his spare time. The letter said her co-executor was to be a lawyer called
Metzger from a firm called Lookat, Meimtrying, Toohard, Tobewacky.

As she mixed herself a whiskey sour and waited for her husband, Wendell 'Mucho' Maas, to return home from FUCK radio, Oedipa allowed herself some anarchic thoughts about Vivaldi's kazoo concerto and how Pierce used to call her in funny voices.

As she mixed herself a whiskey sour and waited for her husband, Wendell 'Mucho' Maas, to return home from FUCK radio, Oedipa allowed herself some anarchic thoughts about Vivaldi's kazoo concerto and how Pierce used to call her in funny voices.

'You're too sensitive,' she said in an access of helplessness as Mucho detailed his latest defeat. 'I'm going to see my shrink.'

'Why are you not taking the pills?' Dr Hilarius asked. 'I need you for my LSD trials.'

'I'm hallucinating already,' Oedipa replied.

'So early in the book.'

She felt the onset of revelation, a shimmer of mystic meaninglessness and lowered her hair, Rapunzel-like, into the studied opacity of chapter two.

Oedipa drove south to San Narcisco, less of a city more a rather dull concept that had been Pierce's domicile, and checked in to the Echo Courts Motel. A drop-out called Miles appeared from behind a statue of a nymphet. 'I'm lead singer with the Paranoids,' he said. 'I'm too old to Frug.'

'You can leave all the enigmatic shit to me,' said another man, who introduced himself as Metzger. 'I live inside my looks. I was once a child actor called Baby Igor. How about we play Strip Botticelli?'

Oedipa went to her room and put on several more layers of clothes. It could have been a good gag but she blew it and went to bed with him anyway. That was the problem with post-modernism. No self-will, no motivation, no character. She wondered if she should confess her infidelity to Mucho, but why bother when he might have been writing the story? Things did not delay in becoming more curious when they came across Pierce's stamp collection, thousands of coloured windows into time and space, ex-rivals for her affections that would be broken into lots. Oedipa sensed a revelation as she drifted into a bar called Scope.

'Join the Peter Pinguid Society,' said Mike Fallopian, a rightwing nutcase. 'We communicate via a rebel mail service using the WASTE system.'

'What's that?'

'I could tell you but it still wouldn't make any sense and you wouldn't care anyway. Best to keep you guessing. That way you might think there's a point.'

'You're right,' Metzger agreed. 'We should go with the Paranoids to check out Pierce's investment at Fangoso Lagoons.'

'I'm your inverse,' said a man called Di Presso. 'I'm a lawyer turned actor. I've no idea what I'm doing here but a load of GI bones got turned into charcoal filters.'

'That's like the Jacobean tragedy that's playing at the Tank theatre.'

They absorbed themselves in The Courier's Tragedy, a play of incest, murder, the Thurn and Taxis mail system and the mysterious breakaway Tristero postal sect. Nobody said an in-joke had to be funny.

'Where's the text?' Oedipa asked. 'There is no text,' the director Randolph Driblette answered. 'This is the text. I made it up.' She longed for meaning. Maybe she could find it in Zapf's bookshop. Who were the Tristero assassins? Had she given them life? Had someone been smoking too much dope? She came across a man drawing the Tristero sign of the horn. Why? She visited John Nefastis, the man who postulated Maxwell's Demon with his perpetual motion machine. 'Entropy connects the laws of thermodynamics to information flow,' he said.

'There's a conspiracy theory,' Genghis Cohen, the stamp expert, explained. 'All Pierce's stamps are deliberate Tristero errors.'

Metzger was not that bothered at Oedipa's leaving, but then why should he be? He'd had enough and he had never existed without her. Besides he had a 15-year-old nymphet to fuck. Oedipa looked at some deaf-mutes, went to a fag club and dropped in on Mucho. He had dropped out on acid. She went to see Dr Hilarius. 'I tortured the Jews at Buchenwald by making them read this kind of crap,' he laughed, firing a gun indiscriminately, before the police arrived.

Oedipa headed to Berkeley to meet Emory Bortz, a world expert in Jacobean tragedy. 'Driblette has committed suicide,' he said.

'Why does everyone leave me?'

'I can't imagine.'

'Now I'll never know the secrets of the Tristero. Did it really exist? Was it Pierce's last elaborate hoax? Am I mad? Or am I just stuck in a dated timewarp of empty counter-cultural allusions to which 60s stoners and reviewers too scared of being thought stupid will attach great depth and revelation?'

Self-absorbed with her own one-dimensionality, Oedipa never heard Pynchon laughing as he scammed the literati once again. Instead she waited for the crying of lot 49 to see who would bid for Pierce's stamps. Oh, look! It's you.

JOHN CRACE

SEAMUS HEANEY · 1939–

USQUEBAUGH

[*partly suggested by Heaney's poem 'Oysters'—'Millions of them ripped and shucked and scattered'*]

Deft, practised, eager.
Your fingers twist the metal cap.

Late into the moth-infested night
We listen to soft scrapings
Of bottle-top on ridged glass,

The plash and glug of amber liquid
Streaming into tumblers, inches deep.
Life-water. Fire-tanged
Hard-stuff. Gallons of it,
Sipped and swigged and swallowed.

Whiskey: its terse vowels belie
The slow fuddling and mellowing,
Our guttural speech slurring
Into warm, thick blather,
The pie-eyed, slug-witted slump

Into soused oblivion—
And the awakening. I long
For pure, cold water as the pump
Creaks in the yard. A bucket
Clatters to the ground. Is agony.

WENDY COPE

CLIVE JAMES · 1939–

LETTER TO MYSELF

*[Clive James's poems include a series of verse-letters to Martin Amis,
Tom Stoppard, and other friends]*

Dear *Clive*, I've meant to scribble you a letter
For some time now. I know you like to get a
Brown-noser now and then, and—well—who better

To do the honours than yours truly, *Clive*?
Over the past few years I think that I've
Proven myself the handiest hack alive

(Or even dead) at pumping up the egos
Of my illustrious *Grub Street amigos*.
It's sometimes said of me, 'Too bad that he goes

Over the top so often. Are his pals
Really the *Goethes, Mozarts, Juvenals,*
Einsteins, Nijinskys, Chaplins, Bluff King Hals,

Elijahs, Pee Wee Russells, Leonardos,   .
Jane Austens, Churchills, Platos, Giottos, Bardots—
This list could grow as long as a *Mikado's*

Great fingernail, if I don't stop it pronto—
Et cetera, of his peer-group? I don't want to
Malign the poor sap, but he sounds like *Tonto*

At times, whose quaint devotion to the *Ranger*
I never understood. He runs the danger
Of taking every passing *Percy Grainger*

For *Beethoven;* or seeing *Botticelli's*
Mind-boggling artistry (or, say, *Crivelli's*)
In some chum's doodle on a *Bertorelli's*

Table-napkin. Good *God,* where will it end?
I like a fellow who sticks by his friend,
But *Clive's* like *Don Quixote,* round the bend!'

I've heard this stuff a zillion times before.
Every great poet meets the kind of bore,
Straight from the *Dunciad,* who feels as sore

As *Grendel* and *Beowulf,* because
He's not in on the act. As if I was
A sort of literary *Wiz of Oz,*

Holding my court, but waiting to be rumbled
By *Judy Garland's* pooch! I bet they grumbled
When *Pope* flashed *Dryden's* name, or *Piero* mumbled

Something about *Veneziano.* Blimey!
These runty characters were sent to try me,
But I'm not *Gulliver* and they can't tie me

Down, sport. I'll lay off writing to my chinas
For now—those *Schopenhauers, Kafkas, Heines*—
And magic up some several-hundred-liners

About myself. The prospect's fairly heady!
Make sure the old adrenal pump is steady:
Not too much juice. Ready when you are . . . Ready!

Actually, *Clive*, I must admit I'm nervous.
I've never had to face the champion servers—
Toe-amputators, any-which-way swervers—

But now I feel the terror of some boy
Alone before the *Wimbledon polloi*,
Waiting for *Hoad* or *Laver* to destroy

Him smash by smash. Will some allusion ace
Me, as I flail about, *gauche*, in disgrace?
Will metaphors bounce up and dent my face?

Or will . . .? But wait a tick; don't let's forget
That's me as well the far side of the net.
Christ, what a bummeroo! I'd better let

This metaphor drop like a hot potato
And settle down to something a bit straighter,
More in the style of *Horace, le grand Maître*.

Clive, you're the greatest poet in the business!
To contemplate your talents brings on dizziness.
Just as a *Bollinger* is full of fizziness—

The mark, I'm told, of any good champagne—
Ideas appear to bubble in your brain.
I'm baffled that your head can take the strain.

Tchaikovsky thought his bonce might topple off.
I don't think his mate *Rimsky-Korsakov*
Suffered the same delusion, but some prof

Might put us right on that one. Anyhow,
I like the splendid eminence of your brow
(*Hokusai's Fuji, Mallory's Jungfrau*

Seem the right names to drop in this connection).
I like your well-used cricket-ball complexion.
I like—and let's waive *Jamesian* circumspection

(I'm talking about me, not *Uncle Harry*)—
I like the whole caboodle. Yes, I'd marry
Me if I could. On honeymoon in *Paris*,

In any other *chic, kulturni* city,
We'd do the local *Hermitage* or *Pitti*
And jot down names of painters for our witty

Verse letters to each other. Life and art?
Both *Proust* and *Aristotle* said some smart,
Quotable things about this, but apart

From them (the *Hobbs* and *Bradman* of their field)
A fair amount remains to be revealed.
Which is where we waltz in. Art has appealed

To us for yonks. We've always nursed a pash
For Russian Lit., Expressionist *gouaches*,
The Blues, *Ming* vases, *Rosewall*'s cross-court smash,

Early *Walt Disney*, madrigals, *Kung Fu*,
Homer, French cooking, *Mahler*'s no. 2,
Dame Sybil Thorndyke, *Pascal's Pensées, Pooh* . . .

The names! The names! They give me such a thrill,
I could run on till Doomsday in this shrill,
Pindaric fashion, and, dear *Clive*, no doubt I will.

CHRISTOPHER REID

J. M. COETZEE · 1940–

YOUTH

[a condensed version of the novel]

He lives in a one-room flat near Mowbray railway station for which
he pays 11 guineas a month. He is at pains not to be late with the rent
because he has obtained the flat under false pretences. He has given his
occupation as library assistant rather than student. It is not quite a lie as
he does man the reading room every weekday evening. Every Sunday he

boils up marrowbones to make enough soup to last a week. He is proving man is an island.

He has a best friend, Paul, also a mathematician, who is having an affair with an older woman named Elinor. Her sister, Jacqueline, takes him for a walk on the beach. He does not resist and goes through with the act. He knows that she will not have enjoyed their lovemaking either, but he knows enough to say nothing. Within a week she has moved in with him. He finds her presence claustrophobic. She finds his diary. She leaves.

He is reading the Cantos of Ezra Pound and dreams of being a poet. He gets a girl named Sarah pregnant. They fail to connect. She has an abortion. They separate. After Sharpeville, he senses revolution in the air. He moves to London.

He gets a job as a computer programmer with IBM and each morning he dons his dark suit, waiting for the weekend when he can see a Bergman film or go to the Reading Room. He joins a poetry group and meets a woman. They get undressed but there is no warmth between them. They say 'sorry' to one another and part. He thinks perhaps he is homosexual. He picks up a man. They say nothing. Is this homosexuality?

He is turned down for a flatshare. He is too boring. His misery is almost complete. His mother writes to him every week, but he replies only rarely. To do otherwise would smack of reciprocation. He meets a Swedish girl named Astrid. They go to bed, but he feels discomforted by her proximity. He pretends to sleep when she lets herself out.

He leaves IBM and attempts to write like Henry James. He fails. He joins International Computers and feels he's sold his soul to the Americans. He reads Beckett. He meets an Indian programmer named Ganapathy and invites him for a meal but he does not turn up. He reflects on his life. He has failed as both a lover and a writer. He sits alone.

JOHN CRACE

CRAIG RAINE · 1944–

LIFE AND TIMES

[*after* History: The Home Movie]

1944: It's a Poet

Baby like hedgehog but
without those pointy bits:
quills. That's it. Quills.

Baby unbearded
as yet, pushes head-first
out of his mummy's pink dressing womb

Like Neil Armstrong
leaving Apollo 9. Or
quite like it, in a way.

Though obviously
Apollo 9 was made of
some sort of metal

And wasn't pink
and it had a control panel
with wires, buttons, levers and so on.

Still one mustn't be
pernickety
when it comes to poetry.

Congratulations, madam,
says the doctor, dressed all
in white, like a

doctor. It's a poet!
A minor poet! Neat on
similes, but we're still checking the

scansion. Baby still
unbearded suckles at
his mother's telephone receiver.

Actually, not her telephone receiver
but her bosoms.
Only they look slightly like

A telephone receiver
as seen from
an unusual angle.

Joyce, Eliot, Pound,
Pasternak, Conrad, Auden,
I thought I'd just

mention them. And also
Haile Selassie and Haile
Mills. And what about

Stalin too? These names
give the poem a swanky ring,
n'est ce pas?

1958: *Sprouts*

Hair begins to sprout
from the poet's skin
in particular

Around his Eiffel
Tower: non-swanks, it
really is that

big. Also from his
chin and around his mouth
the hairiest poet since

Walt Whitman or
Hendrix, Jimi. Mmmmm,
so modern, so very

Modern. Now,
where was I?
Ah, yes. Hitler

Bombs Bristol while
Grandpa Raine brushes his
piano key teeth

In nearby Oxford. Or at
least quite nearby, if
you take the M4.

1972: *The Poet Takes a Pupil*

'Hello' he opened
his pillar-box mouth and
let himself in.

'My name's Amis. Martin
Amis. This your
sock is it then?'

Sock! We speak the same
language! For sock
read office! Great minds!

It must have been something
like this when Wordsworth met
Coleridge. I could murder a

Gitanes, Sam. The biff biff war in
Vietnam continues as
Amis learns at the

Poet's elbowish knee.
And look who Amis
knows! Amis knows

Fenton who knows Barnes who
knows McEwan who knows Motion
who knows Shakespeare

Though not to speak to. The
Shah falls. People die like
goldfish. The Ayatollah,

also bearded, sits in the
Peacock over-throne as the
Poet eases into his Faber sock.

1985: Another dirty bit to keep you reading

Anna Vladimirovna Romanovna
naked. Her breasts unfishy shell-
fish now unshelled.

The poet's great grandpa
naked. His leg of
lamb at the ready.

A condom like a
hot air balloon
only smaller.

Spermatozoa wriggling
on the linoleum like
spilt rice pudding.

Whoops. The poet's
great grandpa has
blown it. Sorry, Anna, love.

1994: Oxford. Major work ahead
The world talks of
nothing else. 'Read all
about it!' yell

The newsvendors. 'Major new
work by Raine!' Crowds
like the collective name for

lots of people stream
from every corner
anxious for an epic

verse history of
Europe, highly praised
by Fenton, Amis,

Raine, Barnes, Raine, Motion,
Raine, McEwan, Raine, Carey,
Morrison, Raine, Raine and

Raine, Raine go away
come again another
thingummy.
                          CRAIG BROWN

Julian Barnes · 1946–

LOVE, ETC.

[a condensed version of the novel, which was published in 2000; the central characters had already appeared in an earlier novel by Julian Barnes, Talking It Over, which was published in 1991]

STUART: Hello. We've met before. Remember? I remember you.

OLIVER: Oh, I remember you. How very Stuartesque. I can tell you remember me.

GILLIAN: You may or you may not remember me.

STUART: Here's the story so far. Gillian and I fell in love, we got married and my best friend, Oliver, stole her off me. He hit her, I went to America, got married, became successful, got divorced (again) and came back to England where I've set up an organic veg business.

OLIVER: Rush not to judgment.

GILLIAN: I knew Stuart was watching, so I made Oliver hit me. To drive Stuart away. It's tough for Oliver now. I'm the one with the job and the money. He's still waiting for things to happen.

OLIVER: Guess who phoned last night? Narcoleptic and steatopygous Stuart. Misprise me not, I'm curious. He could also fund my scriptwriting.

GILLIAN: I just knew Stuart had phoned. Don't ask me how. Did I tell you that Oliver and I rarely have sex these days?

STUART: I offered to take them out, but they couldn't afford a babysitter. Oliver patronised my choice of wine; Gillian had made a delicious lasagne.

GILLIAN: I'd forgotten how thoughtful Stuart is. I also burnt the lasagne.

OLIVER: It all went swimmingly.

STUART: My plan is to move them all back into a house I own. And give Oliver a job driving a van.

GILLIAN: It's the house Stuart and I used to live in.

STUART: Gillian told me Oliver had a breakdown after his father died.

GILLIAN: Do you think I'm deliberately evading things? Oliver's become withdrawn again but the house is quite nice and the kids love it.

OLIVER: Dr Robb says that part of the illness is feeling that you're never going to get better. But how do we know that voice is the illness and not reality.

GILLIAN: I just let Stuart slip into me.

STUART: It was different to how it used to be. Less predictable.

GILLIAN: I've been protecting Stuart. He raped me. And I'm pregnant.

OLIVER: Our lives are a cliché.
STUART: Now we've had sex I'm not sure that I love Gillian as much as I thought.
GILLIAN: Does Stuart still love me? That's the question.

JOHN CRACE

DAVID HARE · 1947–

AN EXTRACT FROM THE DIARY OF DAVID HARE

[*with special reference to Hare's trilogy of plays about British institutions*—Racing Demon, Murmuring Judges *and* The Absence of War]

The State of Britain, Part One: Three days ago, I went to a party. I don't often go to parties, because I'm not that kind of person, I'm a playwright, with more serious concerns. But I went to this one. By bus, of course. I'm not the sort of person who takes taxis. So I hailed a double-decker in the King's Road and told the driver to take me to Islington. He was then to wait for me outside the party for an hour or two and take me back. The instructions were quite clear. But of course this is Thatcher's Britain, so when I left the party—a party I didn't particularly enjoy, by the way, it was hardly serious at all and full of 'amusing' people—the bus was nowhere to be seen (typical) and I was forced to hail, against all my instincts, a black cab. Out of sympathy with the driver I sat with him in the front, observing, observing, observing, my mind racing back to one of those rare defining moments, disproportionately significant but peculiarly illuminating, that had occurred back at the party.

I had been standing in the corner of the room with the dirty paper cup I had specially brought with me, when a man had come over—a tall, flashy type, with an easy smile, wearing a fashionable 'tie'. He said: 'You look a bit lonely, may I introduce myself?' He then introduced himself. I didn't reply, preferring to observe, as most serious playwrights do. He then said—again that fake smile—'And who are you?'

I was outraged, utterly outraged. And flabbergasted. Shocked too. Shocked, outraged and flabbergasted. Not for me, of course, but for my profession, and the whole of British Theatre, from the lowest understudy right up to the most brilliant and dangerous playwright (whether this is me or not is beside the point). Why was this man—this man in his fashionable tie, with his promiscuous smile and his over-attentive handshake—pretending not to know who the hell I was? This was a sign of our inexorable national decline, as significant and painful in its way as the Miners Strike or the Falklands Conflict.

The State of Britain, Part Two: As the hurt and the horror surged within me, I felt driven to speak. 'I'm David Hare,' I said.

'David Hare!' he repeated, 'Goodness! I really enjoy all your plays— you're one of the greatest living playwrights, in my opinion!'

Note that patronising, biassed and artfully demeaning tone in a statement riddled with the foul odour of ruling class condescension: 'ONE OF the greatest LIVING playwrights, IN MY OPINION'. Only in Britain—tired, sick, dislocated, dying Britain—in the 1990s could it be considered 'fashionable' to denigrate a serious playwright in this way. When I got home, I immediately wrote a cool letter to the host of the party, questioning his ethics in inviting me to a function at which there were people who openly hated me, roundly condemning his loathsome hypocrisy in not warning me of his treachery. He eventually replied with some sort of an apology. Which all goes to show that here in Thatcher's Britain, the national pastime—the national characteristic—is to apologise, apologise, apologise. When will we as a nation have the courage to start to stand up for ourselves?

The State of Britain, Part Three: I've tried to bring out something of this and other symptoms of our national decline in my new play *Cardboard Characters*—the first part of my powerful new *Forty Winks* trilogy consisting of *Cardboard Characters*, *Dialogue Dreary* and *An Absence of Interest*—which is currently being staged at The National Theatre. *An Absence of Interest* seeks to analyse the system whereby the ruling classes use the money gained from the working classes to finance other members of the ruling classes to write a trilogy about how they take money from the working classes to finance their systems, a trilogy which will be visited, I hope, not only by other members of the ruling classes but by a few representatives of the working class as well. It is a tremendously strong piece, devastating in its indictment of the inherent hypocrisy of those involved in its creation.

The State of Britain, Part Four: In this truly moving piece of dialogue, the main character is a brilliant yet sensitive playwright, who some people say is based on me but is obviously NOT me at all—I'm not Welsh. In this truly moving piece of dialogue the playwright character, who is called Daffyd Hare, confronts what he sees as the malaise in post-colonial Britain:

JACK: Cigarette?
DAFFYD: No thanks.
JACK: You don't want a cigarette?
DAFFYD: Not at the moment. No thanks.
JACK: Don't smoke?
DAFFYD: Only when I stop to think about the malaise in post-colonial Britain which stems, directly or indirectly, from our national sense of dislocation,

springing, whether consciously or not, from our deeply rooted inability to shed the sense of past glories, a failure which may or may not be rooted in our concurrent inability to face up to the challenges of the future, to develop and expand those institutions that are crumbling around us, unloved and unwanted, fostering an abandoned generation without pride or sense of purpose. *(He frowns. Something is on his mind)*

JACK: Yeah, I keep meaning to give up, too. I did once, for a couple of months, but then I went back. Mug's game, really.

DAFFYD: You're right there, Jack.

JACK: It's not as though I even like the taste, much. How about you?

DAFFYD: I'd relish the taste more if it didn't make me remember the days when hope beat in our hearts, when it seemed as if this country was marching forward into a new age, an age of optimism, an age in which society would look after those who were unable, for whatever reason, to—

JACK *(looking at watch)*: Lordy be, Daffyd—is that the time? I must be going. Cheerio, then. Lovely talking to you.

DAFFYD *(frowns)*: I've always wanted to know the answer. The answer to one question. A question that has haunted me. And the question is. After two and a half hours, is this all it's been about. Is it? Well, is it?

(The lights fade)

Well—is it?

(The sound of 'Land of Hope and Glory' grows louder. Curtain.)

CRAIG BROWN

IAN MCEWAN · 1948–

SATURDAY

[a condensed version of the novel]

Henry Perowne wakes early in a state of near euphoria. He gets up quietly in order not to disturb his wife, Rosalind, who lies sleeping. Like the neurosurgeon he is, he clinically dissects his mood. Has he perhaps become a little too smug and self-satisfied? No, he deserves to be extremely rich and happy.

'Hello birds, hello trees,' he says to himself before he notices an arc of flame cross the sky. He watches as an aeroplane with engines ablaze struggles over his Bloomsbury house, and waits for the explosion that never comes. He is unsettled, wondering if this presages a terrorist attack. How quickly one's life can alter, he thinks, and how curious not to know for sure.

He tiptoes downstairs where his son Theo is drinking a cup of tea. Perowne is as proud of Theo, who is already at just 18 one of the world's leading blues guitarists, as he is of his daughter Daisy, the foremost young poet of her generation, who is returning home from Paris this evening for the first time in six months. He switches on the news to find there was no terrorist incident and that the plane has landed safely. What strange tricks the mind can play, he thinks.

Henry returns upstairs. Rosalind welcomes him and they make love passionately. He loves her now as much as the day his dexterity saved her from blindness more than 20 years ago. 'I love you only,' he whispers. 'I adore you, too,' she replies.

He drives towards his weekly squash match with Strauss. The streets are blocked because of the anti-war march. Henry can see the case both for and against the invasion of Iraq. How complicated life can be, he thinks, when you think so deeply and so philosophically and are yet so happy. A car brushes past him and breaks off his wing mirror. Three men get out and threaten him. One, Baxter, hits him in the chest. Perowne looks him in the eye and diagnoses Huntington's disease. The news confuses Baxter, who backs off.

Bugger, thinks Perowne, upset at having lost to Strauss, as he drives back from his mother's. He should be more disturbed by her Alzheimer's but he's concentrating on his happiness.

The evening is not devoid of tension. Daisy is withholding something and Rosalind's father is drunk, but the mood is mellowing when Baxter breaks in and threatens them with a knife. He orders Daisy to get undressed and Henry observes she is pregnant. Theo tenses his heroic muscular physique and pushes Baxter to the ground.

Henry must perform emergency surgery on Baxter. He harvests two long strips of pericranium and repairs the tear in the dura. He flicks his gloves. Whatever Baxter may have done, he was owed another chance.

He and Rosalind fall into each others arms. 'Everything's going to be happy,' he says. And now the day is over.

JOHN CRACE

MARTIN AMIS · 1949–

SUCCESS

[a digested version of the novel, which was published in 1978]

January

(1) 'Terry speaking,' I said. 'I'm afraid Gregory isn't here, Miranda.'

Gregory was in fact sitting next door. 'Success?' he called. 'It's so tiring when everyone demands you fuck their amber jewel.'

No one wants to fuck me any more. Not even the dwarf with big ears. What a bitch.

Greg is my foster brother. He's six foot one, elegantly handsome with brilliant white teeth and a bit queer; I'm an ugly five-foot-nothing ginger. You could say we're both caricatures, but who really cares when our sole purpose is to shock? Did I mention I was so desperate I'd even fuck a granny?

(2) So you've met Terence, my plebeian foster brother? My father took pity on him after his father murdered his mother and sister. It's a ridiculous idea, I know, but it's all I could come up with at three in the morning after a tough night out, and if Mart doesn't get Terence and me sharing my London bachelor pad then the whole conceit is fucked. Loosen up. It's the late 70s. Suck on the panache of the unpleasant.

'Do wash the effluvia from the palatinate dome of my immense cock,' I said after yet another bout of sexual gymnastics.

April

(1) Guess what? I fucked a beautiful woman. April Fool! I bet you weren't expecting that. Oh, you were. So what can I tell you? Well, I work in some kind of sales job but I'm not sure quite what as Mart doesn't know anything about proley jobs himself other than sales is a proley job which is why I have it. And I'm worried about going broke. There's a rumour going round that some of us will be sacked and Mr Veale the union clerk wants me to get everyone to join. Not sure I can be bothered, though, as I'd rather spend the book worrying if my cock is going to fall off.

'Hello, yobbo.'

That was Ursula, my foster sister. She's even more tonto than me. And even less of a rounded character, if that's possible. I think Greg may have fucked her once. I'm hoping to get a look at her tits.

Things may be looking up. There's a girl at work called Jan who doesn't seem to be put off when we go out for a drink and I end the evening voiding huge quantities of vomit over her enormous breasts. I'm hoping to take her home and fuck her this evening.

(2) Oh dear. I seem to have rather blotted my copybook. Terence had arrived back with a common-looking girl, June I think she was, when the police rang to say Ursula had slit her wrists. There was obviously no point in both of us going to the hospital, so I stayed behind with Jean and buggered her till she bled—not just a Shock Jock but a Shock Cock too!—and booted her out. And, well, Terence wasn't best pleased.

Still, the good news is that Ursula has been staying with me since she got out of hospital, and I'm idly wondering if we will resume fucking again or whether her downy orifices will no longer hold their attraction for me. Come, come, don't get all petit bourgeois with me about incest. Let me tell you, it's a great deal worse being forced to service the ghastly couple, Odette and Jason, whose art gallery I deign to work in. The required tumescence is such an effort.

September

(1) You're getting the hang of this now, aren't you? I mean, come on, you'd need to be a dummy not to see where this is heading. OK, I know I said things were looking up last time, but this time they really are. Sure it was a blow that Greg fucked Jan and I'll admit I moped about the flat for a couple of weeks afterwards, but she left work and I didn't have to see her again and, so, onwards and upwards. Just like my cock.

The good thing about Ursula trying to kill herself is that it's meant she's come to live with us. You may have realised by now that Greg is a liar—No shit! A tricksy unreliable narrator!—and he might say he's out a lot but he spends most of his time alone, and as I've now, thanks to Veale, got loads of money Ursula is all mine. Maybe sex is easy after all. You just insist. I point her to my cock and she sucks it.

(2) I haven't been altogether truthful. I only had sex with Jason and Odette in the hope they wouldn't fire me. But they did anyway, and I'm broke, getting panic attacks and shitting in my pants. Is that extreme enough? I need Ursula. I go to Terence's room to find her passively fucking him.

'You're mine,' I cry. 'I want you to fuck me.'

'I hate you,' she says.

'You can't do that. What will become of us?'

Why is it always the psychological clichés that make you weep?

December

(1) I suppose I ought to feel guilty that Ursula killed herself after that, but I don't.

Then my attempts at pathos when I described my father killing my sister didn't work either. So here I am. I've got loads of money. I've got a hydraulic erection and I'm fucking a lot of women. I even met Jan who told me Greg never fucked her because he couldn't get a hard-on. I'm doing all right.

(2) Ursula's dead. My father's dead. Everything's a mess and the proles are taking over. I should have been a writer. Like Mart.

JOHN CRACE

J. K. ROWLING · 1965–

HARRY POTTER AND THE ROLLING STONE

[The Rolling Stone, as opposed to the Philosopher's Stone]

The boys' uniforms department at Peter Jones was all out of Hogwarts ties, so Harry—who had singed his school tie in a fight with an irksome dragon—decided to try some other stores. He walked down Kings Road, past boutiques of silver suits and orange corduroy jackets, shoe stores that sold platform boots with goldfish in their heels, glitter pumps, and purple suede sandals. Harry smiled as he passed a pub called the Chelsea Potter— perhaps an ancestor had opened it centuries ago, when a group of early Potters had settled in the area.

He continued down the street, marvelling at the colourful and exciting shops, but not finding anything that he could even remotely hope to wear at school.

Then he came across a large modern building that seemed to be entirely covered in mirrors. A sign over the door identified it as the Chelsea Drugstore. Harry walked down the steps and through the shiny doors.

Inside, it didn't look like a drug-store at all. A maze of little stalls sold records and T-shirts, incense and small metal pipes that resembled plumbing supplies. Blaring out of the loudspeakers was a tune Harry recognized from the Top of the Pops, though he couldn't say he liked it much. He began flipping through a pile of magazines of pop stars and film actors as he vaguely noticed a small old shopkeeper beckoning him to come over. Harry ignored him.

'Psssst! Oy, you—come over here.'

The man had long brown hair and huge lips and he seemed to jiggle and throb as he stood behind his stall, as if listening to some sort of secret tune in his head.

'Oy, you with the burnt tie—come 'ere . . .'

Finally Harry went over to the small man in a purple crushed-velvet suit and silver top hat.

'What do you want?'

'Why'd you set fire to your tie?'

'I didn't, I was in a fight with a—' Harry was about to explain how a couch he'd been sitting on had suddenly turned into a dragon, but he thought the better of it. 'It just got burnt.'

'I can help you with that. You don't want to go around looking like that. It gives a bad impression.'

Harry looked at the clothes in the man's stall. There were shiny silk suits, top hats with glittered white stars and red stripes. There were scarves and white jumpsuits with corset strings and uniforms that looked—yes, Harry was sure of it—like they were used for playing American football. But there were no ties.

'What are all these things?'

'These are from my Rock 'n' Roll Circus,' said the man. 'Allow me to introduce myself. I am a man of wealth and taste. Name's Jack Flash.'

'How do you do, Jack Flash?'

'I do fairly well, actually.'

'I'm Harry.'

'Come out back, Harry. I'll see if I can find a tie for you.'

Harry demurred, not so much out of dislike or distrust of Mr Flash (after all, if he had ignored every unlikely offer, he wouldn't be where he was today). But he wasn't sure if he had time.

Sensing Harry's reluctance, Jack Flash quickly reached into the clothing pile and pulled out a couple of brightly coloured, wide psychedelic neckties, holding them up for Harry's inspection. 'Whatcha think of these. Gear, right?'

Harry didn't want to seem unappreciative, but these ties were not right at all. 'I'm not sure they're quite the correct colour,' he said diplomatically.

'Very astute, Harry! That was just a test. We'd better check in the back. I think I've got something that might be a bit more . . . Hogwarts.'

'But how did you know I go to Hogwarts?' inquired Harry.

'Ah! I can always tell a, um, Hogwartian,' said Jack Flash cheerily. 'Come with me.'

Well, that did sound more hopeful, thought Harry. He followed Mr Flash through a small orange door and into a dark, narrow corridor that was lit with odd overhead blue lights that made the white of Harry's shirt look like neon. He noticed that Jack Flash's silver hat glowed bright.

'Totally fab, eh? You should try it on acid.'

Harry didn't say so, but he doubted the thrill could be enhanced by drinking acid.

The blue-light corridor led to another corridor, this one smaller and darker. Harry could hear the dull drone of drums in the distance, which echoed through the walls.

'Charlie's good tonight, ain't 'e?' said Jack Flash with a wicked smile.

Harry had no idea who Charlie was, but he was more concerned with his situation. 'Where am I?' he said.

'Two thousand light-years from home,' said Jack with a laugh, placing his hands on his hips and jutting out his bottom lip. Harry thought that next to Hagrid, this man had the biggest lips he'd ever seen.

'I should like to go home now, please.'

Jack stuck out his tongue and wagged his finger. 'You're very demanding, aren't you? Well you can't always get what you want. And if you try sometime, you just might find, you get what you need.' And with that, he leapt up again and began trotting horselike on the spot. Harry thought this Jack Flash was very odd.

They now came out to a small courtyard with a swimming pool that had a car in it at the bottom.

'What's that?' asked Harry.

'It's a car in a swimming pool, ennit?'

'But what's it doing down there?'

'Brian drove it in. Didn't look where he was going, the silly git. Oops— one of the buttons on my trousers has fallen off. You wouldn't want my trousers to fall down, would you?'

Harry thought he didn't care about Mr Flash's trousers one way or another.

'I should like to see the ties now,' he said. But as he said this, he stepped on something that called out and moaned. 'What was that?'

'Look out where you step!'

Harry looked down and saw he had stepped on a huge pile of putrefying muck. 'Is that a compost heap?' asked Harry.

'No, that's Keith.'

The pile blinked and Harry now saw the two eyes staring frostily at them. The muck parted and formed lips. A groan arose from the muck and then spoke. 'What day is it?'

'It's Tuesday,' said Flash.

'No, it's definitely Monday,' said Harry.

The heap coughed and then closed its eyes. Harry assumed it had gone back to sleep.

'Is that what they teach you at Hogwarts? To step on everything?'

The drums had stopped now and the sudden silence seemed to depress Jack Flash.

'All right, take your clothes off, Harry.'

'What?'

'You heard me. Off with them.' And Harry now noticed the gun in Jack Flash's right hand.

He reached in his pocket for his wand, but it wasn't there. Then he remembered he'd left it in the pocket of his other jacket at school. Curses, he thought. He'd meant to buy another wand at Peter Jones, but had forgotten to do it.

'Hop to it, lad,' said Mr Flash impatiently.

Slowly, Harry began taking off his clothes, tossing the burnt tie aside. Jack Flash began undressing too. Quite soon they were both standing in their skivvies.

'Okay, hand them over.'

Harry handed his jacket, shirt, and shorts to Jack Flash, who tried to squeeze into them.

'You can put mine on if you like.'

Harry didn't much like the thought of wearing Jack Flash's clothes, but he figured it'd be better than standing around half naked in the cold. So he put them on. The silver jacket felt very large.

Jack was now squeezed into Harry's Hogwarts uniform, and Harry thought he looked very silly.

'Hullo! Hullo, I'm Harry Potter!' said Jack Flash in a ridiculously high voice.

'How do you know my name?'

'Oh everyone knows Harry Potter. You have the perfect demographic . . . *Everyone*.' And he laughed, and repeated it: 'Everyone.' He reached into the pocket and a look of disappointment came across his face. 'Where's the wand?'

'It's in my other jacket,' said Harry.

Jack thought for a moment, his face squeezed into a scowl. 'You can help me, little Harry.'

'Help you? How?'

'I once had a merry band of minstrels, but the group fell apart. Charlie went back to his dogs and his wife—his first wife, if you please, whom he never even left in the first place. Bill retired to an old-age pensioners home in Blackpool after his son married his former mother-in-law. Brian drove into his swimming pool, Ronnie got sued by his own haircut, and Keith, as you saw, turned into a compost heap, gathering moss. And you know what they say about a Rolling Stone. Well, it's true. So it's just me now, running on the spot.' Here he began running on the spot again.

'What do you want?'

'I want you to tell me the secret.'

'What secret?'

'You know—the secret of synergy.'

'Synergy doesn't work,' said Harry.

'Oh yes, it does. You're flying proof. Let me have one.'

'One what?'

And here Jack Flash felt so frustrated he almost sneezed. 'A multimedia and cross-marketing deal with AOL–Time Warner!'

Harry turned crimson; talk of marketing always embarrassed him.

Jack was now dancing around the yard, pretending to be sitting on a broomstick. 'Look at me! I'm Harry Potter playing Quidditch!' This was embarrassing too.

Harry thought about Jack Flash pretending to be younger, prancing about in front of people, and it formed an unseemly picture. How could he get this aging Pan with a creative comb-over a cross-marketing deal?

Even Harry was getting a little long in the tooth for the kids these days; every six months they were on to a new action figure or boy band. He was thinking of retiring himself—after all, who wanted a nineteen-year-old boy wizard?

And yet . . . these silver clothes, these platform boots, stirred something within. He'd never had a band of minstrels, he'd never performed live in front of eighty thousand screaming fans. The hell with Hogwarts—he'd go on tour.

Just then a bald geezer with spectacles appeared from behind the shrubbery. 'Oy, Jack. What's with the school threads?'

'Hullo, Charlie. Change of direction. I've decided to become Harry Potter.'

'Does Keith know?'

And the compost heap rose up and shuddered. 'What's the buzz?' said the heap.

The trio was now joined by a skeletal figure with a bird's nest on his head.

'Ronnie-Baby,' said the heap. 'The Flash is going frosty.'

'Aren't we doing America next week?' said Ronnie.

Harry looked on in disbelief as the four men began squabbling. He subtly pointed an index figure at the bickering men and muttered under his breath:

> 'Brown sugar, tumbling dice,
> turn these minstrels into mice.'

There was a sudden thunder crack and then a burst of smoke filled the yard. When it cleared, the men had disappeared, replaced by four small mice clawing at one another and licking their fur.

Harry noticed also that his new clothes fit him better. He did a little jog on the spot. *This is gear,* he thought. He could place an advert in *Melody Maker* and his group could be rehearsing in a couple of weeks. Their emblem would be a burnt tie, and they'd go on Top of the Pops and tour the country. Then Europe and then America, followed by a crazed groupie and drug phase, and then clean up, and then a 'Behind the Music' segment on VH1.

They'd need a name, of course. Harry gave it a good think. Harry and the Potheads? The Chelsea Potters? Harry and the Hogwarts? Hog Harry and the Warts?

No, he'd go by something more poetic, something that would easily roll off the tongues of children around the globe: *World Domination Pop Cultural Event!*

J. B. MILLER

PART TWO

FROM THE WIDER WORLD

FRAGMENT OF A GREEK TRAGEDY

Alcmaeon.   Chorus.

Cho. O suitably attired in leather boots
    Head of a traveller, wherefore seeking whom
    Whence by what way how purposed art thou come
    To this well-nightingaled vicinity?
    My object in inquiring is to know.
    But if you happen to be deaf and dumb
    And do not understand a word I say,
    Nod with your hand to signify as much.
Alc. I journeyed hither a Boeotian road.
Cho. Sailing on horseback or with feet for oars?
Alc. Plying by turns my partnership of legs.
Cho. Beneath a shining or a rainy Zeus?
Alc. Mud's sister, not himself, adorns my shoes.
Cho. To learn your name would not displease me much.
Alc. Not all that men desire do they obtain.
Cho. Might I then hear at what your presence shoots?
Alc. A shepherd's questioned mouth informed me that—
Cho. What? for I know not yet what you will say.
Alc. Nor will you ever, if you interrupt.
Cho. Proceed, and I will hold my speechless tongue.
Alc. —This house was Eriphyla's, no one's else.
Cho. Nor did he shame his throat with hateful lies.
Alc. May I then enter, passing through the door?
Cho. Go, chase into the house a lucky foot.
    And, O my son, be, on the one hand, good,
    And do not, on the other hand, be bad;
    For that is very much the safest plan.
Alc. I go into the house with heels and speed.

Chorus.

In speculation   *Strophe*
I would not willingly acquire a name
        For ill-digested thought,
        But after pondering much
To this conclusion I at last have come:
    Life is uncertain.

This truth I have written deep
In my reflective midriff
On tablets not of wax,
Nor with a pen did I inscribe it there
For many reasons: *Life*, I say, *is not*
A stranger to uncertainty.
Not from the flight of omen-yelling fowls
This fact did I discover,
Nor did the Delphic tripod bark it out,
Nor yet Dodona.
Its native ingenuity sufficed
My self-taught diaphragm.

Why should I mention   *Antistrophe*
The Inachean daughter, loved of Zeus?
Her whom of old the gods,
More provident than kind,
Provided with four hoofs, two horns, one tail,
A gift not asked for,
And sent her forth to learn
The unfamiliar science
Of how to chew the cud.
She therefore, all about the Argive fields,
Went cropping pale green grass and nettle-tops,
Nor did they disagree with her.
Yet, howsoe'er nutritious, such repasts
I do not hanker after.
Never may Cypris for her seat select
My dappled liver!
Why should I mention Io? Why indeed?
I have no notion why.

But now does my boding heart   *Epode*
Unhired, unaccompanied, sing
A strain not meet for the dance.
Yea, even the palace appears
To my yoke of circular eyes
(The right, nor omit I the left)
Like a slaughterhouse, so to speak,
Garnished with woolly deaths
And many shipwrecks of cows.
I therefore in a Cissian strain lament,
And to the rapid,

Loud, linen-tattering thumps upon my chest
    Resounds in concert
The battering of my unlucky head.

Eriphyla (within). O, I am smitten with a hatchet's jaw;
    And that in deed and not in word alone.
Cho. I thought I heard a sound within the house
    Unlike the voice of one that jumps for joy.
Eri. He splits my skull, not in a friendly way,
    Once more: he purposes to kill me dead.
Cho. I would not be reputed rash, but yet
    I doubt if all be gay within the house.
Eri. O! O! another stroke! That makes the third.
    He stabs me to the heart against my wish.
Cho. If that be so, thy state of health is poor;
    But thine arithmetic is quite correct.

A. E. HOUSMAN

APPLYING SEALANT ROUND A BATH WITH
JOHANN WOLFGANG VON GOETHE

[*from* Sartre's Sink: The Great Writers' Complete Book of DIY]

TOOLS:
Mastic gun
Small wedge-shaped piece of wood

MATERIALS:
Silicone sealant
Washing-up liquid

22 May

Oh, my dear friend. What a thing our human destiny is! How happy I am to be embarking on a life in the country at last! Though I cannot say that I have yet met with any society, the solitude here is a balm, and I have already made all manner of acquaintance. A local handyman has become attached to me and will not have cause to regret it. Yesterday I sketched him replacing the guttering on a neighbour's house. I liked his way so spoke to him and asked after his circumstances. Presently we were acquainted and soon, as generally happens to me with this kind of person, intimate. What a serenity has taken possession of my soul since I arrived here in these paradisic parts.

Today he paid me a visit and was kind enough to suggest a large number of improvements to the property, all of which, he assures me, he is more than able to assist with.

25 May

Thank you, my friend, for your warning. Though I well know he can never be my equal, my workman appears an honest type with most pleasing features and attitude. I shall scarcely be able to tell you with what enthusiasm he began work on the house. He is an open man of good heart and I see no reason to keep my distance for the sake of form.

On his suggestion I have paid him in advance and provided him with a set of keys. While I was away riding he removed that old iron bathtub, preparatory to replacing it with a magnificent modern bath and shower unit of such harmonious shape and proportion that my very soul is afire, longing and languishing to try it.

On my return, soaked and dirty from one of those early summer showers that strike with so little notice, the water supply was cut off, but the worthy fellow showed such grace and generosity in sharing with me the contents of his flask of coffee that I was reminded of that magnificent passage in Homer where Odysseus enjoys the hospitality of the excellent swineherd. What fools men are not to see the obstacles that class and privilege place before us.

29 May

How these beautiful spring mornings fill the heart. Today finally the young fellow returned. I cannot express the feelings that overwhelmed me as he busied himself installing the bathtub I described to you in my last letter. Indeed, I should need the gifts of the greatest poets if I were to recount his expressive gestures, the harmony and economy of his movement and the secret fire that shone in his eyes as he set about laying the copper pipes, shaping them to fit so neatly the contours of the room and using his blow torch to such brilliant effect.

The sight delighted me and I sat down on the toilet seat across from him and took great pleasure in drawing this domestic idyll. I added the tiles that formed a backdrop to his work, a towel and the sink, all simply the way it was. And I must congratulate myself on creating a harmonious study. Surely there is more of dignity and honour in one hour of manual labour than in a month of observing protocol and ceremony in the service of the ambassador.

6 June

I no longer know where I got to in my story. It has been more than a week now since I last saw my artisan. A few of his tools still lie abandoned on the bathroom floor, some small wooden wedges, a simple mastic gun and a tube of white silicone sealant. A jar, containing a solution of washing-up liquid, sits still on the window ledge. How their presence haunts me.

I supposed at first that he had perhaps taken ill, until today, when I caught sight of his van in front of another house in the vicinity. I waited for some time to speak with him. When finally, giving up hope, I left a note and walked on, a shout of laughter could be heard from the window. I could tear my heart open and beat my poor head on seeing how little people can mean to each other.

I grind my teeth; the devil take him! Ah, I have snatched up the gun a hundred times thinking to relieve my sorely beset heart.

11 June

Ah this void, this terrible void I feel in my breast. Still no reply or sign of progress. God knows how often I have regretted ever beginning this course of action. Woe! As ever, I fear you are right my friend. Toil and labour, joys and rewards, they cannot be separated.

14 June

The decision is taken. A thousand possibilities and plans raged in my heart but in the end it was there, one last fixed and definite thought. The gun is now in my hand and I am resolved to do whatever is necessary.

15 June

I placed the tube of sealant snugly in the mastic gun and, using only a simple pair of scissors, removed the extremity from the tube's tapered nozzle, so that, when squeezed, the amalgam, as white as the driven snow, was greater in girth than the gap between bath and tiles. What I told you recently concerning painting I can confirm is also true of applying bath sealant; what counts is that one conceives of a line of perfect breadth and straightness, and then dares to give it expression. Applying the steadiest of pressure to the trigger, I began, at one end of the bath, to lay down a steady flow of the sealant, and so to fill the abyss that had tortured me for so long. Then, from among the little wooden wedges I chose one, the width of my little fingernail, and put it to soak in the jar containing the washing-up solution before drawing it with a smooth and steady motion along the little ribbon of white that now joined bath and wall as one. I swear that every man should pass a few moments of each day in such common labour. Its simple pleasure is a balm to the heart.

Farewell. This letter will be to your taste, it is full of practical steps.

That evening I lay soaking in my tub. Through the window, above the chestnut trees illuminated in the moonlight, shone the stars that make up the blade of the Plough, my favourite and the most practical of all the heavenly bodies. But of all this I was hardly sensible. What overwhelmed me with emotion and made the world about me a very paradise, was the blue-white gleam of the sealant in the moonlight, its edges so straight, its surface a smooth and perfect barrier betwixt tile and tub, holding back the splashing foam that burst from the banks of the bath. In such moments the humblest labourer, fatigued by his exertions, surely floats more buoyantly on the waters of the measureless sea, soaks more deeply in the foaming pool of the Eternal and approaches more closely the blessed serenity of Him who makes all things.

MARK CRICK

VICTOR HUGO: FROM *FANTINE*

[Fantine *is a 'condensed novel' based on* Les Misérables]

When a man commits a crime Society claps him in prison. A prison is one of the worst hotels imaginable. The people there are low and vulgar. The butter is bad, the coffee is green. Ah, it is horrible!

In prison, as in a bad hotel, a man soon loses, not only his morals, but, what is much worse to a Frenchman, his sense of refinement and delicacy.

Jean Valjean came from prison with confused notions of society. He forgot the modern peculiarities of hospitality. So he walked off with the Bishop's candlesticks.

Let us consider: candlesticks were stolen; that was evident. Society put Jean Valjean in prison; that was evident, too. Society took away his refinement; that is evident, likewise.

Who is society?

You and I are Society.

My friend, you and I stole those candlesticks!

*

The Bishop thought so, too. He meditated profoundly for six days. On the morning of the seventh he went to the prefecture of Police.

He said: 'Monsieur, have me arrested. I have stolen candlesticks.'

The official was governed by the law of Society, and refused.

What did this Bishop do?

He had a charming ball and chain made, affixed to his leg, and wore it the rest of his life.

This is a fact!

BRET HARTE

VICTOR HUGO: TWO DRAMATIC FRAGMENTS

I

Queen Victoria confesses to her mother that she has surrendered to an illicit passion:

Ce n'était pas un prince; ce n'était pas un milord, ni même *Sir R. Peel.* C'était un misérable du people, un nommé *Wordsworth*, qui m'a récité des vers de son *Excursion* d'une sensualité si chaleureuse qu'ils m'ont ébranlée—et je suis tombée.

II

The opening scene of Sir Brown: *drame en 7 actes et 49 tableaux*

'La Mort du Mari'

The scene is at Osborne's House, Ile de Wigth. The Queen is discovered impatiently expectant of news, seated in her own apartment. 'Entre Brown, Grand costume de Higlander. Il l'embrasse.

LA REINE: C'est fini?
BROWN: Tu l'as dit. Mais embrasse-moi donc aussi, toi, ma reine!
LA REINE: Mon Johny! Mon Jack adoré! Je vais donc enfin être toute à toi!
BROWN: Et tes enfants, Victoria?
LA REINE: Et la Tour de Londres?
BROWN: (*avec un méchant sourire*). En effet—c'est un séjour malsain, à ce qu'on dit, pour les Princes de Galles.'

ALGERNON CHARLES SWINBURNE

Swinburne was a fervent admirer of Hugo, but that did not prevent him rejoicing in the mangled names and melodramatic absurdities of Hugo's ventures into English history. He also saw the ribald possibilities of applying what might be called the Hugo treatment to the court of Queen Victoria: as a young man in the 1860s he produced two jeux d'esprit in this vein—a play, La Sœur de la Reine, *and a novel,* La Fille du Policeman.

Only a few portions of these works are known to have survived (they were printed for the first time in 1964), but a certain amount about them can also be gleaned from memoirs and reminiscences. The Wordsworth fragment above was recorded in 1917: it had been passed on to a literary journalist by an old acquaintance of Swinburne. Sir Brown, *which was never actually written, belongs to a later period in the poet's life. The idea for it was suggested to him by the publication of Queen Victoria's* More Leaves from the Journal of Our Life in the Highlands *in 1884, and sketched out (along with the scene quoted above) in a letter to a friend.*

from THE CHELSEA WAY, OR MARCEL IN
ENGLAND: A PROUSTIAN PARODY

Marcel Proust died in 1922. The Chelsea Way (Le Côté de Chelsea in the original French) presupposes that the narrator of his great novel—who is also called Marcel—lives on; it is an account of a visit which Marcel makes to England in 1928, in the company of Andrée, the friend of his former love Albertine. Initially they stay at the Hyde Park Hotel.

Three days after my arrival the hall-porter (who treated me as a friend, although I was only a guest of no importance, because he spoke French with an exceptionally pure accent, with the consequence that in his eyes I became an opportunity for exhibiting a talent, a circumstance far more effectual in exciting kindly feelings than any mere gratuity) handed me a letter whose typewritten address presented the most amazing appearance, for the lines undulated like a weltering sea, while some characters were blue and others red, without any intelligible reason, yet this disorder and incoherence, far from being unpleasant to contemplate, succeeded on the contrary by an astonishing victory of man over keyboard in bestowing upon this cold and mechanical inscription the intimate, courteous and mystery-laden air of an address written by hand. When I opened this letter I saw with emotion that it was signed: Desmond Farnham, and invited me to lunch on the same day at half past one.

I omitted to mention at the moment of describing my conversation with M. de Norpois how surprised I had been to learn that my favourite novelist was the brother of Lord Shalford. Certainly, I had never nursed that particular prejudice, silly enough as it is though current among persons of intelligence, which consists in supposing that talent or genius are reserved for the labouring classes, and in refusing to recognise them if they make their appearance in a person of exalted birth, or even in a man who frequents society (which would have involved denial in the seventeenth century of the genius of the author of the *Maxims*, and in the eighteenth century of the genius of Saint-Simon), but the name of Farnham and the character of his novels had always led me to imagine a sensitive, timid and solitary man, a temperament which I found it difficult to associate with the name of the Shalfords, who in the time of the Stuarts had been illustrious and gallant cavaliers, and during the last three hundred years had given to England so numerous a levy of ministers, generals, admirals and viceroys. Andrée, who had made *Debrett* her favourite perusal in the reading-room of our hotel, informed me that in fact, after the name of Lord Shalford, GCB, GCMG, GCVO, ninth Viscount and fifteenth Baron, followed the words: '*Living brother:* the Honourable Desmond Farnham, educ. Winchester, first secretary Diplomatic Corps, Colonel, war 1914–1918, DSO.' So apparently the frail and delicate author of *Tiziana Sorelli* was not only the son of a Lord temporal, but also a diplomat and a colonel, and yet (although *Debrett*, with curious modesty, refrained from adding that he was one of the great writers of our time) there could be no doubt as to his identity—a revelation which, compelling me as it did to reconstruct my entire conception of him, was paralleled still more strangely a few days later when I arranged to be taken to the House of Commons, where, a Labour member having stood up to put a few questions to Sir Austen Chamberlain on foreign policy, I indulged myself in imagining this man of the people patiently striving to educate himself during the rare moments he could spare from his manual toil, and studying, as he returned up the mineshaft or left the factory-gates, the map and history of Europe. I had enquired the name of this socialist, and my guide told me without further comment that he was called Arthur Ponsonby, an answer which I had thought perfectly adequate. But a few days afterwards, in the course of a conversation about King Edward the Seventh, M. de Norpois happened to remark: 'His Majesty did not find it easy to forgive Arthur Ponsonby for joining the Opposition, because, as he said, Ponsonby of all people was born in the purple.' I asked the meaning of this expression, and M. de Norpois, with a glance of astonishment, replied: 'What else could it mean, but that Arthur Ponsonby was born in Windsor Castle?'; which proved to me not for the first time that what we see is not reality itself, but what we fancy to be reality, since in complete good faith I had been admiring as the industrious and toil-worn face of a working man what in fact were the hereditary lineaments of a highborn nobleman. I took an immense pleasure, when I came to know them better, in these complicated names of the great English families, and just as Françoise at home never tired of repeating to herself that the son of the Duc de Guermantes was the Prince des Laumes, while the sons of the Duc de La Rochefoucauld were the Duc de Liancourt and the Prince de Marsillac, so I was delighted to learn that the charming Eric Phipps, who once served at the British Embassy in Paris, is a descendant of the Marquess of Normanby, that the eldest son of the Marquess of Headfort is the Earl of Bective whose hobby it is to work as an electrician, his second son is Lord William Taylour, Winston Churchill is a Marlborough, Arthur Balfour a Cecil, and lastly, a piece of information which is not only historical but also topographical, the Duke of Westminster's name is Grosvenor, and the Duke of Bedford's, Russell.

ANDRÉ MAUROIS, translated by GEORGE D. PAINTER

Desmond Farnham] *closely modelled on Maurois's friend, the author Maurice Baring.*

Arthur Ponsonby] *the son of Queen Victoria's private secretary. Originally sat as a Liberal MP; joined the Labour party after the First World War.*

The translator, George D. Painter, was the author of a notable biography of

Proust. In his preface to The Chelsea Way *he writes, 'I have tried, but certainly failed, to make my translation as close a pastiche of the immortal Scott Moncrieff as the original is of Proust.'*

QUICK MISO SOUP À LA FRANZ KAFKA

[*from* Kafka's Soup: A Complete History of Literature in 17 Recipes]

3 dessertspoons fermented miso
150g silken tofu
4–5 small mushrooms
A few leaves of dried wakame
Soy sauce

K. recognised that if a man is not always on his guard this kind of thing can happen. He was looking into the refrigerator and found it to be almost completely bare, apart from some mushrooms, which he began to slice. His guests sat waiting at the table and yet he appeared to have little to offer them. Whether he had invited them or whether they had arrived uninvited was not clear. If it were the first case he was angry with himself for failing to engage a cook for the evening so that he might command some authority at the table; for now his visitors were looking towards him as though he were a subordinate whose inefficiency was delaying their dinner. But in the second case they could hardly expect to be fed, arriving unexpectedly at such a time. The sound of a kettle boiling brought his attention back to the food and at the same time he noticed a jar of fermented miso and a block of silken tofu, perhaps left by his landlady. He placed three spoonfuls of the miso into a saucepan and poured on two pints of hot water, shielding the process from the panel as he did so. He became angry with himself for thinking of the new arrivals as a panel; they had not announced their purpose in calling on him and as yet he did not know what position each of them held. Their manner suggested, perhaps, that they were higher officials but it was also quite possible that he was their superior and they were calling on him merely to create a good impression.

With shame K. realised that he had not offered his guests anything to drink, but when he looked up he saw that a bottle was open on the table and the judges were already enjoying his wine. He found it abominable that they had served themselves without permission, but he knew their impertinence was not without significance. K. decided to shame them for their rudeness. 'How is the wine?' he called. But the ruse backfired. 'It would be better with some food,' they chorused. 'But since you have not even granted us the courtesy of dressing for dinner we do not have high hopes.' K. could scarcely believe it as he noticed with discomfort that he was, indeed, in shirt and drawers.

When the soup was simmering, K. cut the tofu into one-centimetre cubes and dropped it into the steaming pan with the mushrooms and some wakame. Looking out of the window into the darkness he noticed that a girl was watching from the neighbouring house. The girl's severe expression was not unattractive to K., but the thought that she was deriving some pleasure from his situation sent him into a fury and he struck the worktop with his fist. It occurred to him that she might in some way be attached to the interrogation commission or could influence his case, and he looked beseechingly towards her, but she had backed away now and he might already have thrown away any advantages that his situation bestowed upon him. In two minutes the soup was ready. K. poured it into bowls and served his visitors. One of the four chairs around the table had been removed and, not without discomfort, K. saw that the panel was making no effort to make room for him. He added a splash of soy sauce to each of the bowls while the elder of the three judges addressed the others as if K. were invisible. 'He needs to rid himself of a great many illusions; it's possible he imagines that we are subordinates calling on him to win his approval.'

K.'s feeling that he was an outsider at his own dinner party was not unfamiliar. He was sorry that he was not dressed in his grey suit: its elegant cut had caused a sensation among his friends, and it was of the utmost importance to create a good impression in these situations. It was essential for a man in his position not to appear surprised by events and, as the interrogation commission divided the contents of K.'s bowl between them, K. stood still and tried to collect himself, for he knew that great demands would be made upon him and the soup might yet influence the outcome of his case.

MARK CRICK

Nursery Rhymes

VARIATIONS ON AN AIR

composed on having to appear in a pageant as Old King Cole

Old King Cole was a merry old soul,
And a merry old soul was he;
He called for his pipe,
He called for his bowl,
And he called for his fiddlers three.

After Lord Tennyson

Cole, that unwearied prince of Colchester,
Growing more gay with age and with long days
Deeper in laughter and desire of life,
As that Virginian climber on our walls
Flames scarlet with the fading of the year;
Called for his wassail and that other weed
Virginian also, from the western woods
Where English Raleigh checked the boast of Spain,
And lighting joy with joy, and piling up
Pleasure as crown for pleasure, bade men bring
Those three, the minstrels whose emblazoned coats
Shone with the oyster-shells of Colchester;
And these three played, and playing grew more fain
Of mirth and music; till the heathen came,
And the King slept beside the northern sea.

After W. B. Yeats

Of an old King in a story
    From the grey sea-folk I have heard,
Whose heart was no more broken
    Than the wings of a bird.

As soon as the moon was silver
    And the thin stars began,
He took his pipe and his tankard,
    Like an old peasant man.

And three tall shadows were with him
And came at his command;
And played before him for ever
The fiddles of fairyland.

And he died in the young summer
Of the world's desire;
Before our hearts were broken
Like sticks in a fire.

After Robert Browning

Who smoke-snorts toasts o' My Lady Nicotine,
Kicks stuffing out of Pussyfoot, bids his trio
Stick up their Stradivarii (that's the plural)
Or near enough, my fatheads; *nimium*
Vicina Cremonæ; that's a bit too near).
Is there some stockfish fails to understand?
Catch hold o' the notion, bellow and blurt back 'Cole'?
Must I bawl lessons from a horn-book, howl,
Cat-call the cat-gut 'fiddles'? Fiddlesticks!

After Walt Whitman

Me clairvoyant,
Me conscious of you, old camarado,
Needing no telescope, lorgnette, field-glass, opera-glass, myopic
    pince-nez,
Me piercing two thousand years with eye naked and not ashamed;
The crown cannot hide you from me;
Musty old feudal-heraldic trappings cannot hide you from me,
I perceive that you drink.
(I am drinking with you. I am as drunk as you are.)
I see you are inhaling tobacco, puffing, smoking, spitting
(I do not object to your spitting),
You prophetic of American largeness,
You anticipating the broad masculine manners of these States;
I see in you also there are movements, tremors, tears, desire for the
    melodious,
I salute your three violinists, endlessly making vibrations,
Rigid, relentless, capable of going on for ever;
They play my accompaniment; but I shall take no notice of any
    accompaniment;
I myself am a complete orchestra. So long.

After Swinburne

In the time of old sin without sadness
    And golden with wastage of gold
Like the gods that grow old in their gladness
    Was the king that was glad, growing old;
And with sound of loud lyres from his palace
    The voice of his oracles spoke,
And the lips that were red from his chalice
    Were splendid with smoke.
When the weed was as flame for a token
    And the wine was as blood for a sign;
And upheld in his hands and unbroken
    The fountains of fire and of wine.
And a song without speech, without singer,
    Stung the soul of a thousand in three
As the flesh of the earth has to sting her,
    The soul of the sea.

G. K. CHESTERTON

A NURSERY RHYME

as it might have been written by William Wordsworth

The skylark and the jay sang loud and long,
The sun was calm and bright, the air was sweet,
When all at once I heard above the throng
Of jocund birds a single plaintive bleat.

And, turning, saw, as one sees in a dream,
It was a Sheep had broke the moorland peace
With his sad cry, a creature who did seem
The blackest thing that ever wore a fleece.

I walked towards him on the stony track
And, pausing for a while between two crags,
I asked him, 'Have you wool upon your back?'
Thus he bespake, 'Enough to fill three bags.'

Most courteously, in measured tones, he told
Who would receive each bag and where they dwelt;
And oft, now years have passed and I am old,
I recollect with joy that inky pelt.

WENDY COPE

HUMPTY DUMPTY

[as Bret Harte might have written it]

So, stranger, you've come
To my store for a chat,
An' yer settin' right plum
On the wall whar he sat!
Who sat? Why that cuss Humpty Dumpty,
Haven't they told ye o' that?

Made no sort o' fuss,
While he sat on that wall,
But I guess he scart us
When the fool had a fall;
And the way the King sent out his horses
Jes' showed he was someone—that's all.

Yas, they tried hard to git him together,
With putty and tin tacks and glue,
But he'd come to the end of his tether,
What's that you say?—it ain't true!
Why you Pumpkin! You sawed-off assassin!
Why Humpty, you horse-thief! it's you!

PERCY FRENCH

[from 'Humpty Dumpty: The Official Biography']

Humpty Dumpty had a lean summer,
Humpty Dumpty's spring was a bummer
Humpty's winter was no good at all
But Humpty Dumpty had a GREAT FALL!

KIT WRIGHT

[from 'The Harold Pinter Book of Nursery Rhymes']

Humpty Dumpty
Sat on a wall
Humpty Dumpty
Had a great fall.
Serves you fucking right
For being an egg, chum.

CRAIG BROWN

GOOSEY GOOSEY GANDER

[as Kipling might have written it]

And this is the song that the white woman sings,
    When her baby begins to howl;
The song of the goose and its wanderings
    The song of the fate-led fowl.

The song of the chamber of her whom I loved,
    The song of the chamber where—
I met an old reprobate, scented and gloved,
    And hurled him down the stair.

And wherever the Saxon speech is heard,
    By the pig or the polar bear,
We follow the feet of that wandering bird
    As they wobble from stair to stair.

PERCY FRENCH

[censored 'to ridicule the Irish censors']

Goosey Goosey Gander
Where do you mmmmm
Upstairs and mmmmmmm
In a lady's mmmmmmm?

OLIVER ST JOHN GOGARTY

LITTLE BO-PEEP

[as Wordsworth might have written it]

I walked with her upon the hill,
    Her grief was very deep,
Her tears were running like a rill,
    For she had lost her sheep.

'What were they like, my gentle maid,
    Were they some special kind?'
'They all had heads in front,' she said,
    'And all had tails behind!

'Their bodies were between the two,
    Their mouths were full of teeth,
And—this, perhaps, may prove a clue—
    Their legs were underneath.'

'If they have legs,' I cried with joy,
    'Your tears you may refrain,
For 'tis their legs they will employ
    To bring them home again!'

PERCY FRENCH

JACK AND JILL

[as Austin Dobson might have written it]

Their pail they must fill
    In a crystalline springlet,
Brave Jack and fair Jill.
Their pail they must fill
At the top of the hill,
    Then she gives him a ringlet.
Their pail they must fill
    In a crystalline springlet.

They stumbled and fell,
    And poor Jack broke his forehead,
Oh, how he did yell!
They stumbled and fell,
And went down pell-mell—
    By Jove! it was horrid.
They stumbled and fell,
    And poor Jack broke his forehead.

CHARLES BATTELL LOOMIS

[as Walt Whitman might have written it]

I celebrate the personality of Jack!
I love his dirty hands, his tangled hair, his locomotion blundering.
Each wart upon his hands I sing,
Paeans I chant to his hulking shoulder blades.
Also Jill!

Her I celebrate.
I, Walt, of unbridled thought and tongue
Whoop her up!
Her golden hair, her sun-struck face, her hard and reddened hands;
So, too, her feet, hefty, shambling . . .

[*And a good deal more in the same vein*]

CHARLES BATTELL LOOMIS

[*from 'Nursery Rhymes for Little Anglo-Indians'*]

Jack's own Jill goes up to the Hill
Of Murree or Chakrata.
Jack remains, and dies in the plains,
And Jill remarries soon arter.

RUDYARD KIPLING

Murree, Chakrata] *hill-stations.*

*Kipling wrote the Anglo-Indian nursery-rhymes at the age of 19. At around the
same time he also wrote* The Flight of the Bucket, *an energetic version of 'Jack
and Jill'—running to over a hundred lines—in the manner of Robert Browning:*

*Spring water was the needful at the time,
So they must climb the hill for't. Well and good.
We all climb hills, I take it, on some quest . . .*

A NURSERY RHYME

as it might have been written by T. S. Eliot

Because time will not run backwards
Because time
Because time will not run
                    Hickory dickory

In the last minute of the first hour
I saw the mouse ascend the ancient timepiece,
Claws whispering like wind in dry hyacinths.

One o'clock,
The street lamp said,
'Remark the mouse that races towards the carpet.'

And the unstilled wheel still turning

              Hickory dickory
              Hickory dickory

dock

WENDY COPE

RHYMES FOR A MODERN NURSERY

Hey diddle diddle,
The physicists fiddle,
    The Bleep jumped over the moon.
The little dog laughed to see such fun
    And died the following June.

*

Jack and Jill went up the hill
    To fetch some heavy water.
They mixed it with the dairy milk
    And killed my youngest daughter.

*

Two blind mice
See how they run!
They each ran out of the lab with an oath,
For the scientist's wife had injected them both.
Did you ever see such a neat little growth
On two blind mice?

*

Little Miss Muffet
Crouched on a tuffet,
Collecting her shell-shocked wits.
There dropped (from a glider)
An H-bomb beside her—
Which frightened Miss Muffet to *bits*.

*

Ring-a-ring o' neutrons,
A pocket full of positrons,
A fission! A fission!
We all fall down.

PAUL DEHN

Published in 1958. It was at the same period that Paul Dehn wrote a variant on the beautiful Tudor quatrain 'Westron winde, when will thou blow . . .':

> Nuclear wind, when wilt thou blow
>   That the small rain down can rain?
> Oh, that my love were in my arms
>   And I had my arms again.

TORIES AND RADICALS

The Anti-Jacobin *was a weekly magazine which appeared between November* *1797 and July 1798. Unwavering in its support for the government of William Pitt,* *and unyielding in its hostility to the French Revolution, its most gifted contributors* *were two young Tory MPs, George Canning (the future Prime Minister) and John* *Hookham Frere, and a somewhat older one, George Ellis.*

Much of the magazine's content was satirical, and much of its satire took the *form of parody. Its most famous send-up, the joint work of Canning and Frere, was* *provoked by Robert Southey's poem 'The Widow':*

> Fast o'er the bleak heath rattling drove a chariot,
> 'Pity me!' feebly cried the poor night-wanderer.
> 'Pity me, strangers! Lest with cold and hunger
>   Here I should perish.
>
> 'Once I had friends—but they have all forsook me!
> Once I had parents—they are now in heaven!
> I had a home once—I had once a husband—
>   Pity me, strangers!
>
> 'I had a home once—I had once a husband—
> I am a widow poor and broken-hearted!'
> Loud blew the wind, unheard was her complaining,
>   On drove the chariot . . .

Southey had made the mistake of casting 'The Widow' in sapphics, a Latin metre *which wrenches English from its natural accentuation. As Canning and Frere took* *pleasure in pointing out, 'In this poem the pathos of the matter is not a little* *relieved by the absurdity of the metre.' And the incongruity gave their parody its* *starting point.*

SAPPHICS. THE FRIEND OF HUMANITY
AND THE KNIFE-GRINDER

Friend of Humanity

'Needy knife-grinder! whither are you going?
Rough is the road, your wheel is out of order—
Bleak blows the blast;—your hat has got a hole in't,
    So have your breeches!

'Weary knife-grinder! little think the proud ones
Who in their coaches roll along the turnpike-
Road, what hard work 'tis crying all day, "Knives and
　　　　Scissors to grind O!"

'Tell me, knife-grinder, how came you to grind knives?
Did some rich man tyrannically use you?
Was it the squire? or parson of the parish?
　　　　Or the attorney?

'Was it the squire, for killing of his game? or
Covetous parson, for his tithes distraining?
Or roguish lawyer, made you lose your little
　　　　All in a lawsuit?

'(Have you not read the Rights of Man, by Tom Paine?),
Drops of compassion tremble on my eyelids,
Ready to fall as soon as you have told your
　　　　Pitiful story.'

Knife-Grinder

'Story! God bless you! I have none to tell, sir,
Only last night a-drinking at the Chequers
This poor old hat and breeches, as you see, were
　　　　Torn in a scuffle.

'Constables came up for to take me into
Custody; they took me before the justice;
Justice Oldmixon put me in the parish
　　　　Stocks for a vagrant.

'I should be glad to drink your Honour's health in
A pot of beer, if you will give me sixpence;
But for my part, I never love to meddle
　　　　With politics, sir.'

Friend of Humanity

'I give thee sixpence! I will see thee damn'd first—
Wretch! whom no sense of wrongs can rouse to
　　vengeance—
Sordid, unfeeling, reprobate, degraded,
　　　　Spiritless outcast!'

[*Kicks the Knife-grinder, overturns his wheel, and*
exit in a transport of republican enthusiasm and
universal philanthropy.]

Southey was a favourite target of the Anti-Jacobin team. They devoted three other parodies to him. Another of their efforts, a work which can still be read with pleasure, is The Loves of the Triangles, their 'mathematical and philosophical' parody of Erasmus Darwin's botanical and philosophical poem The Loves of the Plants. Darwin was a brilliant scientific pioneer, but as a poet his hackneyed Augustan manner and the tinkling mythological machinery which he employed laid him open to some joyful ridicule:

> Let *Hydrostatics*, simpering as they go,
> Lead the light Naiads on fantastic toe;
> Let shrill *Acoustics* tune the tiny lyre;
> With *Euclid* sage fair *Algebra* conspire;
> The obedient pulley strong *Mechanics* ply,
> And wanton *Optics* melt the rolling eye!

Darwin was also a radical, and the satire of The Loves of the Triangles becomes more political as it proceeds. The poem concludes with a vision of Liberty's final triumph:

> Ye sylphs of *Death*, on demon pinions flit
> Where the tall Guillotine is raised for Pitt:
> To the poised plank tie fast the monster's back,
> Close the nice slider, ope the expectant sack;
> Then twitch, with fairy hands, the frolic pin—
> Down falls the impatient axe, with deafening din;
> The liberated head rolls off below,
> And simpering Freedom hails the happy blow!

A footnote explains 'the monster's back' by referring readers to diatribes in the French assembly against 'le monstre Pitt, l'ennemi du genre humain'.

The most boisterous comedy in The Anti-Jacobin is to be found in The Rover, a wild extravaganza which takes aim at the German romantic drama then coming into fashion in England—Schiller in particular, but Goethe and August von Kotzebue as well. A prologue by Canning and Ellis (based on the prologue written by Alexander Pope for Joseph Addison's tragedy Cato) makes it quite clear who their targets are:

> Tonight our Bard, who scorns pedantic rules,
> His plot has borrow'd from the German schools;
> —The German schools—where no dull maxims bind

The bold expansion of the electric mind.
Fix'd to no period, circled by no space,
He leaps the flaming bounds of time and place:
Round the dark confines of the forest raves,
With *gentle* Robbers stocks his gloomy caves;
Tells how Prime Ministers are shocking things,
And *reigning Dukes* as bad as tyrant Kings . . .

A footnote explains the reference to robbers: 'The Robbers, *a German tragedy* [by Schiller] *in which Robbery is put in so fascinating a light that the whole of a German University went upon the highway in consequence of it.'*

The play itself, which is set in Weimar, more than makes good the promise of the prologue. Its melodramatic clichés are matched by the improbabilities of its plot and surpassed by its surreal anachronisms. One military action involves troubadours who happen to be returning from the Crusades and grenadiers who happen to be returning from the Seven Years War. Two English noblemen put in an appearance. Their names—a nod towards German enthusiasm for Hamlet—*are Puddincrantz and Beefinstern; they are exiles from the tyranny of King John, but return home as soon as they hear that Magna Carta has been signed. And meanwhile the hero, Rogero, languishes in a dungeon in an abbey, where he has been secretly confined for many years, ever since his days as a student. We first meet him, bewailing his lot, in the opening scene:*

> When'er with haggard eyes I view
>   This dungeon that I'm rotting in,
> I think of those companions true
> Who studied with me at the U—
>   —niversity of Gottingen,—
>   —niversity of Gottingen.

After which his lament winds its way, through a series of ingenious rhymes, to a final stanza which is interrupted by him dashing his head repeatedly against the dungeon walls:

> Sun, moon and thou vain world, adieu,
>   That kings and priests are plotting in:
> Here, doom'd to starve on water-gru—
>   el, never shall I see the U—
>   —niversity of Gottingen
>   —niversity of Gottingen.

There is a curious footnote. Rogero's song doesn't qualify as parody—it is pure burlesque; but 140 years later it was parodied itself, or at any rate provided the basis for a serious satirical poem. The occasion was the bicentenary of the University of Göttingen in 1938, an event marked by extensive celebrations on the part of the German authorities:

'Heil Göttingen!'

Now the Third Reich has purged anew
these halls our foes were plotting in,
the learned world is bidden to
our *Kulturfestspiel* at the U-
-niversity of Göttingen.

While democrat and ape-like Jew
our penal camps are rotting in,
the Chairs of Totem and Tabu
take place of honour at the U-
-niversity of Göttingen.

Our plant of Nordic culture true
this nursery we are potting in,
unique for its ensanguined hue,
which smells to heaven at the U-
-niversity of Göttingen.

Intoxicating Brocken-brew
this cauldron we are hotting in,
to rise to Nazi brains like glue
and stick our dogma to the U-
-niversity of Göttingen.

Ach! Groves of learning, fair to view,
with no non-Aryan squatting in,
where racial fetish reigns in lieu
of arts and science at the U-
-niversity of Göttingen-
-niversity of Göttingen!

'SAGITTARIUS' [OLGA KATZIN]

*　　*　　*

George Canning and his collaborators are the best-remembered political parodists of the 1790s. But a generation later, in the era of Peterloo and the repressive 'Six Acts', it was radicals who made the running. The most effective political parodists were now almost all men of the Left.

One practitioner stands out in this respect, partly on account of his work as a writer and publisher, but still more because the Government's attempts to silence him turned him into a popular hero. William Hone found his way into publishing after a number of failed initiatives and false starts. By 1817 he was also a well-known pamphleteer and publicist, firmly identified with the cause of radical reform. It was in that year, after publishing a series of parodies based on the Litany and other sacred texts, that he was charged with blasphemous and seditious libel. He faced trial three times; in each case conducting his own defence with great ability and winning an acquittal. In the course of his trials, he revealed an impressive knowledge of earlier parodists, whom he cited as precedents; he subsequently planned to write a history of parody, but it never materialized.

He did go back to his own work as a satirist, however. For a couple of years he concentrated on publishing; then, between 1819 and 1821, he produced a series of powerful political squibs, with accompanying illustrations by George Cruikshank. The two men's first and greatest success was The Political House that Jack Built, *a pamphlet got up to look like a genuine children's book, which sold over 100,000 copies within a few months of publication.*

In the original 'House that Jack Built', it is the man who married the maiden who is 'all tattered and torn'. In the Hone version, it is the common people. But before we get to them we are shown the wealth of England, the 'vermin' who are plundering it (a lawyer, a court flunkey, a cavalry officer, a clerical magistrate), the 'Thing' which will put them down (a printing press), the 'Public Informer' who is trying to put the Thing down (the Attorney-General) and, most strikingly, 'the Dandy of Sixty'—the Prince Regent, soon to be George IV:

> This is THE MAN—all shaven and shorn,
> All covered with orders—and all forlorn;
> THE DANDY OF SIXTY,
>   who bows with a grace,
> And has *taste* in wigs, collars,
>   cuirasses and lace;
> Who, to tricksters and fools,
>   leaves the State and its treasure,
> And when Britain's in tears,
>   sails about at his pleasure:
> Who spurn'd from his presence
>   the Friends of his youth,
> And now has not one
>   who will tell him the truth;
> Who took to his counsels,
>   in evil hour,
> The Friends to the Reasons
>   of lawless Power;

That back the Public Informer,
    who
Who would put down the *Thing*,
    that in spite of new Acts,
And attempts to restrain it,
    by Soldiers or Tax,
Will *poison* the Vermin,
That plunder the Wealth,
That lay in the House,
That Jack built.

'When Britain's in tears, sails about at his pleasure' alludes to the much-resented fact that while news of the Peterloo massacre was still fresh, the Prince was on his yacht at the Cowes regatta. 'The Friends of his youth' is a reference to the Whig leader Charles James Fox and his associates. It is worth noting that one of the many decorations which Cruikshank shows the Prince wearing is a corkscrew.)

After dispatching their royal victim, Hone and Cruikshank move on to their ultimate target—the Government, as represented by three leading ministers, Sidmouth, Castlereagh, and Canning (who was by now Foreign Secretary). Some of the satire at this point turns on forgotten topicalities, but there can be no mistaking its fierce tone. Canning, for example, is dismissed as 'the Spouter of Froth by the Hour', ready to eulogize colleagues he despised so that he can share their power, while the quotation from William Cowper which is attached to Cruikshank's drawing of him suggests how brutally (in Hone's view) he had misused his wit: 'With merry descants on a nation's woes | There is a public mischief in his mirth'.

Hone was of course well aware of Canning's earlier achievements as a parodist. In the course of one of his trials, arguing for the right to use scriptural quotations in a satirical context, he cited an example of Canning doing just that in a poem in The Anti-Jacobin. He would not call Canning as a witness, he told the court, but he did take a confident guess at what he must be feeling about its proceedings: 'Hone is a poor fellow; I am a parodist too; this prosecution is a nasty thing; I don't like it.'

THE YOUNG JANE AUSTEN

The skits which Jane Austen wrote during adolescence, and even earlier, were the seedbed of her later fiction. One can see her moving forward in them from parody and burlesque to character-study, from pure playfulness to serious involvement.

The element of parody remains uppermost, however. It is directed, not at any particular author, but at the sentimental fiction of the period in general—at the kind of novels the Austen family might have borrowed from a circulating library or encountered in the pages of such widely read publications as The Lady's Magazine. *Her principal targets, in making fun of these novels, have been usefully summarized by the critic and biographer John McAleer: 'facile emotionalism, the cant of sentiment, the flawless hero, the matchless heroine, the foundling child, the exalted pedigree, the shackles of parental authority, youthful defiance, spontaneous attachment, love-at-first-sight, tears, fainting, running mad, fantastic recognition scenes, fortuitous encounters, unmotivated narrative digressions, confidantes, self-revelation, friendship easily given, reckless benevolence, forced difficulties, inept imitations of Richardson, sudden reversals, conduct books, absurd closures, inflated rhetoric, cliché diction, Gothicism, epistolary absurdity, and neglect of time-scale'.*

One should add that Jane Austen pretty obviously took a good deal of pleasure in the novels she lampooned. Why else spend so much time on them? And the exuberance of her parodies suggests something other than stern disapproval.

The most celebrated of the early burlesques, 'Love and Freindship', was written when she was 14. The chapters which follow represent about one-sixth of the story.

LETTER *the* FIRST
From ISABEL *to* LAURA

How often, in answer to my repeated intreaties that you would give my Daughter a regular detail of the Misfortunes and Adventures of your Life, have you said 'No, my freind never will I comply with your request till I may be no longer in Danger of again experiencing such dreadful ones.'

Surely that time is now at hand. You are this day 55. If a woman may ever be said to be in safety from the determined Perseverance of disagreable Lovers and the cruel Persecutions of obstinate Fathers, surely it must be at such a time of Life.

ISABEL.

LETTER 2nd
LAURA *to* ISABEL

Altho' I cannot agree with you in supposing that I shall never again be exposed to Misfortunes as unmerited as those I have already experienced, yet to avoid the imputation of Obstinacy or ill-nature, I will gratify the curiosity of your daughter; and may the fortitude with which I have suffered the many afflictions of my past Life, prove to her a useful lesson for the support of those which may befall her in her own.

LAURA.

LETTER 3rd
LAURA to MARIANNE

As the Daughter of my most intimate freind I think you entitled to that knowledge of my unhappy story, which your Mother has so often solicited me to give you.

My Father was a native of Ireland and an inhabitant of Wales; my Mother was the natural Daughter of a Scotch Peer by an italian Opera-girl—I was born in Spain and received my Education at a Convent in France.

When I had reached my eighteenth Year I was recalled by my Parents to my paternal roof in Wales. Our mansion was situated in one of the most romantic parts of the Vale of Uske. Tho' my Charms are now considerably softened and somewhat impaired by the Misfortunes I have undergone, I was once beautiful. But lovely as I was the Graces of my Person were the least of my Perfections. Of every accomplishment accustomary to my sex, I was Mistress. When in the Convent, my progress had always exceeded my instructions, my Acquirements had been wonderfull for my age, and I had shortly surpassed my Masters.

In my Mind, every Virtue that could adorn it was centered; it was the Rendez-vous of every good Quality and of every noble sentiment.

A sensibility too tremblingly alive to every affliction of my Freinds, my Acquaintance and particularly to every affliction of my own, was my only fault, if a fault it could be called. Alas! how altered now! Tho' indeed my own Misfortunes do not make less impression on me than they ever did, yet now I never feel for those of an other. My accomplishments too, begin to fade—I can neither sing so well nor Dance so gracefully as I once did—and I have entirely forgot the *Minuet Dela Cour*.

Adeiu.
LAURA.

LETTER 4th
LAURA to MARIANNE

Our neighbourhood was small, for it consisted only of your Mother. She may probably have already told you that being left by her Parents in indigent Circumstances she had retired into Wales on eoconomical motives. There it was our freindship first commenced. Isabel was then one and twenty. Tho' pleasing both in her Person and Manners (between ourselves) she never possessed the hundredth part of my Beauty or Accomplishments. Isabel had seen the World. She had passed 2 Years at one of the first Boarding-schools in London; had spent a fortnight in Bath and had supped one night in Southampton.

'Beware my Laura (she would often say) Beware of the insipid Vanities and idle Dissipations of the Metropolis of England; Beware of the unmeaning Luxuries of Bath and of the stinking fish of Southampton.'

'Alas! (exclaimed I) how am I to avoid those evils I shall never be exposed to? What probability is there of my ever tasting the Dissipations of London, the Luxuries of Bath, or the stinking Fish of Southampton? I who am doomed to waste my Days of Youth and Beauty in an humble Cottage in the Vale of Uske.'

Ah! little did I then think I was ordained so soon to quit that humble Cottage for the deceitfull Pleasures of the World.

Adeiu
LAURA.

LETTER 5th
LAURA to MARIANNE

One Evening in December as my Father, my Mother and myself, were arranged in social converse round our Fireside, we were on a sudden, greatly astonished, by hearing a violent knocking on the outward door of our rustic Cot.

My Father started—'What noise is that,' (said he.) 'It sounds like a loud rapping at the door'—(replied my Mother.) 'it does indeed.' (cried I.) 'I am of your opinion; (said my Father) it certainly does appear to proceed from some uncommon violence exerted against our unoffending door.' 'Yes (exclaimed I) I cannot help thinking it must be somebody who knocks for admittance.'

'That is another point (replied he;) We must not pretend to determine on what motive the person may knock—tho' that someone *does* rap at the door, I am partly convinced.'

Here, a 2^d tremendous rap interrupted my Father in his speech, and somewhat alarmed my Mother and me.

'Had we not better go and see who it is? (said she) the servants are out.' 'I think we had.' (replied I.) 'Certainly, (added my Father) by all means.' 'Shall we go now?' (said my Mother,) 'The sooner the better.' (answered he.) 'Oh! let no time be lost' (cried I.)

A third more violent Rap than ever again assaulted our ears. 'I am certain there is somebody knocking at the Door.' (said my Mother.) 'I think there must,' (replied my Father) 'I fancy the servants are returned; (said I) I think I hear Mary going to the Door.' 'I'm glad of it (cried my Father) for I long to know who it is.'

I was right in my conjecture; for Mary instantly entering the Room, informed us that a young Gentleman and his Servant were at the door, who had lossed their way, were very cold and begged leave to warm themselves by our fire.

'Won't you admit them?' (said I.) 'You have no objection, my Dear?' (said my Father.) 'None in the World.' (replied my Mother.)

Mary, without waiting for any further commands immediately left the room and quickly returned introducing the most beauteous and amiable Youth, I had ever beheld. The servant, she kept to herself.

My natural sensibility had already been greatly affected by the sufferings of the unfortunate stranger and no sooner did I first behold him, than I felt that on him the happiness or Misery of my future Life must depend.

Adeiu

LAURA.

LETTER 6th

LAURA to MARIANNE

The noble Youth informed us that his name was Lindsay—for particular reasons however I shall conceal it under that of Talbot. He told us that he was the son of an English Baronet, that his Mother had been many years no more and that he had a Sister of the middle size. 'My Father (he continued) is a mean and mercenary wretch—it is only to such particular freinds as this Dear Party that I would thus betray his failings. Your Virtues my amiable Polydore (addressing himself to my father) yours Dear Claudia and yours my Charming Laura call on me to repose in you, my confidence.' We bowed. 'My Father, seduced by the false glare of Fortune and the Deluding Pomp of Title, insisted on my giving my hand to Lady Dorothea. No never exclaimed I. Lady Dorothea is lovely and Engaging; I prefer no woman to her; but know Sir, that I scorn to marry her in compliance with your Wishes. No! Never shall it be said that I obliged my Father.'

We all admired the noble Manliness of his reply. He continued.

'Sir Edward was surprised; he had perhaps little expected to meet with so spirited an opposition to his will. 'Where, Edward in the name of wonder (said he) did you pick up this unmeaning gibberish? You have been studying Novels I suspect.' I scorned to answer: it would have been beneath my dignity. I mounted my Horse and followed by my faithful William set forwards for my Aunts.'

'My Father's house is situated in Bedfordshire, my Aunt's in Middlesex, and tho' I flatter myself with being a tolerable proficient in Geography, I know not how it happened, but I found myself entering this beautifull Vale which I find is in South Wales, when I had expected to have reached my Aunts.'

'After having wandered some time on the Banks of the Uske without knowing which way to go, I began to lament my cruel Destiny in the bitterest and most pathetic Manner. It was now perfectly dark, not a single star was there to direct my steps, and I know not what might have befallen me had I not at length discerned thro' the solemn Gloom that surrounded me a distant light, which as I approached it, I discovered to be the chearfull Blaze of your fire. Impelled by the combination of Misfortunes under which I laboured, namely Fear, Cold and Hunger I hesitated not to ask admittance which at length I have gained; and now my Adorable Laura (continued he taking my Hand) when may I hope to receive that reward of all the painfull sufferings I have undergone during the course of my attachment to you, to which I have ever aspired. Oh! when will you reward me with Yourself?'

'This instant, Dear and Amiable Edward.' (replied I.). We were immediately united by my Father, who tho' he had never taken orders had been bred to the Church.

Adeiu

LAURA.

Less well-known than 'Love and Freindship' but no less spirited is 'Lesley Castle', written when Jane Austen was 16, in which Margaret and her sister Matilda are left behind in Scotland while their father pursues his pleasures in England—a situation which Margaret enlarges on in a letter to her friend Charlotte:

While our father is fluttering about the streets of London, gay, dissipated, and Thoughtless at the age of 57, Matilda and I continue secluded from Mankind in our old and Mouldering Castle, which is situated two miles from Perth on a bold projecting Rock, and commands an extensive veiw of the Town and its delightful Environs. But tho' retired from almost all the World, (for we visit no one but the M'Leods, The M'Kenzies, the M'Phersons, the M'Cartneys, the M'Donalds, The M'kinnons, the M'lellans, the M'kays, the Macbeths and the Macduffs) we are neither dull nor unhappy; on the contrary there never were two more lively, more agreable or more witty girls, than we are; not an hour in the Day hangs heavy on our Hands. We read, we work, we walk, and when fatigued with these Employments releive our spirits, either by a lively song, a graceful Dance, or by some smart bon-mot, and witty repartee. We are handsome my dear Charlotte, very handsome and the greatest of our Perfections is, that we are entirely insensible of them ourselves . . .

(246)

Ripostes

THE OWL'S REPLY TO GRAY

[*'The moping owl does to the moon complain'*—*'Elegy Written in a Country Churchyard'*]

Who, who has dared to treat us owls so ill?
(With us of course, it's U to use two whos)
To whomsoe'er it was, I take my quill
To twit him for his quite erroneous views.

Doubtless some elegiac poet grey
Too witless and too wooden in the head
To understand a whit of what I say,
Has misconstrued my twilight serenade.

No, I did not complain, I'm not a grouse
(I do not give two hoots when I am blue)
You heard me call my love to share a mouse
For that's our owlish way, to wit, to woo.

F. SINCLAIR

CONTRA BLAKE

[*'The road of excess leads to the palace of wisdom'*]

The Road of Excess
leads, more often than not, to
The Slough of Despond.

W. H. AUDEN

RONDEAU

[*a response to Wordsworth*—

My heart leaps up when I behold
A Rainbow in the sky:
So was it when my life began;
So is it now I am a Man;

So be it when I shall grow old,
 Or let me die!
The Child is Father of the Man;
And I would wish my days to be
Bound each to each by natural piety.]

'The child is father to the man.'
How can he be? The words are wild.
Suck any sense from that who can:
'The child is father to the man.'
No; what the poet did write ran
'The man is father to the child.'
'The child is father to the man'!
How *can* he be? The words are wild.

GERARD MANLEY HOPKINS

HE PRAYETH BEST . . .

[*a response to Coleridge in 'The Rime of the Ancient Mariner'*]

He prayeth best who loveth best
All creatures great and small.
The Streptococcus is the test
I love him least of all.

ANON.

A REPLY FROM THE AKOND OF SWAT

[*in response to Edward Lear—*

Who, or why, or which, or what,
Is the Akond of Swat?]

Mr Lear, I'm the Akond of Swat;
 I'm gracious and fat
 In a very tall hat
And I'm heating a very large pot—
You know why, and for whom, and for what.

ETHEL TALBOT SCHEFFAUER

JENNY ON D. G. ROSSETTI

[*in response to Dante Gabriel Rossetti's 'Jenny'—*

Lazy laughing languid Jenny,
Fond of a kiss, and fond of a guinea . . .]

(*'I wonder what you're thinking of,' D.G.R. on Jenny*)

You think I'm sleeping, Mr R.
That only shows how wrong you are!
Not likely I'd drop off, myself,
Before your guinea's on the shelf.
A girl must live; and who's to blame
If there's no credit in this game?
Still writing? You're *that* kind of man?
Well, let's be cosy while we can.
Though I must say I do not care
For all these poets with long hair,
And painters with their rings and cloaks;
I never really like their jokes.
Look what they done to poor Miss S.
She's like a living ghost, I guess.
Just for a painting, so they say,
They lay her in her bath all day.
There's Mr Swinburne—you should see
The verses what he wrote for me.
They really are—well, not quite nice.
I wouldn't care to read them twice.
Some pictures I could take to. Once
I saw a show of Mr Hunt's,
And Mr Millais' and Rossetti's
At least aren't rude like Mr Etty's.

At last. He's closed his little book.
I've half a mind to take a look.
What, going now?
                Well, there's a ninny!
I never earned an easier guinea!

      'PONTIFEX' (winner of a competition in
                  the *New Statesman*)

KIPPS GIVES HIS VIEWS ON H. G. WELLS

'Mr Wells? Always kindness itself, but not a man you could call "Dad"—
know what I mean?—'E—he'd a way of looking at you—bit pop-eyed he
was, meaning no offence—as if he'd like to cut your liver out. Only to have
a look, mind you, to see if it was the same colour as his own—it was always
"You and me, Kipps," with him, and pretending we'd been boys together.
But it got me fidgeting. Brains was his trouble, I expect; never let him alone,
his brains wouldn't. You know, watching you like a cat, and wanting things
different, and talk! All round the shop. "You're a simple soul, Kipps," he'd
say, and of course I had to play up, even if it meant wood-carving. But a
chap has his feelings, and I could have done without some of his jokes.
Nobody likes to look a fool—you know, slippers at table dote and so on—
and of course I never said "You *be* off" to that bull—not likely! There's one
funny thing, though. I've not read Mr Wells's books meself—got too much
to think about—but they tell me he's no use for chaps like me. Mastodons.
Dodos. You know. "But mind you," they says, "You're the best thing he
ever done, Kipps—he must have loved you like a son." Well, then? See what
I mean? Simple I may be, but I know one thing—you can't 'ave things
both ways.'

L. E. JONES

Wells's novel Kipps *(1905) is the story of an aspiring draper's assistant.*

THE FAT WHITE WOMAN SPEAKS

[*in response to Frances Cornford's 'To a Fat Lady Seen from a Train'—*

O fat white woman whom nobody loves,
Why do you walk through the fields in gloves . . .
Missing so much and so much?]

Why do you rush through the field in trains,
Guessing so much and so much.
Why do you flash through the flowery meads,
Fat-head poet that nobody reads;
And why do you know such a frightful lot
About people in gloves as such?
And how the devil can you be sure,
Guessing so much and so much,
How do you know but what someone who loves
Always to see me in nice white gloves

At the end of the field you are rushing by,
Is waiting for his Old Dutch?

G. K. CHESTERTON

TO YOUNG PESSIMISTS

[*with a glance at T. S. Eliot's 'The Hollow Men'*]

Some sneer; some snigger; some simper;
In the youth where we laughed, and sang.
And *they* may end with a whimper
But *we* will end with a bang.

G. K. CHESTERTON

A RESPONSE TO PHILIP LARKIN'S 'THIS BE THE VERSE'

[*'They fuck you up, your mum and dad . . .'*]

Not everybody's
    Childhood sucked:
There are some kiddies
    Not up-fucked.

They moan and shout,
    Won't take advice.
But—hang about—
    Most turn out nice—

If not better
    Than us, no worse.
Sad non-begetter,
    That bean't the verse.

CAROL RUMENS

ALICE

In his lesser writings, Lewis Carroll was often a highly accomplished parodist. In the Alice *books, he was a parodist of genius. Most of the poems in* Wonderland *and* Through the Looking-Glass *are prime examples of parody being used as a spring-board to something higher—to pure poetry. Countless readers have enjoyed them with-out realizing that they are parodies, and countless others have been no more than dimly aware of the fact. A knowledge of the works they burlesque is at no point essential to appreciating or understanding them. But it does provide an additional pleasure.*

Of the examples which follow, three are of parodies based on heavily moral-izing poems, now largely forgotten, which were schoolroom favourites in Victorian times, and one ('Speak roughly to your little boy') inverts a message of tenderness towards the young which few of the adult characters in the Alice *books can be said to follow. The last example, however ('To the Looking-Glass world it was Alice that said'), does not so much offer a contrast with its original ('Bonnie Dundee') as borrow from its exuberance—appropriately enough, since it celebrates the fact that Alice is now a Queen, on a par with the grown-ups.*

'Against Idleness and Mischief', by Isaac Watts

> How doth the little busy bee
> Improve each shining hour,
> And gather honey all the day
> From every opening flower!
>
> How skilfully she builds her cell!
> How neat she spreads the wax!
> And labours hard to store it well
> With the sweet food she makes.
>
> In works of labour or of skill,
> I would be busy too;
> For Satan finds some mischief still
> For idle hands to do . . .

How doth the little crocodile
 Improve his shining tail,
And pour the waters of the Nile
 On every golden scale!

How cheerfully he seems to grin,
 How neatly spreads his claws,
And welcomes little fishes in
 With gently smiling jaws!

'The Old Man's Comforts and How He Gained Them',
by Robert Southey

'You are old, Father William,' the young man cried;
   'The few locks which are left you are gray;
You are hale, Father William—a hearty old man:
   Now tell me the reason, I pray.'

'In the days of my youth,' Father William replied,
   'I remembered that youth would fly fast,
And abused not my health and my vigour at first,
   That I never might need them at last.'

'You are old, Father William,' the young man cried,
   'And pleasures with youth pass away;
And yet you lament not the days that are gone:
   Now tell me the reason, I pray.'

'In the days of my youth,' Father William replied,
   'I remembered that youth could not last;
I thought of the future, whatever I did,
   That I never might grieve for the past.'

'You are old, Father William,' the young man cried,
   'And life must be hastening away;
You are cheerful and love to converse upon death:
   Now tell me the reason, I pray.'

'I am cheerful, young man,' Father William replied;
   'Let the cause thy attention engage;
In the days of my youth, I remembered my God,
   And He hath not forgotten my age.'

'You are old, Father William,' the young man said,
   'And your hair has become very white;
And yet you incessantly stand on your head—
   Do you think, at your age, it is right?'

'In my youth,' Father William replied to his son,
   'I feared it might injure the brain;
But now that I'm perfectly sure I have none,
   Why, I do it again and again.'

'You are old,' said the youth, 'as I mentioned before,
　And have grown most uncommonly fat;
Yet you turned a back-somersault in at the door—
　Pray, what is the reason of that?'

'In my youth,' said the sage, as he shook his grey locks,
　'I kept all my limbs very supple
By the use of this ointment—one shilling the box—
　Allow me to sell you a couple.'

'You are old,' said the youth, 'and your jaws are too weak
　For anything tougher than suet;
Yet you finished the goose, with the bones and the beak—
　Pray how did you manage to do it?'

'In my youth,' said his father, 'I took to the law,
　And argued each case with my wife;
And the muscular strength, which it gave to my jaw,
　Has lasted the rest of my life.'

'You are old,' said the youth, 'one would hardly suppose
　That your eye was as steady as ever;
Yet you balanced an eel on the end of your nose—
　What made you so awfully clever?'

'I have answered three questions, and that is enough,'
　Said his father; 'don't give yourself airs!
Do you think I can listen all day to such stuff?
　Be off, or I'll kick you downstairs!'

*Readers interested in psychoanalytic interpretations of poetry should note that in
Southey's poem the young man is simply a young man, but that in Carroll's he is
explicitly Father William's son.*

　　　　　'Speak Gently', by G. W. Langford
　　　　　　Speak gently to the little child;
　　　　　　Its love be sure to gain;
　　　　　　Teach it in accents soft and mild;
　　　　　　It may not long remain . . .

　　　　　　Speak gently; 'tis a little thing
　　　　　　Dropped in the heart's deep well;
　　　　　　The good, the joy that it may bring,
　　　　　　Eternity shall tell.

Speak roughly to your little boy,
    And beat him when he sneezes;
He only does it to annoy,
    Because he knows it teases.

I speak severely to my boy,
    I beat him when he sneezes;
For he can thoroughly enjoy
    The pepper when he pleases!

'The Sluggard', by Isaac Watts

'Tis the voice of the sluggard, I heard him complain
'You have waked me too soon, I must slumber again.'
As the door on its hinges, so he on his bed,
Turns his sides and his shoulders, and his heavy head.

I passed by his garden and saw the wild brier,
The thorn and the thistle, grow broader and higher;
The clothes that hang on him are turning to rags;
And his money still wastes till he starves or he begs.

I made him a visit, still hoping to find
That he took better care for improving his mind.
He told me his dreams, talked of eating and drinking;
But he scarce reads his Bible, and never loves thinking. . . .

'T is the voice of the Lobster; I heard him declare,
'You have baked me too brown, I must sugar my hair.'
As a duck with its eyelids, so he with his nose
Trims his belt and his buttons, and turns out his toes.
When the sands are all dry, he is gay as a lark,
And will talk in contemptuous tones of the Shark:
But, when the tide rises and sharks are around,
His voice has a timid and tremulous sound.

I passed by his garden, and marked, with one eye,
How the Owl and the Panther were sharing a pie:
The Panther took pie-crust, and gravy, and meat,
While the Owl had the dish as its share of the treat.
When the pie was all finished, the Owl, as a boon,
Was kindly permitted to pocket the spoon:
While the Panther received knife and fork with a growl,
And concluded the banquet by—

'Bonny Dundee', by Sir Walter Scott

To the Lords of Convention, 'twas Claver'se who spoke,
'Ere the King's crown shall fall, there are crowns to be broke;
So let each cavalier who loves honour and me
Come follow the bonnet of Bonny Dundee:
  Come fill up my cup, come fill up my can,
  Come saddle your horses and call up your men,
  Come open the West Port and let me gang free,
  And it's room for the bonnets of Bonny Dundee!' . . .

To the Looking-Glass world it was Alice that said
'I've a sceptre in hand I've a crown on my head.
Let the Looking-Glass creatures, whatever they be,
Come and dine with the Red Queen, the White Queen,
        and me!'

   Then fill up the glasses as quick as you can,
   And sprinkle the table with buttons and bran:
   Put cats in the coffee, and mice in the tea—
   And welcome Queen Alice with thirty-times-three!

'O Looking-Glass creatures,' quoth Alice, 'draw near!
'Tis an honour to see me, a favour to hear:
'Tis a privilege high to have dinner and tea
Along with the Red Queen, the White Queen, and me!'

   Then fill up the glasses with treacle and ink,
   Or anything else that is pleasant to drink:
   Mix sand with the cider, and wool with the wine—
   And welcome Queen Alice with ninety-times-nine!

Other parodies in the Alice books include 'The Lobster Quadrille' (inspired by Mary Howitt's 'The Spider and the Fly')' 'The Mad Hatter's Song' (which echoes Jane Taylor's 'Twinkle, twinkle little star'), and 'Beautiful Soup' (based on James M. Sayle's 'Star of the Evening'). 'The White Knight's Song' in Through the Looking-Glass satirizes Wordsworth's 'Resolution and Independence'—the poet's attitude in that poem, rather than his style.

Some ten years after Alice in Wonderland, Carroll briefly revisited what is perhaps his most famous parody, in a poem sent to a girl called Adelaide Paine. It is an acrostic, with the first letters of each line spelling out her name:

   'Are you deaf, Father William?' the young man said,
   'Did you hear what I told you just now?

Excuse me for shouting! Don't waggle your head
Like a blundering sleepy old cow!
A little maid dwelling in Wallington Town,
Is my friend, so I beg to remark:
Do you think she'd be pleased if a book were sent down,
Entitled "The Hunt of the Snark"?'
'Pack it up in brown paper!' the old man cried,
'And seal it in olive and dove.
I command you to do it!' he added with pride,
'Nor forget, my good fellow, to send her beside
Easter Greetings, and give her my love.'

James Joyce as Parodist

There is a pervasive element of parody in the major works of James Joyce. Ulysses abounds in mock-heroic devices and wide-ranging verbal mimicry. Finnegans Wake is written in what might reasonably be called a parody of the English language. Yet none of this makes Joyce a great parodist. He is too much his own man for that. His imitations exist to serve his artistic ends, and such limited light as they throw on the authors or styles imitated is purely incidental.

The closest he comes to sustained formal parody in his novels is in the 'Oxen of the Sun' episode in Ulysses. This scene—notable for the first meeting between Leopold Bloom and Stephen Dedalus—is set in a Dublin maternity hospital, where Mrs Mina Purefoy is waiting to be delivered of a child. Like other episodes in the novel, it has its own distinctive narrative technique—in this case a series of parodies of English styles from early Anglo-Saxon to modern trans-atlantic slang, by way of Malory, Pepys, Bunyan, Carlyle, Macaulay, Dickens, and many other celebrated authors. The idea—surely a sadly half-baked one—is that the growth of the language is meant to reflect the growth of the child in the womb.

In practice the parodies not only get in the way of the action; they also lack much parodic point. But then as John Updike has explained, contrasting them with Max Beerbohm's parodies in A Christmas Garland, that wasn't what Joyce was after:

A Christmas Garland *is a program of flawless impersonations by an actor whose own personality is invisible. The 'Oxen of the Sun' episode is a boisterous 'turn' taken in an antic succession of loosely fitting costumes; behind the bobbing masks we easily recognize the vaudevillian himself, Shem the Penman, the old flabbergaster. There is hardly a sentence of this parodic caper that lacks Joyce's own tone—the compacted incantation, the impelling commaless lilt, the love of rubble that turns history itself into a stream of trash. In reading these excerpts, disconnected as they are, we become caught up in the subterranean momentum of Joyce's earnest obsessions, of a narrative we can hardly see; the glimpses of Bloom and Stephen Dedalus take our eye, and the verbal hurly-burly screening them from clear view becomes something of a nuisance. The paragraphs tell us little about the authors imitated—Dickens was sentimental, Carlyle fulminated, etc.—but they strive to tell us everything about things. Their power as fiction mars them as parody—or rather, they are not parody at all but acts of conquest, a multiple annexation, an assimilation of all previous prose into a 'chaffering allincluding most farraginous chronicle' and into Joyce himself.*

There is more pleasure to be had from the simpler parodies in Ulysses—from the sentimental, novelettish prose used to describe the nursemaid Gerty MacDowell, for instance, or from the use of headlines and captions in the 'Aeolus' episode (which is set in a newspaper office). Like the 'Oxen of the Sun' parodies, these stylistic flourishes are primarily intended to amplify the action, to illustrate character and atmosphere. But it is a task they perform with far more success.

As for Finnegans Wake, *it must be left to the experts. But even a non-expert can see that it yields countless separate grains of parody, dozens on every page—distorted echoes, subversive puns, teasing allusions.*

The one place where Joyce was happy to play the parodist pure and unalloyed was in his letters and casual writings. In 1931, for instance, he sent his patroness, Harriet Shaw Weaver, two verses which he had penned celebrating the amorous conquests of Ford Madox Ford. They were based on the Irish ballad 'Father O'Flynn':

> O Father O'Ford, you've a masterful way with you,
> Maid, wife and widow are wild to make hay with you,
> Blonde and brunette turn-about run away with you,
> You've such a way with you, Father O'Ford.
>
> That instant they see the sun shine from your eye
> Their hearts flitterflutter, they think and they sigh:
> We kiss ground before thee, we madly adore thee,
> And crave and implore thee to take us, O Lord.

In an earlier letter to Harriet Weaver, written in 1925, he had cast his account of a family excursion from Rouen to Arcachon, south of Bordeaux, in the form of a parody of The Waste Land:

> Rouen is the rainiest place getting
> Inside all impermeables, wetting
> Damp marrow in drenched bones.
> Midwinter soused us coming over Le Mans
> Our inn at Niort was the Grape of Burgundy
>
> But the winepress of the Lord thundered over that
>   grape of Burgundy
> And we left in a hurgundy.
>   (Hurry up, Joyce, it's time!)
>
> I heard mosquitoes swarm in old Bordeaux
> So many!
> I had not thought the earth contained so many
>   (Hurry up, Joyce, it's time!)
>
> Mr Anthologos, the local gardener,
> Greycapped, with politeness full of cunning
> Has made wine these fifty years

And told me in his southern French
Le petit vin is the surest drink to buy
For if 'tis bad
Vous ne l'avez pas payé
    (Hurry up, hurry up, now, now, now!)

But we shall have great times,
When we return to Clinic, that waste land
O Esculapios!
    (Shan't we? Shan't we? Shan't we?)

The 'Clinic' referred to is one where Joyce was due to have an eye-operation on his return to Paris. 'Shan't we? Shan't we? Shan't we?' is a neatly sarcastic riposte to the serene line of Sanskrit which closes The Waste Land—*'Shantih shantih shantih'; but in* Finnegans Wake *Joyce permitted himself a wilder departure from Eliot: 'Thou in Shanty! Thou in scanty shanty!! Thou in slanty scanty shanty!!!'*

On one occasion he also wrote a parody in Wake-language—appropriately enough, since it was composed in response to a request from his publishers for a blurb for Haveth Childers Everywhere, *a section of the Wake which was brought out as a separate booklet some years before the work as a whole was completed. He chose as his theme Humpty Dumpty, one of the avatars of H. C. Earwicker, the hero of* Finnegans Wake, *but also sometimes identified in the book with the city of Dublin:*

Humptydump Dublin squeaks through his norse,
Humptydump Dublin hath a horrible vorse
And with all his kinks english
Plus his irismanx brogues
Humptydump Dublin's grandada of all rogues.

Joyce's finest informal parody—based on the Irish song 'Molly Brannigan'—was inspired by a dream he had not long after the publication of Ulysses, *in which Molly Bloom appeared to him and bade him farewell:*

Man dear, did you never hear of buxom Molly Bloom at all
As plump an Irish beauty, sir, as Annie Levy Blumenthal,
If she sat in the vice-regal box Tim Healy'd have no room
    at all,
    But curl up in a corner at a glance from her eye.
The tale of her ups and downs would aisy fill a handybook
That would cover the whole world across from Gib right on to Sandy
    Hook,

But now that tale is told, ahone, I've lost my daring dandy look
    Since Molly Bloom has gone and left me here for to die.

Man dear, I remember when my roving time was troubling me
We picnicked fine in storm or shine in France and Spain and Hungary,
And she said I'd be her first and last while the wine I poured went
        bubbling free.
    Now every male she meets with has a finger in her pie.
Man dear, I remember how with all the heart and brain
        of me
I arrayed her for the bridal, but, oh, she proved the bane of me,
With more puppies sniffing round her than the wooers of Penelope
    She's left me on the doorstep like a dog for to die.

My left eye is wake and his neighbour full of water, man,
I cannot see the lass I limned for Ireland's gamest daughter, man,
When I hear her lovers tumbling in their thousands for to court
        her, man,
    If I were sure I'd not be seen I'd sit down and cry.
May you live, may you love like this gaily spinning earth of ours,
And every morn a gallous son awake you to fresh wealth of gold,
But if I cling like a child to the clouds that are your petticoats,
    O Molly, handsome Molly, sure you won't let me die?

COMPOSITES

LUCY AND THE MARINER

(A person from Porlock, who wishes to remain anonymous, discovered the following MS under a primrose by the river's brim half-way between Kendal and Grasmere. Written in two separate hands, the poem seems to be compounded exclusively of material taken either from Wordsworth's 'Lucy' or Coleridge's 'Ancient Mariner'. If Lucy indeed met the Mariner, what more seemly than that both poets should in collaboration have penned a Lyrical Ballad to celebrate the rendezvous?)

> She slept among the untrodden ways
>   Beside the springs of Dove
> With water, water everywhere
>   And very few to love.
>
> Alone, alone, all, all alone
>   In the leafy month of June,
> A violet by a mossy stone
>   Beneath an evening moon.
>
> But in a minute she 'gan stir,
>   With broad and burning face:
> 'What loud uproar bursts from that door?
>   Heaven's mother send us grace!
>
> 'It is an ancient Mariner
>   From lands beyond the sea.
> By thy long grey beard and glittering eye
>   Now wherefore stopp'st thou me?
>
> 'I fear thee, ancient Mariner!
>   I fear thy skinny hand!
> And thou art sportive as the fawn
>   Upon the ribb'd sea sand.'
>
> *'Fear not, fear not! A lovelier flower*
>   *On earth was never sown.*
> *You shall be mine, and I will make*
>   *A lady for my own.'*
>
> 'Hold off! Unhand me, greybeard loon,
>   Here in this happy dell . . .'

Yet vital feelings of delight
    Her virgin bosom swell.

Her beams bemock the sultry main
    Like April hoar-frost spread.
What fond and wayward thoughts will slide
    Into a lover's head!

The bridegroom's doors are open wide:
    'Come near and nearer still!'
(Oh, mercy! To myself I cried,
    The Mariner hath his will.)

PAUL DEHN

THE LOVE SONG OF J. OMAR KHAYYAM

Awake! for Morning in the Pan of Night
Has dropped the Egg that puts bad Dreams to Flight;
And Newspapers and empty Bottles gleam
Encircled by a Hangman's Noose of Light.

I sometimes think there's none so red a Nose
As when some *fin de siècle* Poet goes;
That every Hyacinth the Garden wears
Through a blank Pair of female Sockets blows,

Come fill the Tea-cups and the Ices bring
So little time to hear the Mermaids sing,
The Footman waits already with my Hat;
I shall be Seventy in the Fire of Spring.

The Moving Finger writes; and, having writ,
Some other Finger comes to cancel it,
And out of a single word and half a line
Makes Verses of profundity and Wit.

ROY FULLER

GOD AND THE JOLLY BORED BOG-MOUSE

Jake Strugnell's entry for the Arvon/Observer Poetry Competition in 1980, the year in which the competition was judged by Ted Hughes, Philip Larkin, Seamus

Heaney, and Charles Causley. (Strugnell is the central character or supposed author of a number of Wendy Cope's poems. See p. 177.)

God tried to teach Mouse how to sing.
'Piss off! I'm not the sort.'
Mouse squelched away across the bog.
'It's jolly cold,' he thought.

Stone-numb, Mouse watched the ice-bright stars,
Decided they were boring.
Cradled in roots and sodden turf,
Soon he was jolly snoring.

Mouse dreamed a Universe of Blood,
He dreamed a shabby room,
He dreamed a dank hole in the earth,
(Back to the jolly womb).

Mouse tried to vomit up his guts
Then got up for a pee.
A comet pulsed across the sky—
He didn't jolly see.

WENDY COPE

STAGE AND SCREEN

THE ART OF EXPOSITION

[*from* The Spanish Armada, *the play-within-a-play in Sheridan's* The Critic]

The curtain rises and discloses Tilbury fort. Two sentinels asleep.
Enter Sir Walter Raleigh and Sir Christopher Hatton

SIR CHRISTOPHER:
                 True, gallant Raleigh!
But O, thou champion of thy country's fame
There *is* a question which I yet must ask;
A question which I never asked before—
What mean these mighty armaments?
This general muster? And this throng of chiefs?
Alas, my noble friend, when I behold
Yon tented plains in martial symmetry
Arrayed.—When I count o'er yon glittering lines
Of crested warriors, where the proud steeds neigh,
And valour-breathing trumpet's shrill appeal,
Responsive vibrate on my list'ning ear;
When virgin majesty herself I view
Like her protecting Pallas veiled in steel,
With graceful confidence exhort to arms!
When briefly all I hear or see bears stamp
Of martial vigilance, and stern defence,
I cannot but surmise.—Forgive, my friend,
If the conjecture's rash—I cannot but
Surmise.—The state some danger apprehends!

SIR WALTER:
O, most accomplished Christopher, I find
Thy staunch sagacity still tracks the future,
In the fresh print of the o'ertaken past.
Thy fears are just.

SIR CHRISTOPHER:
               But where? Whence? When? And what
The danger is—Methinks I fain would learn.

SIR WALTER:
You know, my friend, scarce two revolving suns,
And three revolving moons, have closed their course,
Since haughty Philip, in despite of peace,
With hostile hand hath struck at England's trade.

SIR CHRISTOPHER:
I know it well.

SIR WALTER:
Philip, you know, is proud Iberia's king.

SIR CHRISTOPHER:
He is.

SIR WALTER:
  —His subjects in base bigotry
And Catholic oppression held,—while we
You know, the Protestant persuasion hold.

SIR CHRISTOPHER:
We do.

SIR WALTER:
  You know beside,—his boasted armament,
The famed Armada,—by the Pope baptized—
With purpose to invade these realms—

SIR CHRISTOPHER:
        Is sailed,
Our last advices so report.

SIR WALTER:
While the Iberian Admiral's chief hope,
His darling son—

SIR CHRISTOPHER:
    Ferolo Whiskerandos hight—

SIR WALTER:
The same—by chance a pris'ner hath been ta'en
And in this fort of Tilbury—

SIR CHRISTOPHER:
      —Is now
Confined,—'tis true, and oft from yon tall turret's top
I've marked the youthful Spaniard's haughty mien
Unconquered, though in chains!

SIR WALTER:
    You also know—

SIR CHRISTOPHER:
Enough, enough,—'tis plain—and I no more
Am in amazement lost!

        RICHARD BRINSLEY SHERIDAN

STAGE DIALOGUE WE CANNOT DO WITHOUT

[*or which we couldn't do without in 1947, when this was written*]

John, d'you think it's going to be all right . . . about us,
I mean?

*

O God, Mary, what a blind fool I've been all along.

*

But Clive, that's . . . that's nothing short of blackmail!
Oh come, my dear, that's a very nasty word.
Oh Clive, don't you see—I'm trying to help you, but
you won't let me.

*

You were always the lucky one, John. It's been like that
as long as I can remember. It was you who was sent to
St Paul's, while I . . . what's the use of talking about it?

*

Mary, do you think you are being very fair to your
mother? You know what she feels about lipstick and all
this newfangled gallivanting and . . . what d'ye call the
stuff . . . boogie-woogie and so on . . .

*

I was in love with an artist once, Mary . . . *before* I met
your father . . . in Paris . . . we had the maddest time in
the Artists' Balls in the Latin Quarter, dancing all through
the night, . . . life was one long glorious dream . . . and
yet, I'm glad I didn't marry Gaston . . . I'm glad I came
to live in Alperton.

PETER USTINOV

TWO DIALOGUES

[*a review of two books published in 1960,* A Life in the Theatre,
by Tyrone Guthrie, and Mid-Century Drama, *by Laurence Kitchin*]

The Guthrie

SOCRATES: Good morning, Guthrie! How glad I am to see you! I am
depressed this morning.

GUTHRIE: What! A rational man like you, Socrates? You must not give way to it.

SOCRATES: You see, I dined last night with some theatrical friends and came away deeply ashamed of my ignorance in dramatic matters. Oh, Guthrie, I am sick of parties where everyone talks about the theatre and where I, alone, have nothing intelligent to say. Silence, as you know, has never been my forte.

GUTHRIE: There is nothing for it, Socrates, but to educate you. Let us begin at the beginning. What is a play?

SOCRATES: I don't know.

GUTHRIE: A play is something that happens in the theatre. Now, what is the theatre?

SOCRATES: Why, it is that round place with those stone seats.

GUTHRIE: That is *a* theatre, Socrates. *The* theatre is quite different. It is 'the direct descendant of fertility rites, war-dances, and all the corporate ritual expression by means of which our primitive ancestors, often wiser than we, sought to relate themselves to God, or the gods. . . .'

SOCRATES: My dear Guthrie, what a power of backsight you enjoy! So, a play is a sort of religion, is it? I would never have thought that. Is it also the same thing as the theatre?

GUTHRIE: No. A play is always a play, but the theatre is always a mystery.

SOCRATES: I shall never get to first base at this rate. Is a play, then, not something that is written by an author?

GUTHRIE: No. It is something that is interpreted by actors and produced by me. It has no existence before that.

SOCRATES: But, Guthrie, surely Euripides has written it first?

GUTHRIE: Yes, he has written it, Socrates, but it still has no existence.

SOCRATES: Oh. Has it been written in invisible ink?

GUTHRIE: Of course not! It is quite legible, but it does not become a play until I have acted it.

SOCRATES: Oh, I see! You mean that there is greater pleasure in seeing it acted than in reading it?

GUTHRIE: If I had meant that, Socrates, I would have said that.

SOCRATES: I pray you will not be angry with me, Guthrie: I am only trying to understand the mystery of the theatre. Do you mean that if I were to read a play, it would not be a play that I was reading?

GUTHRIE: That is correct, Socrates. You would merely be reading what I call 'the expressor's original idea'. Until this idea is 'interpreted' by 'artists'—that is to say, by people who have been initiated into the theatre mystery—nobody knows what the play is.

SOCRATES: Yes, since the play has not been made public, only the author can know what it is.

GUTHRIE: No, even the author does not know what it is.

SOCRATES: But, Guthrie, Aristophanes wrote a dangerous play about the dictator, Cleon. All the artists, as you call them, were so frightened by it that they refused to interpret it. Aristophanes had to play Cleon's part himself. Surely he knew what he was doing?

GUTHRIE: He knew, *because* he had ceased to be the author and had become an artist. That is the very point I am trying to make.

SOCRATES: Ah, I begin to see! Has an author, then, no knowledge at all of what he is about?

GUTHRIE: The better his play, the less he will know about it. I have estimated the degree of knowledge mathematically and concluded that an author of the first rank will know only one-tenth of what he is doing.

SOCRATES: By Zeus, what a puzzle! And why is this, Guthrie? Why have the gods loaded you and your fellow artists with such powers of comprehension, yet withheld all but a tittle from the original expressor?

GUTHRIE: We cannot say why. It is the very heart of the theatre mystery. Indeed, were it otherwise, there might be no theatre mystery at all.

SOCRATES: And have you and your fellow artists the power instantly to interpret the author's sibyl utterance?

GUTHRIE: No, Socrates. We artists must struggle long with the appointed text before we can draw sense from it.

SOCRATES: And how is this drawing done?

GUTHRIE: By a delicate selecting of those words and lines that speak to the artist in us, or which draw large numbers to the theatre, eager to witness what is new and strange.

SOCRATES: And whence comes your guidance in this selecting?

GUTHRIE: It is of the gods, Socrates, tempered by current fashion.

SOCRATES: And what of those words which defy your interpretation?

GUTHRIE: We utter them otherwise than their expressor wrote them, or, failing that, must expunge them utterly.

SOCRATES: Oh, what a labour! And is it for all those reasons that a play cannot be a play until it is enacted?

GUTHRIE: It is so, Socrates.

The Kitchin

KITCHIN: Whence come you, Socrates, so wide-eyed?

SOCRATES: I am straight from Guthrie, Kitchin.

KITCHIN: 'He is the first *régisseur* to have established himself as such in the main stream of English drama.'

SOCRATES: How richly you speak, Kitchin! Guthrie has been explaining the theatre mystery to me. Must all utterance concerning this mystery be mysterious, too?

KITCHIN: Yes, it must, Socrates. The mystery of the theatre is too deep for simplicity. Only figures, similes, and metaphors can express it. For this is 'the golden age of the Lambretta', and a 'negative attitude to speech, arrived at in deference to the limitations of the mid-century audience, has been abetted by the positive trend of the last two decades towards balletic ensemble, a thing of intrinsic beauty and vitality.'

SOCRATES: Heavens, Kitchin, how your prose proves this! But are you never self-conscious about speaking so?

KITCHIN: 'Self-conscious grapples with a resistant medium bring out a sweat of theorizing and other by-products easily mistaken for the end-product. . . .'

SOCRATES: Yes, we must avoid that. But tell me, Kitchin, are you able to use this mysterious language for discussing performances of plays? For, as you know, it is performance makes the play, and not the play the performance.

KITCHIN: Without stint. I can say of the author, Osborne: 'He is coming to grips with the new drama's most dangerous enemy, which . . . is the sterile conformism implicit in the values of mid-century consumer society and fostered by commercial interests with the powerful aid of psychologists and the mass media.' Better still, I can say of a play by the author, Beckett: 'It communicates its Pascalian interrogation as pithily as a Biblical strip-cartoon at more levels than one.'

SOCRATES: I love your prose, Kitchin, but I regret that you should waste it on authors, who are only aware of one-tenth of what they are up to. The simplest words should be good enough for them, and your choicest arabesques of tongue reserved for those who can be called artists. For, as Guthrie has explained to me, there is no play save in the interpretation of it by artists.

KITCHIN: I have expressed that far more beautifully, saying: 'Reading a play is like trying to visualize a statue by measuring the gap left in the quarry.'

SOCRATES: Oh, Kitchin, that is felicity itself! And can you so adapt your golden tongue as to be able to apply your similes to all that is by nature theatrical?

KITCHIN: Without difficulty. I can say of the artist, Callas: 'Reinforced by a generous mouth, she has the magnetism of the ancient world, at once enigmatic and blatant, as caught by Botticelli in *Primavera*.' In hedgerow vein, I can say of the artist, McCowen: 'He has big hands, expressive in repose as the roots of a beech.' 'The comic Shakespearean subsoil' is another of my rustic phrases.

SOCRATES: And all these phrases, Kitchin, serve as it were as veils, to render the theatre mystery more mysterious still?

KITCHIN: That is so, Socrates.

SOCRATES: Am I right, then, in defining a play in these words: It is a text which comes to the theatre falling short of comprehension by nine-tenths. This all but total inadequacy is rectified by the balletic Guthrie and his ensemble of fellow artists, after which the utter density of the performed mystery is made absolute by yourself?

KITCHIN: One might so say it, Socrates.

SOCRATES: How marvellous is the way of the Muses, how inscrutable the decisions of Zeus! In all other walks of life, the gods favour that which is clear, simple, and unaffected by the frenzy of grandeur. Only the theatre mystery stands without the general rule—priestly, extravagant, purple, and apart. Yet tell me, good Kitchin, do you and Guthrie and the other artists not find this grandeur a bitter and intolerable burden, driving you half mad with a sense of singular greatness?

KITCHIN: No, Socrates, for though in our priestly appointments we are mysterious and splendid, we are at heart simple, ordinary men, much as you are yourself.

SOCRATES: Why, Kitchin, something tells me that it is true—so true that my eyes begin to brim with tears. Farewell, generous-mouthed priest! May your subsoil engender beech roots.

KITCHIN: Doubt it not, Socrates. Farewell!

NIGEL DENNIS

PETER BROOK'S D'IK

[*from* I, An Actor, *the autobiography of the actor Nicholas Craig*]

'Why not have everyone swinging about on trapezes?' I had said to Peter in a cold rehearsal room one morning in 1970.

'What, *all* of them?' Peter had replied incredulously. 'Puck? Titania? Bottom?'

'Yes, and the Lovers. You know—swinging about.'

'I suppose we could give it a try, Nick,' he had said, thoughtfully popping a Sweetex into his coffee. And the rest, as they say, is history.

As a relatively junior member of that company (I was understudying Toadflax, as a matter of fact) it was immensely gratifying to see a suggestion of mine have such an enormous impact on World Theatre. The production is always referred to as 'Brook's Dream', which is quite right since he was the director and no one was more delighted than I at the plaudits which were lavished upon that wise, slightly balding head. Naturally, Peter was tremendously grateful to me for putting him on the theatrical map, so to speak, and I knew it would only be a short time before we were working together again.

I read with great interest about his move to Paris and his search for an internationally accessible narrative form. Clearly this was a product of the discussions we had had during those early *Dream* rehearsals. Remarkably, he was following an almost identical path to me in his development as an artist. I had to be with him.

'I'm coming out,' I told him when I eventually got through to his *atelier*. He made all sorts of protestations about not having a suitable 'biggy' for me, but I swept them aside and, within twenty-four hours of putting the phone down, I was standing in a disused abattoir in the 10*ième arrondissement* daubing myself with mud.

Oh, what a door was opened to me that first morning! Here, at long last, was the kind of theatre I had been seeking: primal, epic story-telling in humble classless surroundings; a theatre for everyone. It was exhilarating, liberating. I was discovering my inner-storyteller; Nicholas Craig the gipsy pedlar of spells and dreams; the vagabond troubadour who takes life as he finds it and bites his thumb at danger; the *beau chevalier* who dines with the Duchess and laughs with the scullion and probably beds the pair of them; the gay dog who hunts with the Bishop and brawls with the tar; the singer of songs, the clown, the dark-eyed illusionist. It didn't matter at all when some tramps told me that I had got the wrong derelict building, for I had discovered something infinitely more precious—I had discovered Nicholas Craig the Global Artist.

Peter seemed surprised but obviously delighted to see me when I arrived at his office and he broke off a conversation he was having in Manx with a Tamil actor to give me big hugs. It was the first time we had met since the *Dream* and I think we were both a bit weepy. We talked in broad terms of how our ideas had developed over the last few years and I could see that he was bursting to tell me about his latest project.

It was to be an adaptation of the ancient Indonesian legend *D'ikwi Ting-ton*. I was immediately seized with enthusiasm and bombarded Peter with questions about stylistic approach, ritual catharsis formulae and whether he had cast the main part yet.

He shrugged his shoulders. 'All I've got at this stage, Nick, is a wonderful group of internationally talented actors and four hundredweight of potting compost. The project could go in any direction. It is very, *very* exciting.'

There was no doubt that Brook had assembled a remarkable array of talent (living proof—if it were needed—that China has its Peter Bowleses just as Yugoslavia boasts its Googie Witherses). There were Swiss, Kiwis, Derrymen—all tremendously exciting. There was an immaculate Solomon Islander very much in the Nigel Patrick mould and several Faeroese actors who would, frankly, make the current RSC crop look like a bunch of amateurs. Then there was a half-Finnish, half-Madagascan actor who could do things with a bone which brought tears to your eyes. There were Bretons, Springboks, Walloons and a wonderful gamin Prussian. I palled up with a Pathan lass who shared my passion for Victorian chamber-pots.

Peter conducted the early rehearsals with painstaking thoroughness. There were language difficulties of course—it once took him thirty-five minutes to say 'Coffee-time, girls and boys' in ways that everyone could understand—but we were soon producing some immensely interesting work. It was a time of stripping off our preconceptions and revealing our emotional nudity to each other. Using gravel and feathers, we were learning to explore and love ourselves all over again—to *re*-love ourselves. It was tremendously stimulating, though rather messy of course.

In order to be truly international, and to be understood by our simple peasant audiences the world over, we invented a completely new language in which to perform the *D'ik*. It was composed of Church Latin, Persian, Welsh and Maori. We called it Horghczitt and within a few months we were jabbering away to each other like natives. Horghczitt had a strange poetry all of its own and it suited the primal myth perfectly—when the Narrator stepped out of his mud mound and delivered the first line, 'Ha-lo k'Ids. Hav agoo d'Krismus diju?' the effect was electric.

I was playing the Bird of Paradise, whom D'ik meets on his travels to the South Seas. No wings, no Kirby wire, just a cardboard beak, a feather and my talent. I invented as never before, preening, strutting, having baths and doing my best to avoid the sudden assaults of Brunhilde who was playing the cat.

There was a big set-piece scene at the end of Part Four in which D'ik dreams of his homeland and his sweetheart, the daughter of the wicked Al-Damahn Fitswahan. He imagines his helpless love searching the countryside for him, wailing as she does so, 'Nien myls fromlon don-ands tilnoh syn of D'ik.' It was a very moving section and of course it was vital that it should work properly. But no matter how much energy we put into it, it still seemed curiously lifeless. What the trouble was we couldn't tell. Peter ordered a month's meditation in Kashmir but when we came back it was no better. Then, one day in about the eighth month of rehearsal, Peter came up with a typically international and innovative approach to the problem. Just before we began to play the scene for the umpteenth time he stopped us and said simply, 'Do nothing.'

I twigged immediately but some of the others were a bit slow to comprehend the maestro. 'Faites rien,' he continued, 'ποιετε 'ουδεν. . . . Ddoliog nos,' etc. At the end of the day we tried it. We actually *did nothing*—and it was the most exciting moment I have ever had in a disused abattoir. Fifteen of us standing there doing absolutely bugger-all and it was riveting.

Suddenly the show was in terrific shape, all that remained was to find some simple mountain peasants to perform it to. We scoured Montmartre but nary a one could we find. Then there was the additional snag that Peter would only allow the *D'ik* to be performed on the south side of a volcano at dawn during Ramadan. So our joy over the brilliance of the production was tempered by the knowledge that our chances of performing it were steadily receding.

Peter found the Mexican and Javanese arts councils to be entirely unhelpful in the matter of a venue, while the Neapolitans, predictably, wanted to make all kinds of idiotic conditions. We spent several tense weeks in Paris practising cries and squawks while Peter jetted further and further afield in search of somewhere to put his *D'ik*. And all the time Ramadan was getting closer.

Finally, the message came telling us to get ourselves on a plane to Iceland asap. The newly formed volcanic island of Surtesy was, Peter said, the perfect setting. As for the audience, he had found a small community in the Cahchapoyas region of Peru who were as poor and unsophisticated as they were desperate for good theatre. He had made arrangements for the entire village to be flown out to Reykjavik.

He was right about the setting. Apart from some rather dry acoustics, there was no doubt that the *D'ik* had found its spiritual home. The day before the performance we busied ourselves mixing up the special muds and improvising good luck prezzies out of pumice.

At three a.m. on March 23rd 1981, the first and only performance of the *D'ik* began. At four a.m. we heard the news that the Peruvian peasants' charter flight was grounded at Luxembourg. But it didn't matter because at five p.m. the following day the sun sank behind the volcano and the audience, consisting of Nicholas De Jongh, the crew of a herring trawler and a girl from *City Limits*, wept openly. There was no question that Peter Brook's *D'ik* was the theatrical event of the decade.

It will always be my proudest boast that I was a vital element in that extraordinary mixture of Horghczitt, mud and international talent. It is a tragic reflection of the state of the world theatre now that not a single nation possessing an area of high vulcanicity has come forward to fund another performance.

NICHOLAS CRAIG (with the co-operation of
NIGEL PLANER and CHRISTOPHER DOUGLAS)

THE LIFE OF JOAN CRAWFORD

For Barbara Barry

She was a working girl from a small town
but the town wasn't so small
that it didn't have a railroad track
dividing the right side from the wrong side.
On the right side was the Hill

where the swells lived in big houses,
and on the wrong side, the Hollow where the proletariat
spent their greasy and unrewarding lives.
(For in those days the American town
was a living demonstration of Marxist theory.)

Joan of course lived in the Hollow
in one of those shacks with sagging porches
the mill put up rows of for the workers.
Her father, Tim Crawford, was the town drunk
living on relief and odd jobs
ever since the mines closed down when Joan was a baby.
He had been waiting for them to reopen for twenty years.
Joan never knew what had happened to her mother:
Joan's birth, her mother's disappearance or death, the mine's
       closing,
that was in a time of violence no one would discuss.
Just mention it and her father went on a binge,
not that he was ever sober.

She sighed, and went off to work in the five-and-ten
wearing her made-over dress with little washable collar and cuffs.
Even with her prole accent and the cheap bag and shoes
she was a good looker.
Men used to come by in their flashy suits and big cigars,
call her tootsie and ask for a date,
but she knew a poor girl didn't stand a chance with them.
She wasn't one of those innocents
who think a guy loves you if he gets a hard-on.
Yet she wouldn't go with any of the boys from the Hollow
because with them the future was sleazy with kids
and the ruin of her figure before she was thirty—
and no fun after the honeymoon
except the Friday-night fight
when he would come home stinking, having drunk up the paycheck
and beat her black and blue
when she threw the stack of overdue bills at him
and then screw her viciously on the dining-room table.
Some fun.
That was life in the Hollow and she wasn't having any.
She had turned down a job working in the mill
where the pay was better but life closed like a trap on you
and chose the more ladylike job at the five-and-ten

where people called her Miss and she could pose genteelly
behind the Tangee cosmetic display and the ribbon counter.
For Joan had the makings of a lady
if she could ever get some dough to fix herself up with
and a speech teacher to correct her dreadful accent.

But Nature had its way with Joan at last:
Spring came and handsome John Wainrich
(of the best family in town—they owned everything,
the five-and-dime, the shut mines, and the mill),
John Wainrich came in one day to collect the receipts or something
and found a million dollar baby in his own five and ten cents store.
Well Joan fell hard
and went out with him in his big car
and of course in the moonlight she let him have his way with her.
She used to meet him on the sly
when he could get away from the country club
and the milk-white debutante he was engaged to,
and they would drive out to roadhouses
where he wouldn't be seen by his swell friends.
Joan had pride,
but what is a woman's pride when she's in love.
What it came to, a few months later,
was that she got pregnant,
and just as she was about to break the good news,
he told her he was going to be married
and would have to stop seeing her until after the wedding,
that it was just a marriage of convenience
and wouldn't make any difference to them.
So she couldn't tell him then, she would have died first.

My great love, she muttered sarcastically,
he didn't even use a scum-bag.
And she went off to the city
where she got a job as receptionist in an office.
Her boss, Mr Harris, was an older but dignified man
with a wife at home on Park Avenue, the victim of neurosis and
        wealth—
with all that money she could buy neither health nor happiness.
Joan used to listen to Mr Harris's troubles
when she brought him his alka-seltzer mornings.
    And when she was promoted to secretary, they would have
        dinner out

and she'd advise him on business,
she being a girl with a good head on her shoulders.

In Mr Harris's company she saw the world and learned fast.
She lost her small-town look and learned to dress,
wearing hat and gloves, to fluff out her hair
and drink vermouth cocktails.
And while retaining the colorful idiom of the Hollow,
her grammar improved and her voice lost its nasal whine.
Joan was a knockout in every way
from honest eyes and square shoulders
to the narrow hips of a tango dancer.

Nothing showed yet in the baby department.
At night Joan looked critically at herself in the mirror:
Not a bulge, but baby was in there all right,
and her eyes went bitter as she thought of its father—
her great love, hmph.
'Well young feller, at least we'll have each other.
But I'd better be making preparations.
A working girl can't leave things to the caterer.'

Then her boss proposed: He'd divorce his wife and marry her.
'Gee Mr Harris, I think you're swell but I can't.
There is a real big favor you could do for me, though,'
and she told him how she gave her all for love
and her lover turned out to be a louse.
So Mr Harris set her up in a little flat until the baby came.
He didn't make any demands on her or anything,
not yet anyway: It was sort of a promissory note
to be paid off later when she grew to love him out of gratitude.

But her ex-lover, John Wainrich, came to town
with his new wedding ring on, and tracked her down;
and misunderstanding the arrangement, called her a few names,
but swore she was his and he'd never give her up.
Joan still loved him but had the courage
to flee to a cheap hotel.
She got a job as dance-hall hostess, dime-a-dance,
six months pregnant, but with a brave smile
as the customers stepped on her toes.
They found her a good joe and a willing ear
as they told her their troubles

while rubbing off against her to a slow foxtrot.
One of her customers, impressed by her dancing,
got her to enter a dance marathon with him for prize money—
she needed that dough for the little stranger—
but the strain was too much for her,
marathon-dancing in her seventh month!

She came to on a hospital bed
with no makeup on and a white cloth over her forehead like a nun
to see her griddle-faced father looking down on her,
his mouth boozy as ever, but in his heart
vowing to go on the wagon if God would spare her life:
'Come home with me, Joanie, I'll take care of you.'
'And baby too, papa?'
'Didn't they tell you, Joanie? The baby . . .'
'Oh no . . .'
And tears of mourning still in her eyes
she went back home to the Hollow and kept house for her father.

She had two visits shortly after returning home:
First, John's pale bride came by, big with child,
neglect driving her to seek out her rival.
When she saw Joan so sweet and good
instead of some tramp homewrecker type,
she burst into tears and confessed she knew John didn't love her
but hoped he would when the baby was born, his heir.
The bitterness in Joan's heart turned to pity—
weren't they both women who had suffered?—
so she forgave her and they wept together:
Joan never could resist being a pal.

The other visit was from old Mr Wainrich, John's father.
(Never had the Hollow seen so many long cars drive through.)
The old capitalist had a confession to make:
'When I saw you at the window watering the geraniums
I could have sworn you were your mother.'
'You knew my mother, Mr Wainrich?' asked Joan astonished.
'Yes. Bette wasn't like the other women in the Hollow.
She was a Davis you know. Her parents
had been plantation people down in Georgia
and even if they did end up here in the Hollow
she never forgot that she was a thoroughbred.'
'Are you trying to tell me that you loved my mother?' Joan gasped.

'Yes, I loved her, but the heir to an industrial empire
isn't free to marry whom he chooses,
so my family chose an appropriate bride for me.
At that time I was running our coal mines here,
where Tim Crawford worked.
He was the biggest and toughest man in the Hollow
so naturally he was spokesman for the boys.
He had loved your mother for years
but she knew what it meant for a woman to marry a miner
and live in constant fear of a cave-in.
And she hated his coarse language and crude manners: she was
          a lady.
And besides, she loved me.
But when I broke the news of my engagement to her
(I explained it was just a marriage of convenience
and it wouldn't make any difference to us)
she married Tim just to spite me.
But it wasn't enough for her: right on my wedding day
she got Tim Crawford to call the men out on strike,
and, with violence surging around the Hill,
I had the biggest wedding ever seen in these parts.
I was coal and my bride was steel: what a merger!
The President came, and there were reporters from Chicago,
and your mother, already big with child, leading a picket line.
That strike went on for months, and you were born in the middle
          of it.
But we couldn't go on apart, your mother and I.
We knew we were sinners, but we managed to meet on the sly,
although the strike had turned the town into a battlefield
and we belonged to opposing armies.
Finally we decided to run away together, but just at that time
a load of scabs I was importing to work the mines arrived,
and there was a tremendous battle between them and the miners,
led by Tim Crawford of course.
The miners had lead pipes and dynamite,
but we had the National Guard in full battle dress.
Your mother and I, eloping, got caught in the middle
and took refuge in a deserted mine;
and I don't know which side did it, but a stick of dynamite
was thrown down the shaft, and your mother
was buried by a ton of falling rock.'
(Joan moaned and hid her face in her hands.)
'It was useless to do anything so I left her there.

Why say anything when no one knew?
She was destroyed by the strike she had started.
The mines were shut down for good of course,
I couldn't bear the memory.
They would have had to be shut anyway,
we were losing money on them.'
'And that's why daddy never knew what happened to mother,
raising me all by himself, and took to drink . . .'
'Yes, and I went back home to my wife and our little John was born
and I tried to forget . . .'
'Promise me one thing, Mr Wainrich,' Joan said,
'for the sake of my mother's memory,
that you'll open the mines again and give daddy back his old job.'
Joan had a lot to think about in the days that followed.
One day she got a call to come up right away to the big house,
and arriving, found John's wife dying,
having given birth to a child, and asking for her.
The pale bride lay holding her child, the Wainrich heir,
but seeing Joan, she sat up with her last strength and said,
'I give him to you,' and fell back dead.
Joan fainted away, and when she came to,
it seemed a long time later, after the funeral and the mourning,
John Wainrich held her in his arms and was saying over and over,
'I am yours now, she gave me to you.'
'But she meant the child,' Joan cried.
'Both of us are yours, my darling.'

So Joan found her place in life at last.
They always said she'd make it up there, surrounded by the help,
a lady, moving gracefully among the guests.
And what a difference now:
The miners in tuxes standing around the punchbowl with the swells,
the colored butler joining in the fun with loud yaks,
a new era, the classless society,
brought about by the smartest little woman in the U.S.A.,
Ladies and Gentlemen: Miss Joan Crawford.

                                        EDWARD FIELD

ARTISTIC ENDEAVOURS

MY TURNER PRIZE DINNER

It was a real privilege to find myself invited to the Turner Prize dinner after the glamorous award ceremony.

I was delighted to be placed between the Director of the Tate, Sir Nicholas Serota, and his Communications Director, Simon Wilson. As ever, Sir Nicholas was the perfect host. 'May I fill your glass?' he asked, with a very real sense of urgency coupled with restraint.

Sir Nicholas then reached for an empty bottle of wine, and poured its lack of contents into my glass. Simon leant forward and whispered, 'He is making a very important statement about something and nothing, and how nothing can emerge out of something. In this case, the bottle is some-thing—but inside it is nothing. The whole process of pouring "nothing" from a bottle into a glass raises extremely disturbing questions about the whole nature of emptiness in today's society.'

The waiters and waitresses then arrived with our first course—or, to be more accurate, they did not arrive, and there was no first course. While everyone at the table was asking searching and relevant questions about where it was, Sir Nicholas smiled quietly to himself. 'This calls into ques-tion the whole nature of the so-called "first course". Is it first—or is it in some extraordinary way second? And is it really a course at all? Can a first course that isn't served really count as a first course in any valid meaning of the phrase? Our bold decision not to serve a first course at all has generated a lot of argument and discussion . . .'

'. . . and that must be a good thing,' added Simon.

'To be honest,' I said, 'I was feeling a bit peckish.'

At this point, the leading art critic Diana Meacher butted in. 'Passing judgement on the first course does not seem to me to be either a relevant or an adequate response,' she said. 'The whole absence-of-a-starter concept is a valid and powerful statement about the nature of consuming in the twenty-first century.'

Suddenly, there was a rumble. It came from the stomach of the prize-winning artist, Martin Creed. Obviously, this made those of us around the table tremendously excited. We all listened very, very carefully. 'His stom-ach is really out there on the edge of things,' whispered Simon Wilson. 'It's coming out of the whole tradition of noise-related body art. Martin's stomach is making an important statement about hunger and about food, and about the connection between the two.'

After twenty-five minutes, our empty soup plates were taken away, and a large trolley bearing the main course was brought on. 'I'm tremendously excited about this main course,' Sir Nicholas confided to me. 'It's full of all sorts of resonances and meanings.' He pointed to the empty trolley. 'It is—quite literally—nothing.'

'B-b-but,' I said, 'I was looking forward to something.'

'Absolutely marvellous!' said Sir Nicholas. 'You see, this very important main course has, in a very real way, been playing with your sense of expectation. In denying your expectation of a meal, it seems to me not only audacious, bold and witty—but it also succeeds in overturning the traditional discredited premise upon which a meal is judged—namely food.'

Did I notice a hint of self-satisfaction playing upon his lips?

Across the table, the art critic Diana Meacher was staring with her customary disarming intensity at her empty plate. 'It's bleak. And it's honest,' she said, 'but more than that—it's bleakly honest.'

Twenty minutes later, our empty plates were removed, to cluckings of approval from the critics. 'Uncompromising minimalist!' said one. 'And so bleakly nutritious!' cooed another. There was then a choice of sweets: soufflé of nothing, or no fruit salad. Most people opted for neither, or both. An expectant hush fell upon the room as the winner of the Turner Prize broke wind. Immediately, there was a sense of something very real, almost pungent in the air. 'Breathtaking!' murmured Simon Wilson, approvingly. 'It not only has resonance—but reverberation too.'

We all listened intently while Creed offered both a theory of the concept, and, more importantly, a concept of the theory. 'I was attempting to activate the whole space,' he explained. 'On one level, it entirely occupies the space, and so in a sense it's a really big work. But at the same time on another level there is nothing there.'

A few minutes later, the lights in the room began to flash on and off. 'We have come, in a very real way, to the end of dinner,' announced Sir Nicholas.

But was it dinner? And was it the end? If the dinner never began, how could it end? 'Ultimately, it makes people ask questions,' said Sir Nicholas.

'And that must be a good thing,' added Simon.

CRAIG BROWN

from 'OPERA SYNOPSES: SOME SAMPLE OUTLINES
OF GRAND OPERA PLOTS FOR HOME STUDY'

DIE MEISTER-GENOSSENSCHAFT

SCENE: *The Forests of Germany.*
TIME: *Antiquity.*

CAST

STRUDEL, *God of Rain*		Basso
SCHMALZ, *God of Slight Drizzle*		Tenor
IMMERGLÜCK, *Goddess of the Six Primary Colours*		Soprano
LUDWIG DAS EIWEISS, *the Knight of the Iron Duck*		Baritone
THE WOODPECKER		Soprano

ARGUMENT

The basis of 'Die Meister-Genossenschaft' is an old legend of Germany which tells how the Whale got his Stomach.

ACT 1

The Rhine at Low Tide Just Below Weldschnoffen.—Immerglück has grown weary of always sitting on the same rock with the same fishes swimming by every day, and sends for Schwül to suggest something to do. Schwül asks her how she would like to have pass before her all the wonders of the world fashioned by the hand of man. She says, rotten. He then suggests that Ringblattz, son of Pflucht, be made to appear before her and fight a mortal combat with the Iron Duck. This pleases Immerglück and she summons to her the four dwarfs: Hot Water, Cold Water, Cool, and Cloudy. She bids them bring Ringblattz to her. They refuse, because Pflucht has at one time rescued them from being buried alive by acorns, and, in a rage, Immerglück strikes them all dead with a thunderbolt.

ACT 2

A Mountain Pass.—Repenting of her deed, Immerglück has sought advice of the giants, Offen and Besitz, and they tell her that she must procure the magic zither which confers upon its owner the power to go to sleep while apparently carrying on a conversation. This magic zither has been hidden for three hundred centuries in an old bureau drawer, guarded by the Iron Duck, and, although many have attempted to rescue it, all have died of a strange ailment just as success was within their grasp.

But Immerglück calls to her side Dampfboot, the tinsmith of the gods, and bids him make for her a tarnhelm or invisible cap which will enable her to talk to people without their understanding a word she says. For a dollar and a half extra Dampfboot throws in a magic ring which renders its wearer insensible. Thus armed, Immerglück starts out for Walhalla, humming to herself.

ACT 3

The Forest Before the Iron Duck's Bureau Drawer.—Merglitz, who has up till this time held his peace, now descends from a balloon and demands the release of Betty. It has been the will of Wotan that Merglitz and Betty should meet on earth and hate each other like poison, but Zweiback, the druggist of the gods, has disobeyed and concocted a love-potion which has rendered the young couple very unpleasant company. Wotan, enraged, destroys them with a protracted heat spell.

Encouraged by this sudden turn of affairs, Immerglück comes to earth in a boat drawn by four white Holsteins, and, seated alone on a rock, remembers aloud to herself the days when she was a girl. Pilgrims from Augenblick, on their way to worship at the shrine of Schmürr, hear the sound of reminiscence coming from the rock and stop in their march to sing a hymn of praise for the drying-up of the crops. They do not recognize Immerglück, as she has her hair done differently, and think that she is a beggar girl selling pencils.

In the meantime, Ragel, the paper-cutter of the gods, has fashioned himself a sword on the forge of Schmalz, and has called the weapon 'Assistance-in-Emergency.' Armed with 'Assistance-in-Emergency' he comes to earth, determined to slay the Iron Duck and carry off the beautiful Irma.

But Frimsel overhears the plan and has a drink brewed which is given to Ragel in a golden goblet and which, when drunk, makes him forget his past and causes him to believe that he is Schnorr, the God of Fun. While labouring under this spell, Ragel has a funeral pyre built on the summit of a high mountain and, after lighting it, climbs on top of it with a mandolin which he plays until he is consumed.

Immerglück never marries.

ROBERT BENCHLEY

THE WRITTEN WORD

Edward Copleston's Advice to a Young Reviewer *(1807) presupposes that Milton's* L'Allegro *has just been published for the first time, and subjects it to a review written in the slashing style favoured by conservative critics of the day. The review concludes with a curious anticipation of the jibes against Keats which appeared in* Blackwood's Magazine *in 1818 ('back to the shop, Mr John, back to the plasters, pills and ointment boxes'):*

Upon the whole, Mr Milton seems to be possessed of some fancy and talent for rhyming; two most dangerous endowments, which often unfit men for acting an useful part in life, without qualifying them for that which is great and brilliant. If it be true, as we have heard, that he has declined advantageous prospects in business, for the sake of indulging his poetical humour, we hope it is not yet too late to prevail upon him to retract his resolution. With the help of Cocker and common industry he may become a respectable scrivener; but it is not all the Zephyrs, and Auroras, and Corydons, and Thyrsis's, aye, nor his junketing Queen Mab, and drudging Goblins, that will ever make him a poet.

Cocker] *a standard arithmetic book for over a hundred years.*

LE TRAITEMENT SUPERBE

'Book-handling', as offered to interested parties by the Irish columnnist Myles na Gopaleen, is 'a new service which enables ignorant people who want to be suspected of reading books to have their books handled and mauled in a manner that will give the impression that their owner is very devoted to them'.

As part of 'Le Traitement Superbe', the most expensive form of the service, 'suitable passages in not less than fifty per cent of the books are to be underlined in good-quality red-ink, and an appropriate phrase from the following list inserted in the margin'—

Rubbish!
Yes, indeed!
How true, how true!
I don't agree at all.
Why?
Yes, but cf. Homer, Od., iii, 151.
Well, well, well.
Quite, but Bossuet in his Discours sur l'histoire Universelle has already established the same point and given much more forceful explanations.

Nonsense, nonsense!
A point well taken!
But *why* in heaven's name?
I remember poor Joyce saying the very same thing to me.

In addition, 'not less than six volumes are to be inscribed with forged messages of affection and gratitude from the author of each work, e.g.'—

'To my old friend and fellow-writer, A.B., in affectionate remembrance, from George Moore.' 'In grateful recognition of your great kindness to me, dear A.B., I send you this copy of The Crock of Gold. Your old friend, James Stephens.'

'Well, A.B., both of us are getting on. I am supposed to be a good writer now, but I am not old enough to forget the infinite patience you displayed in the old days when guiding my young feet on the path of literature. Accept this further book, poor as it may be, and please believe that I remain, as ever, your friend and admirer, G. Bernard Shaw.'

'From your devoted friend and follower, K. Marx.'

'Dear A.B.,—Your invaluable suggestions and assistance, not to mention your kindness, in entirely re-writing chapter 3, entitles you, surely, to this first copy of "Tess". From your old friend T. Hardy.'

'Short of the great pleasure of seeing you personally, I can only send you, dear A.B., this copy of "The Nigger". I miss your company more than I can say . . . (signature undecipherable).'

Under the last inscription, the moron who owns the book will be asked to write (and shown how if necessary) the phrase 'Poor old Conrad was not the worst.'

'MYLES NA GOPALEEN' (FLANN O'BRIEN)

THE POET OF BRAY

Back in the dear old thirties' days
When politics was passion
A harmless left-wing bard was I
And so I grew in fashion:
Although I never really *joined*
The Party of the Masses

I was most awfully chummy with
   The Proletarian classes.
      This is the course I'll always steer
        Until the stars grow dim, sir—
      That howsoever taste may veer
        I'll be in the swim, sir.

But as the tide of war swept on
   I turned Apocalyptic:
With symbol, myth and archetype
   My verse grew crammed and cryptic:
With New Romantic zeal I swore
   That Auden was a fake, sir,
And found the mind of Nicky Moore
   More int'resting than Blake, sir.

White Horsemen down New Roads had run
   But taste required improvement:
I turned to greet the rising sun
   And so I joined the Movement!
Glittering and ambiguous
   In villanelles I sported:
With Dr Leavis I concurred,
   And when he sneezed I snorted.

But seeing that even John Wax might wane
   I left that one-way street, sir;
I modified my style again,
   And now I am a Beat, sir:
So very beat, my soul is beat
   Into a formless jelly:
I set my verses now to jazz
   And read them on the telly.

Perpetual non-conformist I—
   And that's the way I'm staying—
The angriest young man alive
   (Although my hair is greying)
And in my rage I'll not relent—
   No, not one single minute—
Against the base Establishment
   (Until, of course, I'm in it).
      This is the course I'll always steer
        Until the stars grow dim, sir—

That howsoever taste may veer
I'll be in the swim, sir.

JOHN HEATH-STUBBS

Apocalyptic] *The New Apocalypse was a poetry movement of the 1940s; Nicholas Moore was a member;* The White Horseman *(1941) was an anthology of their work.*

SOME POSTMODERN POOH

In The Pooh Perplex *(1963) and its sequel* Postmodern Pooh *(2001), Frederic Crews subjects* Winnie-the-Pooh *and related writings by A. A. Milne to the scrutiny of some representative modern critics.* Postmodern Pooh *records the proceedings of a panel at a conference of the Modern Language Association of America: those taking part include a Cultural Theorist, a Negotiationist, a Radical Feminist, a Poststructuralist Marxist, and a disciple of Jacques Derrida.*

The passage which follows comes from a paper delivered at the conference by a leading figure in the field of psychoanalytically oriented Postcolonial literary studies, Das Nuffa Dat. In an introductory note Crews tells us that Dat was born in Calcutta and educated at Eton and Oxford, and that after winning acclaim as a teacher in Australia, Canada, and Scotland he has recently been appointed to a distinguished professorial chair at Emory University in Atlanta, Georgia—an occasion marked by a press release in which the university's president declared that 'with this appointment, marginality now takes center stage at Emory'.

Dat begins by politely but firmly disagreeing with the speakers who preceded him. A follower of Michel Foucault is informed that Foucault's 'paradigmatic European prison and asylum cannot begin to explain how a despised indigeneity gets catachrestically imbricated in a dominant'; a Marxist is warned that 'we must insist on a more concrete mode of inquiry purged of essentialist abstractions'. After which he proceeds to his own interpretation of the matter in hand:

Our outgoing MLA president, Edward Said, did not exaggerate, I fear, when he declared that 'every European, in what he could say about the Orient, was . . . a racist, an imperialist, and almost totally ethnocentric'.* Even the most eminent of French Orientalists, Louis Massignon, was exposed by Said as merely 'a kind of system for producing certain kinds of statements, disseminated into the large mass of discursive formations that together make up the archive, or cultural material of his time'.† Why, the bounder was scarcely a person at all! Happily, though, we who have gathered today *are* persons, and deeply caring ones. And what we presently care about is seeing whether a rigorous postcolonial hermeneutic can afford us a non-racist, nonchauvinistic purchase on the major writings of A. A. Milne.

* Edward Said, *Orientalism* (New York: Pantheon, 1978), p. 204.
† Said, *Orientalism*, p. 274.

You are doubtless hoping (generous souls that you are) that I will absolve the beloved Milne of any association with the crimes and cruelties of empire. After all, the fellow is well known to have been a pacifist in the period between the two world wars. Straight off, however, I must let the penny drop. To up sticks and embrace pacifism in the twenties, when the imperial row of dominoes was beginning to teeter before all discerning eyes, was simply to deny one's obvious complicity in the extortion of wealth from victim lands. And this is precisely what we find, among other harrowing yet predictable revelations, when we turn to Milne's various writings in prose and verse for his pampered son and other apprentice sahibs.

In one of his poems Milne tells those impressionable children:

> Don't be afraid of doing things
> (Especially, of course, for Kings.)

Milne even dares to fancy *himself* an imperial ruler who can enlist the dark-skinned natives in satisfying his perverse tastes:

> If I were King of Timbuctoo,
> I'd think of lovely things to do.

And with Britannia still ruling the waves in the loot-laden twenties, dreams of endless conquest proved as irresistible to Milne as to John Bull in general. Sailing his chimerical ship 'through Eastern seas', and taking possession of whatever island struck his fancy,

> I'd say to myself as I looked so lazily down on the sea:
> 'There's nobody else in the world, and the world was made for me.'

Here is Western solipsism in its most grandiose and ominous mood. 'There's nobody else in the world'? You're off by quite a stretch, A.A., old chum. For one thing, there's the problem of having to contend with fellow imperialists from rival European nations. Mussolini, for example, who had come to power in 1922, was already casting covetous eyes on North Africa when Milne, perhaps anticipating a clash of territorial aims between Italy and England, wrote, 'They went on hunting, and they caught three wopses.'

Though killing a few unarmed Italians may be jolly sport, a face-off with third-worlders in their own forests and jungles would be a stickier wicket altogether. Milne offers us a number of stanzas that place a British voyager—himself, thinly disguised—in harm's way as he strives to hold down a mounting panic. What if the island he has assumed to be uninhabited actually teems with 'savages'?

Sitting safe in his hut he'd have nothing to fear,
Whereas now they might suddenly breathe in his ear!

The horror, the horror!—namely, of coming face-to-face with some people who already live in peace with the surroundings that one is dashed-all bent on despoiling.

Hearing the tom-toms getting louder as he longs to be back in his country manor sipping amontillado and reading *Blackwood's* at the fireside, what can a stout Englishman like Milne do but try to switch off his terrified imagination? The effort of banishment to the unconscious is especially evident in the queasy poem 'Nursery Chairs', in which Milne conceives of himself as leading his 'faithful band' up the Amazon River. Ominously, Indians 'in twos and threes' begin clustering on the banks. But is he worried? Not a bit of it! Why, with English *sang-froid* he will simply wave his hand,

And then they turn and go away—
They always understand.

Don't they, though—but I wouldn't wager a farthing on it if I were you. In the real world, daft apotropaic verses of this kind can do precious little to stay the arching bows and poison-tipped arrows of traduced but not yet conquered tribesmen.

It can't be an accident that Milne's prototypical subalterns are characterised as 'Indians'. For a Britisher who has been weaned on colonialist propaganda, all Indians are alike, and they're all from Asia. You surely won't have forgotten Milne's poem about bad King John, whose yearned-for *India* rubber ball arrives out of the blue from a Santa Claus whose worker-elves would hardly have been growing their own rubber in the Arctic Circle. Less conspicuously, but even more tellingly, we learn from the concluding chapter of *Winnie-the-Pooh* that India rubber—which, remember, is nothing but booty pinched from Sumatra and other 'Indies'—works well 'for rubbing out anything which you had spelt wrong.' Isn't this a trope for repression, and specifically for repression of what 'trade' with South Asia was actually like? If so, we can expect that *Pooh* itself, which cannot fail to show the same politicocognitive connotations as the poems, will have India and the Indies constantly tugging at its guilty conscience.

But a nationalist freedom fighter such as myself—one who inhaled a staunch Fabianism from his natal soil of Bengal—cannot run blithely to analysis of *Pooh* without first coping with a grave misgiving. As my grandfather the maharajah never tired of pointing out, the founding movement of 'English' as an academic field occurred when the imperialist historian Thomas Macaulay brazenly urged that Indians be rendered 'English in taste, in opinions, in morals, and in intellect' through compulsory exposure to *his* nation's literature.* A rum job, that. As the most widely read text in the master tongue—a text, moreover, that we shall find more indoctrinating than most—*Pooh* continues to serve Macaulay's program not just in India but everywhere. How, then, can I presume to discuss it without swelling its pernicious influence even further?

A possible riposte could be that one neutralises *Pooh's* ideological effect in the very act of exposing and denouncing it. That's one up on the Empire, true enough, and I shall be doing a spot of such neutralising myself in just a twinkling. Yet the mode of indignant alarm grows precious thin after a while. If, instead, we make full use of *postmodern* postcolonial conceptions—among others, 'aporia, ambivalence, indeterminacy, the question of discursive closure, the threat to agency, the status of intentionality, the challenge to "totalizing" concepts'†—our critique can be immeasurably more efficacious, even revolutionary . . .

FREDERIC CREWS

---

* Thomas Babington Macaulay, 'Minute on Indian Education', in *Selected Writings*, ed. John Clive and Thomas Pinney (Chicago: Univ. of Chicago Press, 1972), p. 249.

† Homi K. Bhabha, *The Location of Culture* (London and New York: Routledge, 1994), p. 173.

DRAYNEFLETE

Osbert Lancaster's Drayneflete Revealed *is the history of a small English town from Roman times until 1949 (when the book was published). In a chapter entitled 'Poet's Corner', Lancaster gives an account of a literary dynasty with long-standing connections with the town.*

A little more than a mile from the bridge there was a cross-roads at which stood a single humble inn opposite the recently completed walls of Lord Littlehampton's great park. The second Earl, 'Sensibility Littlehampton' as he was known, at the time of the second rebuilding of Drayneflete Castle conceived the kindly idea of building a small Gothic Lodge at this corner of his estate for his friend and protégé, the poet Jeremy Tipple. It was the long residence of this celebrated bard in this villa

Jeremy Tipple, Esq., poet. From a portrait by Knapton, now in the Art Gallery.

which first gained for the cross-roads the appellation 'Poet's Corner', and it was here that he wrote his immortal *The Contemplative Shepherd*, a poem of some fifteen thousand lines of which we can, alas, only quote a small selection. The passage chosen is of particular topographical interest as the landscape described is today almost entirely covered by the municipal sewage farm.

> Th'enamelled meadows that can scarce contain
> The gentle windings of the limpid Drayne
> Full oft have seen me, wandering at dawn
> As birds awaken and the startled fawn
> Leaps from her mossy bed with easy grace
> On catching sight of my indulgent face.
> Deep in some crystal pool th'enamoured trout
> Frolics and wantons up a lichened spout
> By which the stream, in many a sparkling rill,
> Is made by art to turn a water-mill.
> At last the sluggard Phoebus quits his bed
> And bares the glory of his fiery head;
> Now all the world assumes an aspect new
> And Nature blushes neath the mantling dew.
> E'en yonder mossy walls and em'rald sward
> The home of Littlehampton's puissant lord,
> The ancient fastness of a warrior race
> Regards these marches with a kindlier face. . . .

By 1820 both the poet and his patron were dead. Owing to the slump at the end of the Napoleonic Wars, coupled with a bad run of luck at Crockfords, the nephew and successor of the second Earl ('Sensibility Littlehampton' had never married) had been forced to sell land for development and a row of gentlemen's villas to the design of Mr Papworth had been erected alongside Poet's Corner, while a bailiff's cottage in the Rustic style was erected on the further side of the inn some years later. The Gothic Villa itself was now in the possession of Miss Amelia de Vere, the only child of the poet's married sister, Sophonisba, who had long kept house for her brother. Along with the house Miss Amelia had inherited much of her uncle's poetic gift, although at first this was only revealed to a small circle of intimate friends. After, however, the anonymous publication of her *Lines on the Late Massacre at Chios*, which sounded like a tocsin throughout Liberal Europe, her fame was assured. It is not, alas, possible, nor indeed is it probably necessary, to quote this celebrated work in full, but the two opening verses will serve to demonstrate both the fearless realism of the gentle poetess and her exceptional command of local colour, a command the more extraordinary in that she never, save for a brief visit to Tunbridge Wells, travelled more than ten miles from Drayneflete in all her life.

Miss Amelia de Vere. From a miniature by Sir George Richmond,
formerly in the possession of Bill Tipple, Esq.

O hark to the groans of the wounded and dying,
Of the mother who casts a last lingering look
At her infant aloft, understandably crying,
Impaled on the spear of a Bashi Bazook

O see where the vultures are patiently wheeling
As the scimitars flash and the yataghans thud
On innocent victims, vainly appealing
To dreaded Janissaries lusting for blood.

Amelia de Vere died in 1890. By this time Draynflete had grown considerably—it
was now an important railway link—and the villas adjacent to Poet's Corner had
been turned into shops.

Casimir de Vere-Tipple, Esq. From a drawing by Jacques Émile Blanche.
Reproduced by kind permission of the Trustees of the Tate Gallery.

On the death of Miss de Vere, Poet's Corner passed to her nephew, Mr Casimir De Vere-Tipple, in whom the poetic gift, so constant in this remarkable family, burnt, if not with renewed vigour, certainly with a 'hard gem-like flame'. His contributions appeared regularly in *The Yellow Book*, and were published in a slim volume by the Bodley Head under the title *Samphire and Sardonyx*. Unfortunately he did not long enjoy his property as he was forced, for private reasons, to live abroad from 1895 onwards and thenceforth resided on Capri in a charming villa where his great social gifts and exquisite hospitality will still be remembered by many visitors.

After the departure of Mr de Vere-Tipple the Poet's Corner was let on a long lease to a firm of monumental masons. A further great change in the appearance of the neighbourhood occurred when, shortly before the 1914 war, Messrs Pinks, the drapers, entirely rebuilt their premises and a confectioner's acquired the space between them and the Poet's Corner. The secluded quiet of this once shady nook was further interrupted by the

substitution of trams for horse-buses at the turn of the century, and the
subsequent increase in traffic due to the coming of the internal combustion engine.

However, the poetic tradition of the locality was not even yet extinct. On
his death in 1929 Mr de Vere-Tipple left this valuable site to his favourite
nephew, then at Oxford, Guillaume de Vere-Tipple, who had already made
a name for himself by the publication of *Feux d'artifice* (Duckworth 1927),
a collection of verse astonishing in its maturity, from which we quote a
single poem, *Aeneas on the Saxophone*.

> . . . Delenda est Carthago!
> (ses bains de mer, ses plâges fleuries,
> And Dido on her lilo à sa proie attachée)

> And shall we stroll along the front
> Chatting of this and that and listening to the band?

> The plumed and tufted sea responds
> Obliquely to the trombone's call
> The lecherous seaweed's phallic fronds
> Gently postulate the Fall.

> But between the pebble and the beach rises the doubt,
> . . . Delenda
> Between the seaside and the sea the summons
> . . . est
> Between the *wagon* and the *lit* the implication,
> . . . Carthago.

In the years between the wars the whole character of the district was still
further altered. In 1930 Messrs Watlin acquired the *Duke of York*, which was
at once rebuilt in a contemporary style which, although it at first struck
those accustomed to the brassy vulgarity of the old 'pub' as strangely
austere, was soon generally agreed to be both socially and aesthetically
an immense improvement. Two years later another even more daring
example of 'the Modern Movement', as it had come to be known, arose in
the shape of the Odium Cinema. While some of the more old-fashioned
residents might find fault with the functional directness of this great building, nothing but praise could be accorded to the modified Georgian style
in which the new Council flats across the road were built at much the same
date.

The coming of a new age, of which the buildings round Poet's Corner
were a portent, found a reflection in the poet's verse. Guillaume de
Vere-Tipple was socially conscious to a remarkable degree and had long

entertained doubts as to the security of capitalist society, doubts which received striking confirmation when International Nickel, in which he had inherited a large holding, slumped to 11½. Making a clean break with the past, his next volume of poetry, *the liftshaft* (Faber and Faber 1937) appeared above the signature Bill Tipple, and, as may be seen from the poem quoted below, this reorientation is reflected in the contents:—

crackup in barcelona

among the bleached skeletons of the olive-trees
stirs a bitter wind
and maxi my friend from the mariahilfer strasse
importunately questions a steely sky
his eyes are two holes made by a dirty finger
in the damp blotting paper of his face
the muscular tissues stretched tautly across the scaffolding of bone
are no longer responsive to the factory siren
and never again will the glandular secretions react

Bill Tipple. From a still from the film 'Whither Democracy', reproduced by kind permission of the C. of I.

to the ragtime promptings of the palais-de-danse
and I am left balanced on capricorn
the knife-edge tropic between anxiety and regret
while the racing editions are sold at the gates of football grounds
and maxi lies on a bare catalan hillside
knocked off the tram by a fascist conductor
who misinterpreted a casual glance.

The late war dealt hardly with Poet's Corner. Fortunately the house itself is still standing, but the confectioner's next door was totally demolished and extensive damage was caused to much of the surrounding property.

After the end of the conflict, in a misguided effort to relieve the considerable local housing shortage, an estate of pre-fabricated dwelling-houses was erected by the Borough Council in what had been erstwhile the shady groves and green retreats of the Littlehampton Memorial Park.

Today Poet's Corner is up for sale: its owner, Bill Tipple, who on the outbreak of war had been a conscientious objector, but who, on hearing the news of the invasion of Russia, experienced a complete change of heart and immediately joined the Drayneflete section of the National Fire Service, is absent for long periods abroad in his capacity of organising secretary of the World Congress of International Poets in Defence of Peace . . .

In Osbert Lancaster's book, the development to the once-charming spot known as Poet's Corner is in many ways a microcosm of the growth of Drayneflete as a whole. Interspersed with the literary parodies, a series of brilliant panoramic drawings (too extensive and elaborate to be reproduced here) portray the gradual transformation of a tranquil rural cross-roads into a crowded urban traffic junction. They are packed with detailed satirical observation of changing styles in architecture, transport, street furniture and social customs, of everything from the habits of pedestrians to the lettering over shops.

AFFAIRS OF STATE

from THE DECLARATION OF INDEPENDENCE IN AMERICAN

[*H. L. Mencken undertook this 'translation' in 1921. What follows is the opening section, preceded by the same passage in the original version:*]

When, in the course of human events, it becomes necessary for one people to dissolve the political bands which have connected them with another, and to assume among the powers of the earth the separate and equal station to which the laws of nature and of nature's god entitle them, a decent respect to the opinions of mankind requires that they should declare the causes which impel them to the separation. We hold these truths to be self-evident; that all men are created equal; that they are endowed by their creator with certain inalienable rights; that among these are life, liberty and the pursuit of happiness; that to secure these rights, governments are instituted among men, deriving their just powers from the consent of the governed; that whenever any form of government becomes destructive to these ends, it is the right of the people to alter or to abolish it, and to institute new government, laying its foundation on such principles, and organizing its powers in such form, as to them shall seem most likely to effect their safety and happiness. Prudence, indeed, will dictate that governments long established should not be changed for light and transient causes; and accordingly all experience hath shewn, that mankind are more disposed to suffer while evils are sufferable, than to right themselves by abolishing the forms to which they are accustomed. But when a long train of abuses and usurpations, pursuing invariably the same object, evinces a design to reduce them under absolute despotism, it is their right, it is their duty, to throw off such government, and to provide new guards for their future security.

When things get so balled up that the people of a country got to cut loose from some other country, and go it on their own hook, without asking no permission from nobody, excepting maybe God Almighty, then they ought to let everybody know why they done it, so that everybody can see they are not trying to put nothing over on nobody.

All we got to say on this proposition is this: first, me and you is as good as anybody else, and maybe a damn sight better; second, nobody ain't got no right to take away none of our rights; third, every man has got a right to live, to come and go as he pleases, and to have a good time whichever way he likes, so long as he don't interfere with nobody else. That any government that don't give a man them rights ain't worth a damn; also, people ought to choose the kind of government they want themselves, and nobody else ought to have no say in the matter. That whenever any government don't do this, then the people have got a right to give it the bum's rush and put in one that will take care of their interests. Of course, that don't mean having a revolution every day like them South American yellow-bellies, or every time some jobholder goes to work and does something he ain't got no business to do. It is better to stand a little graft, etc., than to have revolutions all the time, like them coons, and any man that wasn't a anarchist or one of them I.W.W.'s would say the same. But when things get so bad that a man ain't hardly got no rights at all no more, but you might almost call him a slave, then everybody ought to get together and throw the grafters out, and put in new ones who won't carry on so high and steal so much, and then watch them.

I.W.W.s] *members of the revolutionary labour union Industrial Workers of the World.*

REX V. PUDDLE: A CASE OF BLACKMAIL

[*A. P. Herbert published his collection of legal parodies,* Misleading Cases, *in 1929. 'Rex* v. *Puddle' is from its sequel,* More Misleading Cases, *which came out the following year*]

The Hammersmith Blackmail Case was concluded at the Old Bailey to-day.

Mr Justice Trout, addressing the jury, said: Gentlemen, this is a very grave case. The prisoner in the dock, a Collector of Taxes for the district of South Hammersmith, stands charged with the odious crime which is commonly described as blackmail. That expression dates from very early times, when it was the custom to pay tribute to men of influence who were allied with certain robbers and brigands for protection from the devastations of the latter. The practice was made illegal by a statute of Queen Elizabeth's time, and ever since it has been classed by our Courts among the most contemptible and dangerous offences. A person, who, knowing the contents, sends or delivers a letter or writing *demanding with menaces and without reasonable cause* any chattel, money, or other property, commits felony and is liable to penal servitude for life. The menace, the 'putting in fear', as our ancestors expressed it, is of the essence of the crime. The spectacle of one man demanding money from another must always be painful to the civilized mind; but when in addition that other is made to fear for his safety, liberty, or reputation the law steps in to protect and punish.

Now Mr Haddock, the prosecutor in this case, received a letter from the prisoner demanding money. The letter was printed in ink of a bright red colour, and that is a circumstance which you may well take into account when you come to consider the intention of the letter and the effect which it may have had upon the mind of the recipient. For red is notoriously the colour of menace, of strife, of bloodshed and danger; and it is worthy of note that the prisoner's previous communications to Mr Haddock had been printed in a quiet and pacific blue. The letter was as follows:

'Previous applications for payment of the taxes due from you on the 1st day of January, 1930, for the year 1929–1930, having been made to you without effect, DEMAND is now made for payment, and I HEREBY GIVE YOU FINAL NOTICE that if the amount be not paid or remitted to me at the above address within SEVEN DAYS from this date steps will be taken for recovery by DISTRAINT, with costs.

'E. PUDDLE, *Collector*'

'Collector', I may observe in passing, was in other centuries a word commonly used to denote a highwayman. But you will not allow that point to influence you unduly.

Now the 'demand' is clear; indeed the word, as you will notice, is printed in block capitals. And you have to say, first of all, whether or not that 'demand' is accompanied by menaces. You will take everything into consideration, the terseness, I had almost said the brutality, of the language, the intimidating red ink, the picking out in formidable capitals of the words 'DEMAND', 'SEVEN DAYS' and 'DISTRAINT', and any other circumstance which may seem to you calculated to cause alarm in the mind of the recipient. You will observe in particular the concluding words, 'Steps will be taken for recovery by DISTRAINT, with costs.'

'DISTRAINT.' What is the exact meaning of that? It means the forcible seizure of a person's goods; it means the invasion of his home by strangers; it amounts to licensed burglary; it means the loss not only of favourite possessions but of reputation; it means distress to wife and family, and it is significant that the correct and common term for the process is 'Distress'. Evidence has been given that a threat 'to put the bailiffs in' brings terror to any home. The prosecutor has sworn that at the sight of that one red word he experienced alarm; that he understood from the letter that, without opportunity to state his case in a court of law, his goods would be seized and his wife and family alarmed by the prisoner. The prisoner says that that was not his intention; that the words 'steps will be taken for recovery' indicated a preliminary summons to the Court. You may think that in that case he would have done better to print those words in the same large type as the word 'DISTRAINT'; and you may think, as I do, looking at all the circumstances, that the letter was deliberately planned and worded with the intention of creating alarm, and through that alarm extracting money from Mr Haddock, who is a sensitive man.

You will then have to ask yourselves, Was this menacing demand for money made with reasonable cause? You will bear in mind that Mr Haddock is not a debtor or criminal; he has not taken another's property or done any disgraceful thing. His only offence is that by hard work he has earned a little money; and the suggestion is now made that he shall give away a fifth part of that money to other people. That being his position, you might well expect that he would be approached not with brusquerie but with signal honours, not with printed threats but with illuminated addresses. But the whole tenor of the prisoner's communications suggests that in his opinion Mr Haddock is a guilty person. Observe the strange use of the word 'recovery'—as if Mr Haddock had *taken* money from the prisoner. Mr Haddock has made repeated protests to the Collector and to his confederate, the Inspector, urging that even under the strange customs of our land the sum demanded of him was excessive, that due allowance had not been made for the particular hardships and expenses of his professional calling, and that in his judgment the prisoner and his principals have taken from him during the past years money which they ought in conscience to restore. While this dispute was still proceeding the prisoner sent this letter. Mr Haddock, a public-spirited man, conveyed the letter to the police, and it is for you to say whether he was right. An official from the Inland Revenue Department has drawn your attention to the difficulties of a Mr Snowden, the prisoner's principal, it appears, who is in need of money. You will pay no attention to that. We are all in need of money; and if Mr Snowden has an insufficient supply of money he must spend less money, as the rest of us have to do. Neither his avarice nor his extravagance can excuse a breach of the law.

The jury eagerly found the prisoner guilty of blackmail, and he was sentenced to penal servitude for life, and solitary confinement for ten years, the sentences to run consecutively. The Court congratulated Mr Haddock.

The particular hardships and expenses of his professional calling] *Mr Haddock, who figures in many of the misleading cases, is an author.*

Mr Snowden] *Philip Snowden was Chancellor of the Exchequer at the time.*

CONSPIRATORS

Writing in 1938, George Orwell tried to explain what had been happening in the Soviet Union by translating the show trials staged by Stalin into English terms. 'Make the necessary adjustments, let Left be Right and Right be Left, and you get something like this':

Mr Winston Churchill, now in exile in Portugal, is plotting to overthrow the British Empire and establish Communism in England. By the use of unlimited Russian money he has succeeded in building up a huge Churchillite organisation which includes members of Parliament, factory managers, Roman Catholic bishops and practically the whole of the Primrose League. Almost every day some dastardly act of sabotage is laid bare—sometimes a plot to blow up the House of Lords, sometimes an outbreak of foot-and-mouth disease in the Royal racing-stables. Eighty percent of the Beefeaters in the Tower are discovered to be agents of the Comintern. A high official of the Post Office admits brazenly to having embezzled a postal order to the tune of £5,000,000 and also to having committed *lèse majesté* by drawing moustaches on postage stamps. Lord Nuffield, after a 7-hour interrogation by Mr Norman Birkett, confesses that ever since 1920 he has been fomenting strikes in his own factories. Casual half-inch paras in every issue of the newspapers announce that fifty more Churchillite sheep-stealers have been shot in Westmorland or that the proprietress of a village shop in the Cotswolds has been transported to Australia for sucking the bull's-eyes and putting them back in the bottle. And meanwhile the Churchillites (or Churchillite-Harmsworthites as they are called after Lord Rothermere's execution) never cease from proclaiming that it is *they* who are the real defenders of Capitalism and that Chamberlain and the rest of his gang are no more than a set of Bolsheviks in disguise.

GEORGE ORWELL, review of *Assignment*
in Utopia by Eugene Lyons

TONY BLAIR: A CONFERENCE SPEECH

Look, I'm listening.

And listen: I'm looking.

Listening. Looking. Every day I'm listening. And every day I'm looking.

Because I owe it to you. I owe it to the British people.

I am listening to pensioners. Pensioners tell me, look we like what you're doing. We like the way you're listening.

And let. Me say this. I'm also listening to our lorry drivers. And you know what? British lorry drivers are the best in the world. The skill and dedication. They put into driving their lorries. Is second. To none.

In fact, to me they're not just lorry drivers. They're much, much more than that. To me, they're *road hauliers*.

And we thank them for that.

I am listening. I am hearing. And I will act. Today, I make this solemn pledge. This year, the Government will set bold new targets for listening and hearing:

We pledge 32 per cent more listening per year *over and above the rate of inflation*.

And an immediate 28 per cent to go straight into a network of new Listen-and-Hear Network Initiative Centres the length and breadth of this country.

A lot more listening. A lot more hearing. In five years' time, our mission for Britain is to have more listeners and hearers than *any other country in the world*.

But for many families life's still. A struggle. It's tough, balancing work. And family. There's the mortgage to pay. The holiday to save for. The odd pint. And—can you believe it—the bulb in the downstairs toilet's gone again.

Inflation may be lower but the kids' trainers don't get any cheaper. The stair carpet needs a good going-over. There's ketchup and old cabbage strewn all over the kitchen floor. And the dog's raided that bin again.

But let me say this.

You—all of you, every single one—have responded magnificently to being listened to. You're quite simply the best. The best teachers. The best doctors and nurses. The best road hauliers. World-class film directors and actors. The best scientists and inventors. The best people any nation could wish for.

Hi! How are you? Hey, you're looking great.

Smashing to have you with us.

We should be proud. Not self-satisfied. Never that. Never self-satisfied. Just very, very satisfied. With ourselves.

The Dome. There. I've said it. And—believe me—that took some guts. You can't win them all. There are those on the far right who try to put it about that you can win them all. But, you know, I recently received a letter from an elderly woman living in sheltered housing on the outskirts of Bradford.

And she told me this: you can't win them all.

So to the euro. At issue—bless you—at issue is not whether we join. At issue—bless you again—is this. Do we rule out joining? Of course, there'll always be those who want to rule out ruling out joining. To them I say this. Let's not rule out ruling it out. Though nor is it something I'd rule out.

You know why? That's not standing up for Britain. That's not strong.

You know what I call strong? This is what I call strong. I say to Milosevic. You lost. Go. The world has suffered enough. And the same applies to you, Mao Tse-Tung and Joseph Stalin. Don't tell me you were once great figures on the world stage. You're not any more. It's time to stand up to you. Your time has passed. Go.

But, you know, speaking totally off the cuff for a moment, I want to tell you something from the bottom. End page 10.

Start page 11. Of my heart. Pause. There are certain things I cannot do. If you ask me to put tax cuts before education spending, I'm sorry, I can't do it.

If you want me to send our economy into a downward spiral, throwing literally millions into poverty, I'm sorry, I simply can't do it. Pause.

And if you want me to go outside this Conference Hall and poke fun at the elderly and the infirm, I'm sorry, but that's not the kind of guy I am.

There are those in the Conservative Party who say we should do away with pet cats. Abolish garden implements. Crack down on Zimmer frames. And bring in draconian anti-knitting laws.

To them I say: no. That's not our kind of country. That's not our vision of Britain. The British are a nation of animal lovers. We love to potter about in our gardens. Some of us are forced—through no fault of our own—to rely on our Zimmer frames.

And, for pity's sake, where's the harm in a little knitting?

If we want to reach our journey's end, there are choices we have to make.

Tough choices.

Hard choices.

Choices that are tough and hard. In the road ahead there are many forks. Some urge me to take every fork. But then where would we end up? Right back at the beginning. No: you do not reach the journey's end by taking the road that gets you there.

But we still have a long way to go.

And that is an achievement we can be proud of.

CRAIG BROWN

THE SOKAL HOAX

In May 1996 a leading American journal of cultural studies, Social Text, pub-lished an article with an impressive, not to say daunting title—'Transgressing the Boundaries: Toward a Transformative Hermeneutics of Quantum Gravity'. It was the work of Alan Sokal, a mathematical physicist at New York University.

It soon turned out that the article was a hoax—a beautifully executed parody of the kind of thing which Sokal had calculated (correctly) that the editors of Social Text would be happy to print. And as the resulting furore showed, it was a hoax with a serious purpose. Sokal had set out to expose the dubious or fraudulent aspects of the whole cultural studies approach to science—the approach, that is to say, of cultural studies in its radical, deconstructionist mode. He was particularly concerned to throw cold water on the claim that the laws of nature are man-made 'social constructions'.

His position with respect to this last issue—or rather, his ironical pseudo-position—is set down firmly in the opening paragraphs of his article:

> Transgressing disciplinary boundaries . . . [is] a subversive undertak-ing since it is likely to violate the sanctuaries of accepted ways of perceiving. Among the most fortified boundaries have been those between the natural sciences and the humanities—Valerie Greenberg, *Transgressive Readings*

> The struggle for the transformation of ideology into critical science . . . proceeds on the foundation that the critique of all presup-positions of science and ideology must be the only absolute principle of science—Stanley Aronowitz, *Science as Power*

There are many natural scientists, and especially physicsts, who con-tinue to reject the notion that the disciplines concerned with social and cultural criticism can have anything to contribute, except perhaps periph-erally, to their research. Still less are they receptive to the idea that the very foundations of their worldview must be revised or rebuilt in the light of such criticism. Rather, they cling to the dogma imposed by the long post-Enlightenment hegemony over the Western intellectual outlook, which can be summarized briefly as follows: that there exists an external world, whose properties are independent of any individual human being and indeed of humanity as a whole; that these properties are encoded in 'eternal' physical laws; and that human beings can obtain reliable, albeit imperfect and tentative, knowledge of these laws by hewing to the 'object-ive' procedures and epistemological strictures prescribed by the (so-called) scientific method.

But deep conceptual shifts within twentieth-century science have under-mined this Cartesian-Newtonian metaphysics (Heisenberg 1958; Bohr 1963); revisionist studies in the history and philosophy of science have cast further doubt on its credibility (Kuhn 1970; Feyerabend 1975; Latour 1987; Aronowitz 1988b; Bloor 1991); and, most recently, feminist and poststruc-turalist critiques have demystified the substantive content of mainstream Western scientific practice, revealing the ideology of domination concealed behind the facade of 'objectivity' (Merchant 1980; Keller 1985; Harding 1986, 1991; Haraway 1989, 1991; Best 1991). It has thus become increasingly appar-ent that physical 'reality,' no less than social 'reality,' is at bottom a social and linguistic construct; that scientific 'knowledge,' far from being objec-tive, reflects and encodes the dominant ideologies and power relations of the culture that produced it; that the truth claims of science are inherently theory-laden and self-referential; and consequently, that the discourse of the scientific community, for all its undeniable value, cannot assert a privi-leged epistemological status with respect to counterhegemonic narratives emanating from dissident or marginalized communities. These themes can be traced, despite some differences of emphasis, in Aronowitz's analysis of the cultural fabric that produced quantum mechanics (1988b, esp. chaps. 9 and 12); in Ross's discussion of oppositional discourses in post-quantum science (1991, intro. and chap. 1); in Irigaray's and Hayles's exegeses of gender encoding in fluid mechanics (Irigaray 1985; Hayles 1992); and in Harding's comprehensive critique of the gender ideology underlying the natural sciences in general and physics in particular (1986, esp. chaps. 2 and 10; 1991, esp. chap. 4).

Here my aim is to carry these deep analyses one step further, by taking account of recent developments in quantum gravity: the emerging branch of physics in which Heisenberg's quantum mechanics and Einstein's gen-eral relativity are at once synthesized and superseded. In quantum grav-ity, as we shall see, the space-time manifold ceases to exist as an objective physical reality; geometry becomes relational and contextual; and the foundational conceptual categories of prior science—among them, exist-ence itself—become problematized and relativized. This conceptual revo-lution, I will argue, has profound implications for the content of a future postmodern and liberatory science . . .

The remainder of the article runs to over 10,000 words, along with a further 10,000 words or so of notes and references. It abounds in non sequiturs, twisted facts, false analogies, 'acceptable' ideological gestures and general mumbo jumbo. The finest examples of obfuscation it contains have the added charm of being taken from life, so to speak: they are direct quotations from Jacques Derrida and other deconstructionist pundits.

In comparison, the opening paragraphs quoted above are straightforward. It is quite easy to be lulled by their rhetoric—provided you don't think too hard about what they are actually saying, that is. In a short piece which he published soon after the hoax had been revealed, Sokal professed puzzlement at the fact that the editors of Social Text *had not realized almost at once that they were dealing with a spoof. For example,*

in the second paragraph I declare, without the slightest evidence or argument, that 'physical "reality" [note the scare quotes] . . . is at bottom a social and linguistic construct.' Not our *theories* of physical reality, mind you, but the reality itself. Fair enough: Anyone who believes that the laws of physics are mere social conventions is invited to try transgressing those conventions from the windows of my apartment. (I live on the twenty-first floor.)

Two Tributes

(from *The Times* of AD 2027)

It is a hundred years ago to-day since Forster died; we celebrate his centenary indeed within a few months of the bicentenary of Beethoven, within a few weeks of that of Blake. What special tribute shall we bring him? The question is not easy to answer, and were he himself still alive he would no doubt reply, 'My work is my truest memorial.' It is the reply that a great artist can always be trusted to make. Conscious of his lofty mission, endowed with the divine gift of self-expression, he may rest content, he is at peace, doubly at peace. But we, we who are not great artists, only the recipients of their bounty—what shall we say about Forster? What can we say that has not already been said about Beethoven, about Blake? Whatever shall we say?

The Dean of Dulborough, preaching last Sunday in his own beautiful cathedral, struck perhaps the truest note. Taking as his text that profound verse in Ecclesiasticus, 'Let us now praise famous men,' he took it word by word, paused when he came to the word 'famous,' and, slowly raising his voice, said: 'He whose hundredth anniversary we celebrate on Thursday next is famous, and why?' No answer was needed, none came. The lofty Gothic nave, the great western windows, the silent congregation— they gave answer sufficient, and passing on to the final word of his text, 'men,' the Dean expatiated upon what is perhaps the most mysterious characteristic of genius, its tendency to appear among members of the human race. Why this is, why, since it is, it is not accompanied by some definite outward sign through which it might be recognized easily, are questions not lightly to be raised. There can be no doubt that his contemporaries did not recognize the greatness of Forster. Immersed in their own little affairs, they either ignored him, or forgot him, or confused him, or, strangest of all, discussed him as if he was their equal. We may smile at their blindness, but for him it can have been no laughing matter, he must have had much to bear, and indeed he could scarcely have endured to put forth masterpiece after masterpiece had he not felt assured of the verdict of posterity.

Sir Vincent Edwards, when broadcasting last night, voiced that verdict not uncertainly, and was fortunately able to employ more wealth of illustration than had been appropriate in Dulborough Minster for the Dean. The point he very properly stressed was our writer's loftiness of aim. 'It would be impossible,' he said, 'to quote a single sentence that was not written from the very loftiest motive,' and he drew from this a sharp and salutary lesson for the so-called writers of to-day. As permanent head of the Ministry of Edification, Sir Vincent has, we believe, frequently come into contact with the younger generation, and has checked with the kindliness of which he is a past-master their self-styled individualism—an individualism which is the precise antithesis of true genius. They confuse violence with strength, cynicism with open-mindedness, frivolity with joyousness—mistakes never made by Forster who was never gay until he had earned the right to be so, and only criticized the religious and social institutions of his time because they were notoriously corrupt. We know what the twentieth century was. We know the sort of men who were in power under George V. We know what the State was, what were the churches. We can as easily conceive of Beethoven as a Privy Councillor or of Blake as, forsooth, an Archbishop as of this burning and sensitive soul acquiescing in the deadening conditions of his age. What he worked for—what all great men work for—was for a New Jerusalem, a vitalized State, a purified Church; and the offertory at Dulborough last Sunday, like the success of Sir Edward's appeal for voluntary workers under the Ministry, show that he did not labour in vain.

The official ceremony is for this morning. This afternoon Lady Turton will unveil Mr Boston Jack's charming statue in Kensington Gardens, and so illustrate another aspect of our national hero: his love of little children. It had originally been Mr Boston Jack's intention to represent him as pursuing an ideal. Since, however, the Gardens are largely frequented by the young and their immediate supervisors, it was felt that something more whimsical would be in place, and a butterfly was substituted. The change is certainly for the better. It is true that we cannot have too many ideals. On the other hand, we must not have too much of them too soon, nor, attached as it will be to a long copper wire, can the butterfly be confused with any existing species and regarded as an incentive to immature collectors. Lady Turton will couple her remarks with an appeal for the Imperial Daisy Chain, of which she is the energetic Vice-President, and simultaneously there will be a flag collection throughout the provinces.

Dulborough, the Ministry of Edification, the official ceremony, Kensington Gardens! What more could be said? Not a little. Yet enough has been said to remind the public of its heritage, and to emphasize and define the central essence of these immortal works. And what is that essence? Need we say? Not their greatness—they are obviously great. Not their profundity—they are admittedly profound. It is something more precious than either: their nobility. Noble works, nobly conceived, nobly executed, nobler than the Ninth Symphony or the Songs of Innocence. Here is no small praise, yet it can be given, we are in the presence of the very loftiest, we need not spare or mince our words, nay, we will add one more word, a word that has been implicit in all that have gone before: like Beethoven, like

Blake, Forster was essentially English, and in commemorating him we can yet again celebrate what is best and most permanent in ourselves.

E. M. FORSTER

THE PASSING OF SHERLOCK HOLMES

[an obituary, first published in 1948]

The death is announced at North Friston, near Eastbourne, of Mr Sherlock Holmes, the eminent Criminologist and Investigator, President of the South Sussex Apiarist Society, and Corresponding Secretary to the National Beekeepers' Union. He was in his ninety-third year; and there is little doubt that but for his characteristic disregard of the occupational risks of this last hobby he would have lived to become a centenarian.

'The creatures know my methods,' he would often observe to visitors as he walked without veil or gloves between the orderly rows of his hives. Yet he over-estimated their obedience, and it was an irritant poison caused by one of these dangerous insects, possibly an Italian Queen, that under-mined his iron constitution in the end, and was the immediate occasion of his demise.

His white hair and only slightly stooping figure had long been objects of veneration both to the passing motorist and to all residents of the country-side between Birling Gap and Newhaven.

He was particularly interested in the formation and history of dew ponds, and might often have been seen returning to his little farmhouse with a bundle of fossils taken from the chalk, or a nosegay of downland flowers.

His later years were but little disturbed by occurrences either terrible or bizarre, but we must except from this statement the sudden appearance (narrated by himself) of *Cyanea Capillata*, the giant jellyfish, which, at the foot of the Seven Sisters, stung to death Mr Fitzroy Macpherson and came very near to baffling the old Investigator's deductive powers. Otherwise his closing years were passed in quietude. Every evening he was accustomed to listen to the Third or the Home Programme of the BBC, especially the musical portions. For Light Programmes, and especially for the feature entitled 'Dick Barton', he was wont to express a profound contempt.

Sherlock Spencer Tracy Holmes was born in 1855, the second son of Sir Stateleigh Holmes of Carshalton in Surrey. The family was descended from a long line of country squires, and Sir Stateleigh's mother was the sister of Vernet, the French artist. Sherlock himself was educated at St Peter's School and Pembridge College, Camford, where the rooms he occupied (now held by the Director of Theological Studies in that college) are often pointed out with pride and gratification by the present Master.

He took little part in the academic or sporting life of his contemporaries and made few friends; but those whom he did know never forgot him and lived to be thankful for the fact. Two of the most eminent were the late Colonel Reginald Musgrave, MFH, of Hurlston, and Admiral Victor Trevor, KCB, both of whom he had assisted at critical junctures in their youth, and it is safe to say that but for these early acquaintanceships neither the whereabouts of the lost crown of Charles I nor the log-book of the *Gloria Scott* would ever have been made known to the public. It was, indeed, Admiral Trevor's father who actually suggested to Holmes in his early days the vocation which he afterwards so brilliantly followed, using the following remarkable prophetic words: 'I don't know how you managed this, Mr Holmes, but it seems to me that all the detectives of fact and of fancy would be children in your hands. That's your line of life, sir; and you may take the word of a man who has seen something of the world.'

He spoke no more than the truth. Dying a few months later, with little more time than to say that the papers were in the back drawer of the Japanese cabinet, Mr Trevor could not foresee that his son's friend was destined to become almost a legendary figure, the hero and idol of two generations of mankind, and the scourge of evil-doers throughout what was once called the civilized globe.

No detective can have travelled more widely than the late Mr Holmes, nor on errands so mysterious, not to say sinister, and verging on the grotesque. Summoned to Odessa to unravel the Trepoff murder, he was equally successful in solving the tragedy of the Atkinson brothers at Trincomalee. Rome knew him at the inquiry into the sudden death of Count Tosca. Lyons, when he had penetrated the colossal scandals of Baron Maupertuis in connection with the Netherland Sumatra Company. In the interval between his supposed death in Switzerland and his reappearance in London he made journeys through Persia, looked in at Mecca, rendered assistance to the Khalifa of Khartoum, visited Lhasa, and spent some time with the Grand Lama of Tibet. It is a pity that the details of these expeditions are for the most part wrapped in a veil of impenetrable secrecy, which, unless the great tin box bequeathed to the British Museum is opened by Mr Attlee or some future Prime Minister, may never be lifted.

But in spite of these foreign pilgrimages, Holmes was able to undertake in this country a series of investigations which made him for more than twenty years, and later at intervals, the terror of the metropolitan underworld, the knight-errant of suburban London, and the constant corrector of the stupidities of Scotland Yard.

This department, especially during the middle 'nineties, appears to have had only two consistent policies, of which the first was complacent error and the second unutterable bewilderment. Holmes revolutionized its procedure, and we may note as evidence of this that the old daguerreotypes of Athelney Jones, Gregson, and Lestrade, which once adorned its portrait gallery, have long ago had their faces turned to the wall. It is a pity that the projected work by Assistant Commissioner Stanley Hopkins, OBE, entitled 'My Master's Voice' remained uncompleted at the time of the Nether Wallop Mystery, when that able officer met his end after a dastardly assault from the blow-pipe of a Nicaraguan dwarf.

If ever a man was called for to meet the hour, Sherlock Holmes, in the heyday of his triumphs, was that man. For England, during the last decade of the nineteenth century, was in danger of submersion beneath an almost unprecedented wave of crime. Criminals of Herculean strength and stature, gifted with a well-nigh super-human cunning, had spread a network of villainy throughout the land.

Blackmail and forgery were rife. The robbery of the most famous piece of jewellery in the world was an almost hourly occurrence. Agents of mysterious secret societies, thirsting for revenge, haunted the docks and the purlieus of Soho. Wills and the plans of submarines were constantly disappearing, and no treaty with a foreign Power was safe for more than a moment in its desk.

To all these manifestations of the villainous and the macabre, Holmes opposed a technique, entirely novel and entirely his own. It may be subdivided and tabulated as follows:

1. Chemical Analysis; 2. Analytical Deduction; 3. Tobacco; 4. Bouts of Contemplation; 5. Feverish Energy; 6. The Minute Examination of Scratches; 7. Omniscience; 8. Cocaine.

And to these should possibly be added the cross-indexing of important cases, the music of the violin, the employment of a horde of street Arabs as agents, and the constant use of the agony columns of the daily Press. The result was a purer air in the streets of London, a sense of relief in the suburbs from Kensington to Whitechapel, from Hampstead to Norwood, and the rescue of many an ill-used girl from death or worse than death in the Home Counties and the more distant provinces.

Repeatedly also the government of the day was saved from ruin. We need only mention in this connection the temporary loss of the Bruce Partington Submarine plans in 1895, and the fear that they might have been sold to a foreign Power. 'You may take it from me,' said Mr Holmes' brother in speaking of them, 'that naval warfare becomes impossible when in the radius of a Bruce Partington's operation.' Happily for the future of this country, Mr Holmes succeeded in recovering the plans.

By the close of the century, the agency which he established had become world-famous. Many were the nights when the feet of a flustered client would patter along the flagstones of Baker Street, or the spirited horse of some hastily driven four-wheeler would be reined to its haunches at his door.

The sound of his violin would float out into the foggy atmosphere, punctuated by the pistol shots with which he pock-marked the pattern VR from his sofa on the opposite wall of his sitting-room.

A bundle of letters from the sister of his landlady (recently discovered on a bomb-site) is ample evidence of the admiration not unmingled with awe which he inspired in the whole of her family.

But it is impossible to deal adequately with the great detective's achievements unless we acknowledge the peculiar debt that he owed during the greater part of his active career to his old friend and colleague, the late Lord Watson of Staines. Lord Watson, it will be remembered, died suddenly last year, after a particularly violent attack in the House of Lords upon certain provisions of the National Health Bill. Eminent alike as a physician and an orator, he is none the less even more likely to incur the gratitude of posterity as the constant companion and intermittent (though mystified) biographer of Mr Sherlock Holmes.

'How do you know that?'
'I followed you.'
'I saw no one.'
'That is what you may expect to see when I follow you.'

Yet indeed it was Lord Watson himself, wondering, shadowy, yet observant, who followed Holmes. Without him, Holmes would have remained a mysterious, almost a visionary character: known to the police forces of the world, familiar to the courts and the aristocracies of Europe, the condescending patron of Prime Ministers, and of the humbler clients whom he chose to assist, yet occult from the observation of the public at large. For publicity was a thing he disdained, and only in the case of Lord Watson, especially in the privacy of the rooms which they shared, did he throw off the mantle of obscurity that screened his personal habits from the eyes of men.

Never, we think, has so great a privilege been so enthusiastically enjoyed. Lord Watson was par excellence a hero-worshipper. He had nothing to learn of Plato or Boswell in this respect. To be baffled was his glory, to be astounded his perennial delight. Sitting with his medical dictionary just out of the line of pistol fire, he revelled in the deductive processes by which the great detective inferred the whole of a visiting client's character from a button, a whisker, a watch, or a boot. There are many who say that Lord Watson was an inaccurate historian. There are cavillers (and Holmes himself was one of them) who have suggested that he embellished fact with fiction, and dipped his brush in melodrama instead of depicting the portrait of a living man. It is impossible to pursue all these charges in detail. Yet one or two comments are not out of place.

Curiously enough, his biographer's presentation does not always redound to the advantage of Holmes. Lord Watson was bemused by metaphors. His mind was influenced beyond all reason by images of the chase. Time after time, for instance, he seems to have been obsessed with the idea that Mr Holmes was a kind of dog.

'As I watched him I was irresistibly reminded of a pure-blooded well-trained foxhound as it dashes backwards and forwards through the covert, whining in its eagerness until it comes across the lost scent. . . .'

'His nostrils seemed to dilate with a purely animal lust for the chase, and his mind was so absolutely concentrated upon the matter before him that a question or remark fell unheeded upon his ears, or at the most only provoked a quick impatient snarl in reply. . . .'

'He was out on the lawn, in through the window, round the room, and up into the bedroom, for all the world like a dashing foxhound drawing a cover. . . .'

'Like an old hound who hears the View Holloa. . . .'

Hard indeed it is to reconcile these phrases with the picture of the tall, dignified, sombrely-attired figure whom we know so well from his portraits in *The Strand Magazine*, dressed in frock coat or ulster; the finely chiselled features, the pale intellectual forehead surmounted by the silk or Derby hat. Even the deerstalker of his more rustic peregrinations does not warrant the perpetual comparison of Mr Holmes to a denizen of the hunting kennel: and we can only feel that idolatry has here overstepped its bounds, and trespassed on the realm of caricature.

On the other hand, Holmes (as stated in a previous paragraph) was omniscient. Lord Watson must have known this. Yet he denies it. He makes Holmes attribute this particular gift (or 'specialism' as he called it) to Sir Mycroft, the detective's elder brother, but Sherlock (as a hundred instances will testify) had it, too. Let a single example suffice.

From what motive one cannot guess, whether from envy or for the sake of whimsical exaggeration, Lord Watson in one memoir states that Sherlock's knowledge of literature was *nil*. In another he makes Holmes quote Goethe twice, discuss miracle plays, comment on Richter, Hafiz and Horace, and remark of Athelney Jones: 'He has occasional glimmerings of reason. *"Il n'y a pas des sots si incommodes que ceux qui ont de l'esprit!"* '

It has even been conjectured, though wrongly, from this evidence of wide culture that Mr Holmes was attracted by the decadent aesthetic movement of the 'nineties. But a careful search through the pages of the *Yellow Book* fails to reveal any poem or prose contribution from his pen, and the whole tenor of his life seems to remove him entirely from the world in which Dowson, Symons and Aubrey Beardsley and the other ghosts of the old Café Royal lived and moved. He is never mentioned by Sir William Rothenstein or Sir Max Beerbohm in any of their reminiscences of the period. As a literary figure he remains enigmatic and aloof. Yet from Lord Watson's narrative, however melodramatic, however inaccurate, there does emerge the definite picture of a man; and (if we are prepared to make allowances for the occasional eccentricities of the writer) a man who must be very like the real Holmes.

To continue the actual narrative of his known career, Sherlock Holmes was offered a knighthood in 1902 but refused it. He took up government work in the period immediately preceding the First World War, and was instrumental in foiling the notorious Von Bork, one of the most devoted agents of the Kaiser. For this he was again offered a knighthood which he again refused.

He had a profound knowledge of chemistry, and a grip of iron, was an expert boxer and swordsman, and a voluminous writer. His most popular and widely-read works are those on *The Polyphonic Motets of Lassus*, his two short *Monographs on Ears*, originally published in the *Anthropological Journal*, his brochures on *The Tracing of Footsteps, with some Remarks upon the Uses of Plaster as a Preserver of Impresses*, his *Influence of a Trade on the Form of a Hand*, his *Essay on the Distinction of the Ashes of Various Tobaccos*, and his *Handbook of Bee Culture, with some Observations upon the Segregation of the Queen*.

It is one of fate's ironies that a failure to observe some of his own precepts, laid down in the last book, may have brought about the close of a life ever devoted to his country's good. His form and lineaments, together with those of Lord Watson, have long been familiar in waxen effigy at Madame Tussaud's Exhibition, not far from his old lodgings. A sturdy moralist, if not a devout churchman, he was also an ardent Democrat, a believer in the close union of the English-speaking races, a hater of the colour bar, and a despiser of the trappings of pomp and power. He may well have been said, in the words of Kipling, to have walked with kings nor lost the common touch. He was unmarried.

E. V. KNOX

A MIXED ASSEMBLY

A BRIEF STATEMENT OF OUR CASE

A response to the New Testament section of the New English Bible *on its publication in 1961—a summing-up of the Sermon on the Mount in the style of the NEB, using only phrases which appear in that translation:*

When he realised how things stood, Jesus held a meeting to look into the matter. It was no hole in the corner business. He went up the hill and began:

'And now, not to take up too much of your time, I crave indulgence for a brief statement of our case. How blest are those that know that they are poor. You are light for all the world. If a man wants to sue you for your shirt, let him have your coat as well. I also might make bold to say that you cannot serve God and Money. Do not feed your pearls to pigs, and be ready for action, with belts fastened and lamps alight. Thank you for giving me a hearing.'

He then went to lunch with some distinguished persons.

DWIGHT MACDONALD

THE EVIL DAYS

[reflections of an ageing man of letters – after Ecclesiastes]

While the years draw nigh when the clattering typewriter is a burden, likewise a parcel of books from the postman, and he shall say, I have no pleasure in them; for much study is a weariness of the flesh;

Also when the cistern shall break, and the overflow be loosed like a fountain; when the lights are darkened, and the windows need cleaning,

And the keeper of the house shall tremble at rate bills, and be afraid of prices which are high; and almonds are too much for the grinders, and beers shall be out of the way;

Yet desire may not utterly fail, and he shall rise up at the sight of a bird, when the singsong girls are brought low;

In the day when he seeks out acceptable words; when the editors are broken at their desks, and the sound of the publishers shall cease because they are few.

Then shall the dust return to the earth as it was, and the spirit also, whether it be good or evil, shall look for its place.

D. J. ENRIGHT

A HYMN, A CAROL AND MATINS — PLAYGROUND VERSIONS

[*collected by Iona and Peter Opie in* The Lore and Language of Schoolchildren, *1959*]

I

(*to the tune of 'Gentle Jesus'*)
Charlie Chaplin meek and mild
Took a sausage off a child.
When the child began to cry
Charlie sloshed him in the eye.

II

Good King Wenceslaus walked out
In his mother's garden.
He bumped into a Brussels sprout
And said 'I beg your pardon.'

III

Dearly beloved brethren,
The Scripture moveth us in sundry places,
For to go and seek the donkey races,
For to confess our manifold sins,
And to see which donkey wins.

SPACETIME

[*Stephen Hawking discusses his book* The Universe in a Nutshell (*2000*)]

Apparently, a large number of the many millions who bought *A Brief History of Time* got stuck on page one. Oh dear. I expected more of my readers. With this in mind, I have now simplified some of the ideas in the hope you will make it to page two. But since you had no idea of what I was talking about first time round, this is almost certainly a total waste of time.

Still, as Einstein pointed out, there is no universal quantity called time. Instead, everyone has his or her own personal time and mine, dare I say it, is more valuable than yours. This is one of the postulates of the theory of relativity—so called because it implied that only relative motion was important.

Relativity was not compatible with Newton's law of gravity, and from this Einstein inferred that it is not space that is curved, but spacetime itself. This led us to understand that the universe is expanding. Sadly, relativity breaks down at Big Bang because it is not compatible with quantum theory. Alas, despite having worked on this problem myself, we still don't have a grand unified theory of the origin of the universe.

But back to time. Although I have my own personal time, I cannot actually say what it is. I can only describe the mathematical model for it.

The singularity theorems of Roger Penrose and myself established that spacetime is bound to the past by regions in which quantum gravity is important. So to understand the universe we need a quantum theory of gravity.

Supersymmetries provided a natural physical mechanism to cancel the infinities arising from ground-state fluctuations. This led to the discovery of supergravities and superpartners. However, in 1985, people realised there was no reason not to expect infinities and this led to one-dimensional extended object superstring theories.

But that wasn't it; Paul Townsend found there were other objects that could be extended in more than one dimension. He called them p-branes – or pea brains, as I like to call them. Ho ho. And these could be found as the solutions of the equations of supergravity theories in 10 or 11 dimensions.

Which leads us to time measured in imaginary numbers. Did you know that Richard Feynman proposed the idea of multiple histories of the universe? Just imagine it: there's even a history in which you understand this book.

JOHN CRACE

A LEXICOGRAPHER

Sir James Murray, the venerable founding editor of the Oxford English Dictionary, *was frequently ill at ease with scientific terms, or rather with the problem of whether or not they were widely used enough to warrant inclusion in the Dictionary. In 1902, for instance, he decided not to include 'radium', a misjudgement which led one of his assistants, H. J. Bayliss, to devise a spoof OED entry for the word in the best Murray style:*

Radium (reˈdiˈum). Forms : See Suppl. [mod.L. *radium* (B. Balius *Add. Lex.*: not in Du Cange). The orig. source is Preh. *-adami-, spadi-* to dig :— Antediluv. *randam-* (unconnected with PanArryan *randan*). Cognate with OHHash. *mqdrq*, OPj. *rangtum*, MHGug. *tsploshm*, MUlr. *dndrpq*; Baby. *daddums* and MPol. *rad* are unconnected.]
The unknown quantity. *Math.* Symbol *x.* Cf. EUREKA.

Aristotle *De P. Q.* li. xx says it may be obtained from the excrement of a squint-eyed rat that has died of a broken heart buried 50 feet below the highest depths of the western ocean in a well-stopped tobacco-tin; but Sir T. Browne says this is a vulgar error : he also refutes the story that it was dug in the air above Mt. Olympus by the ancients.

[Not in J., the Court Guide, or the Daily Mail Yrbk. before 1510.]

*c*925 *Vesp. Ps.* xcii. 315 Sleӡe hem wiþ þy wraðiu. *c*1386 CHAUCER *Dustm. T.* 31 Brynge . . forthe yowre waystid wrathym. **1470–85** MALORY *Arthur* XVII. 7. 935 Hauyng a swerde wiþ a blayde of rathio. **1626** BACON *Sylva* §627 Experiment extraordinary. Radiom will not washe clothes. **1669** PEPYS *Diary* 31 June, And so to bed. Found radium an excellent pick-me-up in the morning. **1678** BUNYAN *Pilgr.* 317 When I had affixed a pinch of radium to the tail of Apollyon, he went on his way and I saw him no more. **1766** GOLDSM. *Inhab. Vill.* 29 The toper still his wonted radium quaffs. **1873** *Hymns A. & M.* 2517 Thy walls are built of radium. **1905** [My son writes : I well remember introducing Radium as an illuminant into Slushton, last July.]

b. *attrib.* and *Comb.*

1600 *Hakluyt's Voy.* IV. 21 The kyng was attyred simply in an hat of silke and a radium-umbrella. *a***1704** NEWTON *Optics* IV. 29 These rays are radium-coloured. **1747** MRS. GLASSE *Cookery* 761 Radium cutlets. **1856** KANE *Arct. Explor.* III. 57, I hurled a radium-bootjack at the beast. **1879** *Jrnl. R. Soc.* CLXX. 315 Prof. Bigass exhibited a radium-filled tooth of a cave-dweller.

A RESTAURANT CRITIC

In Posy Simmonds's graphic novel Gemma Bovery, *the heroine falls in love with Patrick Large, who writes restaurant reviews for a magazine called* CitiZone.

Widgeons
2 Brinkley Street, London W1

Another below par restaurant which seeks to impress with its over-long menu, napkins like blankets, Brobding-nagian wine glasses. The decor's red and overstuffed like the (mostly male) punters. The carpet pattern looks like a series of nose-bleeds. The food's a mess too. My pasta and woodland mushrooms had a whiff of marsh gas. My com-panion's lobster was a very nasty package – an overkill of coriander in the vinaigrette – and the cuttlefish-ink risotto was dried out. Sweetbreads and capers were OKish but they came, unaccountably, with a tumulus of flaccid chips. We gave the pud a miss. Two bottles of sumptuous (nicely over-oaked) Chardonnay were the sole excitements. Wine included, £120 for 2.

MY GOODNESS!

Many advertisers have made use of parody, none more abundantly or imagina-
tively than the Guinness company. The Alice books were particular favourites with
Guinness artists and copywriters, especially in the 1930s, 1940s, and 1950s. This
sometimes involved producing a parody of a parody – the Guinness version of
'How doth the little crocodile', for instance:

> How doth the goodly Guinness glass
> Improve each dining hour!
> No other drink is in its class
> For strength and staying-power.
>
> How cheerfully it seems to grin,
> How creamily it flows!
> How does that ruby gleam get in?
> Ah, Guinness only knows!

That advertisement carried a scrupulous double-credit, 'with acknowledgments to
Isaac Watts and Lewis Carroll', just as the Guinness version of 'Father William'
carried acknowledgements to Carroll and Robert Southey.

Carroll's prose proved as fruitful a source for the firm's advertising depart-
ment as his verse—in a satisfying variant on the Lion and the Unicorn episode in
Through the Looking-Glass, *for instance:*

'What are the Lion and the Unicorn fighting for?' said Alice.
'They both want a Guinness,' said the King, 'and there's only one left.'
'Does the one that wins get the Guinness?' asked Alice.
'Dear me, no!' said the King. 'The one that's had the Guinness wins.'

Another famous feature of Guinness advertising owed its presence, not quite to a
parody, perhaps, but to an ingenious transmutation. In 1935 a leading Guinness
artist came up with a drawing of a pelican balancing seven pints of the noble brew
on its beak. By way of copy, he added the well-known lines:

> *A wonderful bird is the pelican,*
> *Its bill can hold more than its belly can.*
> *It can hold in its beak*
> *Enough for a week:*
> *I simply don't know how the hell he can.*

The firm found this rhyme too coarse for its purposes, and one of the copywriters
at its advertising agency was asked to tone it down. Instead, she hit on the idea of
changing the pelican into a toucan, a bird which soon became the most celebrated
creature in the Guinness menagerie, even more familiar than the ostrich and the

seal. She also came up with the pun which was to accompany it through many subsequent advertisements:

> If he can say as you can
> Guinness is good for you
> How grand to be a Toucan
> Just think what Toucan do

The copywriter in question was Dorothy L. Sayers, creator of Lord Peter Wimsey and future translator of Dante.

'IN THE MANNER OF . . .'

We are the poets who by choice
Eschew the individual voice,
The parodists, the pastiche-makers,
The copyists, the honest fakers.
We take a published verse and bend
Its purpose to a different end;
We have our sport, but come the day
That minor talent slips away
Or ever-lurking Father Time
Draws the blind on life and rhyme,
They'll look upon our works and say,
'Another's labours smoothed his way.'

PHILIP A. NICHOLSON

SOURCES AND ACKNOWLEDGEMENTS

THE items by Alexander Pope, Samuel Johnson, Lewis Carroll, and Gerard Manley Hopkins can be found in their collected poems (though most of the Carroll items are more easily accessible in *Alice in Wonderland*). The poems by Algernon Charles Swinburne can be found in his collected poems; his prose parodies of Victor Hugo were first published in *New Writings by Swinburne*, ed. Cecil Y. Lang (Syracuse University Press, 1964).

Anon.: 'To a Gentleman who Desired Proper Materials for a Monody', published anonymously in the *Political Calendar*, 1763, reprinted in *The New Oxford Book of Eighteenth-Century Verse*, ed. Roger Lonsdale (1984).

Jane Austen: 'Love and Freindship' and 'Lesley Castle', first published in *Love and Freindship* (1922), reissued in vol. vi of the Oxford Jane Austen (*Minor Works*, 1954).

Ambrose Bierce: 'Our Tales of Sentiment', from *The Sample Counter*, in *The Collected Works of Ambrose Bierce* (1909–12).

C. S. Calverley: 'Of Propriety', from *Verses* (1861), 'Ballad' and 'The Cock and the Bull', from *Fly Leaves* (1872).

Henry Carey: *Namby-Pamby*, from *Poems on Several Occasions* (1729).

George Colman the elder: his parody of Johnson's Dictionary is quoted in James Boswell's *Life of Johnson* (1791).

Hartley Coleridge: 'He lived among the untrodden ways', from *Poems* (1851).

Edward Copleston: *Advice to a Young Reviewer, With a Specimen of the Art* (1807).

George du Maurier: limerick inspired by 'Break, break, break', from 'Vers nonsensiques' in *A Legend of Camelot* (1898).

Catherine Maria Fanshawe: 'Fragment in Imitation of Wordsworth', from *Literary Remains* (1876).

Owen Felltham: parody of Ben Jonson, first published in *Parnassus Biceps* (1656).

Percy French: parody-versions of nursery rhymes, from *Chronicles and Poems of Percy French* (Dublin, 1922).

Bret Harte: parodies of Dickens and Victor Hugo, from *Condensed Novels* (1867).

Robert Hichens: *The Green Carnation* (1894).

A. C. Hilton: 'Octopus' and 'The Heathen Passee', first published in *The Light Blue*, an undergraduate magazine, in 1872.

A. E. Housman: 'Fragment of a Greek Tragedy', first published in the *Bromsgrovian*, a school magazine, in 1883; reached a wider public when it was published in the *Cornhill* magazine in 1901.

H. S. Leigh: ''Twas ever thus', from *Carols of Cockayne* (1882).

Charles Battell Loomis: 'Jack and Jill' in versions by Walt Whitman and Austin Dobson, from *Just Rhymes* (1899).

James Clerk Maxwell: 'Rigid Body Sings' and 'John Alexander Frere', in L. Campbell and W. Garnett, *The Life of James Clerk Maxwell with Selections from his Correspondence and Occasional Writings* (1884).

William Shenstone: *The Schoolmistress*, first published in 1737 and expanded and revised in 1742 and 1748.

James and Horace Smith: parodies of Crabbe, Cobbett, and Thomas Moore, from *Rejected Addresses* (1812).

J. K. Stephen: 'A Grievance', 'Imitation of Robert Browning', and 'Sincere Flattery of W.W. (Americanus)', from *Lapsus Calami* (1891).

Bayard Taylor: 'Camerados' and 'Cimabuella', from *Diversions of the Echo Club* (1871).

William Whitehead: 'New Night Thoughts', from *Gentleman's Magazine*, 1747, reprinted in *The New Oxford Book of Eighteenth-Century Verse*, ed. Roger Lonsdale (1984).

Gilbert Adair: from *The Act of Roger Murgatroyd* (Faber, 2006), copyright © Gilbert Adair 2006, reprinted by permission of the author c/o Blake Friedmann Agency Ltd.

Alan Alexander: 'Little Jack Horner', *New Statesman*, 19.12.1975, copyright © New Statesman Ltd. 2009, reprinted by permission of *New Statesman*. All rights reserved.

Anonymous parody of Ted Hughes: 'Lines on the Queen's 60th Birthday' published in *Poetry Corner* (Private Eye/Corgi, 1992), reprinted by permission of *Private Eye* magazine.

W. H. Auden: 'Contra Blake' from *Collected Poems* (Faber, 1976), copyright © 1976 by Edward Mendelson, William Meredith and Monroe K. Spears, Executors of the Estate of W. H. Auden, reprinted by permission of the publishers, Faber & Faber Ltd. and Random House Inc.

Michael Barsley: 'Whenas in slacks my Julia goes': copyright holder not traced.

H. J. Bayliss: spoof *Oxford English Dictionary* entry for the word 'radium' published in *The Treasure House of Language* by Charlotte Brewer (Yale University Press, 2007), reprinted by permission of the Secretary to the Delegates at Oxford University Press.

Max Beerbohm: 'Savonarola Brown' from *Seven Men and Two Others* (Heinemann, 1919), 'After Tom Moore' and 'A Luncheon' from *Max in Verse* (Heinemann, 1964), and 'A Mote in the Middle Distance', 'A Recollection', 'P.C. X, 36' and 'Some Damnable Errors About Christmas' from *A Christmas Garland* (Heinemann, 1912), reprinted by permission of Berlin Associates. 'In the Shades', a caricature of Johnson and Boswell drawn in 1915, published in *A Catalogue of the Caricatures of MB* edited by Rupert Hart-Davis (Macmillan, 1972), reproduced by permission of Berlin Associates and Dr Johnson's House Trust.

Hilaire Belloc: 'Imitation' from *The Complete Verse* (Pimlico, 1991), copyright © Hilaire Belloc 1970, reprinted by permission of PFD (www.pfd.co.uk) on behalf of the Estate of Hilaire Belloc.

Robert Benchley: 'Die Meister-Genossenschaft' from 'Opera Synopses: Some Sample Outlines of Grand Opera Plots for Home Study' in *The Benchley Roundup* (Cassell, 1956), reprinted by permission of Nathaniel R. Benchley.

Alan Bennett: from *Forty Years On* (Faber, 1969), copyright © Alan Bennett 1969, reprinted by permission of Chatto & Linnit Ltd. on behalf of the author.

Nicolas Bentley: 'To Lady A—' from *Second Thoughts* (Michael Joseph, 1939), reprinted by permission of the heirs of Nicolas Bentley.

D. C. Berry: 'Godiva' from *Jawbone* (Thunder City Press, 1978), reprinted by permission of the author.

John Betjeman: 'Longfellow's Visit to Venice' from *Collected Poems* (John Murray, 1988) and 'The Old Land Dog' from *Uncollected Poems* (John Murray, 1982), reprinted by permission of John Murray (Publishers) Ltd.

Malcolm Bradbury: 'Voluptia', 'Last Things', and 'A Jaundiced View' from *Who Do You Think You Are? Stories and Parodies* (Secker & Warburg, 1976/Picador, 2000), reprinted by permission of Pan Macmillan, London.

John Malcolm Brinnin: 'A Thin Façade for Edith Sitwell', first published in the *New Yorker*, 1953: copyright holder not traced.

Anthony Brode: 'Breakfast with Gerard Manley Hopkins' first published in *Punch*, reprinted by permission of Punch Ltd.

Craig Brown: 'Humpty Dumpty' from 'The Harold Pinter Book of Nursery Rhymes', *Private Eye*, 22.8.2008; and 'From the Diary of Anthony Powell: 22nd January 1995', 'From the Diary of David Hare: The State of Britain' and 'Life and Times' from *The Private Eye Book of Craig Brown Parodies* (Private Eye/Corgi, 1995), reprinted by permission of the author; 'The BT History of England in Verse' and 'Tony Blair: A Conference Speech' from *The Tony Years* (Ebury Press, 2007), 'The Night Train' and 'My Turner Prize Dinner' from *This is Craig Brown* (Ebury Press, 2003), reprinted by permission of the publishers, The Random House Group Ltd.

A. Y. Campbell: 'Murie Sing' from *Yet More Comic and Curious Verse* edited by J. M. Cohen (Penguin, 1959), reprinted by permission of the heirs of A. Y. Campbell.

Charles Causley: 'Betjeman, 1984' from *Collected Poems* (Macmillan, 1975), reprinted by permission of David Higham Associates.

John Clarke: 'There was an old man with a beard . . .' and 'The Emperor's New Album' from *The Even More Complete Book of Australian Verse* (Text Publishing, 2003), reprinted by permission of the author.

Cyril Connolly: from *Bond Strikes Camp* (Shenval Press, 1963) and from 'Told in Gath' in *The Two Natures* (Picador, 2002), copyright © Cyril Connolly, reprinted by permission of the author c/o Rogers. Coleridge & White Ltd., 20 Powis Mews, London WII IJN.

Wendy Cope: 'Waste Land Limericks', 'Mr Strugnell', 'A Policeman's Lot', 'Usquebaugh', 'The skylark and the jay sang loud and long', 'Because time will not run backwards', and 'God and the Jolly Bored Bog-Mouse' from *Making Cocoa for Kingsley Amis* (Faber, 1986), reprinted by permission of the publishers, Faber & Faber Ltd. and United Agents on behalf of Wendy Cope.

Noel Coward: 'Let's Do It' from *The Lyrics of Noel Coward* (Methuen, 1983), reprinted by permission of Methuen Drama, an imprint of A. & C. Black Publishers Ltd.

John Crace: 'The Crying of Lot 49', *The Guardian*, 13.9.2008, copyright © Guardian News & Media Ltd. 2008, and 'Success', *The Guardian*, 7.2.2009, copyright © Guardian News & Media Ltd. 2009, reprinted by permission of Guardian News & Media Ltd.; 'Youth', 'Love, etc', 'Saturday', and 'Stephen Hawking discusses his book *The Universe in a Nutshell* (2001)' from *The Digested Read* (Guardian Books, 2005), reprinted by permission of the publishers.

'Nicholas Craig': see Christopher Douglas.

Frederick Crews: from '. . . Das Nuffa Dat' in *Postmodern Pooh* (Profile Books, 2002), reprinted by permission of the publisher.

Mark Crick: 'Clafoutis Grandmère à la Virginia', 'Lamb with Dill Sauce à la Raymond Chandler' and 'Quick Miso Soup à la Franz Kafka' from *Kafka's Soup: A Complete History of Literature in 17 Recipes* (Libri Publications, 2005/Granta, 2007), copyright © Mark Crick 2005, reprinted by permission of the author c/o Jill Hughes–Foreign

Rights. 'Applying Sealant Round a Bath with Johann Wolfgang von Goethe' from *Sartre's Sink: The Great Writers' Complete Book of DIY* (Granta, 2008), copyright © Mark Crick 2008, reprinted by permission of Granta Books.

John Davenport: see Dylan Thomas.

Russell Davies: 'Pleasurebubble Hubbyhouse' from *The Antibooklist* edited by Brian Redhead and Kenneth MacLeish (Hodder & Stoughton, 1981), reprinted by permission of United Agents Ltd. on behalf of Russell Davies.

Paul Dehn: 'Whenas in jeans . . .' first published in *Punch*, 'Lucy and the Mariner', *Punch*, 8.1.1958, 'Rhymes for a Modern Nursery', *Punch*, 5.2.1958, 'Jenny kiss'd me' and 'Nuclear Wind' from *A Leaden Treasury of English Verse*, *Punch*, 12.2.1958, lines from 'Tennysoniana—"The splendour falls from castle walls . . ."', *Punch*, 19.2.1958, reprinted by permission of Berlin Associates.

Nigel Forbes Dennis: 'The Guthrie' and 'The Kitchin' from *Dramatic Essays* (Weidenfeld & Nicolson, 1962), copyright © Nigel Forbes Dennis 1962, reprinted by permission of the publishers, an imprint of The Orion Publishing Group, London and of A. M. Heath & Co, Ltd. Author's Agents.

Christopher Douglas and Nigel Planer: 'Peter Brook's D'ik' from *I, An Actor* by Nicholas Craig (Methuen, 2001), reprinted by permission of The Writers' Company for Christopher Douglas and United Agents for Nigel Planer.

D. J. Enright: 'The Evil Days' from *Collected Poems* (OUP, 1987), reprinted by permission of Watson, Little Ltd.

Gavin Ewart: 'A Wordsworthian Sonnet for Arnold Feinstein, Who Mended My Spectacles in Yugoslavia' and 'Audenesque for an Initiation' from *Collected Poems* (Hutchinson, 1991), reprinted by permission of Margo Ewart.

Sebastian Eleigh: see Hugh Greene.

Anne Fadiman: 'Clarissa Harlowe On-line' from *At Large and At Small* (Penguin Books, 2007), copyright © Anne Fadiman 2007, reprinted by permission of Penguin Books Ltd. and Farrar, Straus & Giroux, LLC.

Edward Field: 'The Life of Joan Crawford' from *After the Fall: Poems Old and New* (University of Pittsburgh Press, 2007), copyright © Edward Field 2007, reprinted by permission of the author and the publisher.

E. M. Forster: 'My Own Centenary' from *Abinger Harvest* (Edward Arnold, 1936), copyright 1936 and renewed 1964 by Edward M. Forster, reprinted by permission of The Provost and Scholars of King's College, Cambridge and the Society of Authors as the literary representatives of the Estate of E. M. Forster, and of Houghton Mifflin Harcourt Publishing Company.

Roy Fuller: 'The Love Song of J. Omar Khayyam', *The New Statesman*, 2.2.1973, reprinted by permission of John Fuller.

Oliver St John Gogarty: 'Ode' and 'Goosey Goosey Gander censored "to ridicule the Irish censors" ' from *Poems* edited by Norman Jeffares (Colin Smythe, 2001), reprinted by permission of Colin Smythe Ltd.

Hugh Greene: from a competition entry for the *New Statesman*, published in Graham Greene, *Yours Etc: Letters to the Press* (Reinhardt Books, 1989), extract copyright © Hugh Greene 1989, reprinted by permission of PFD (www.pfd.co.uk) on behalf of the Estate of Sir Hugh Greene.

Bill Greenwell: 'William Blake Rewrites T. S. Eliot's "The Hollow Men"' from *How to be Well Versed in Poetry* edited by E. O. Parrott (Penguin, 1990), copyright © Bill Greenwell 1990, reprinted by permission of Campbell Thomson and McLaughlin on behalf of the author.

E. V. Knox: 'Upon Julia's Clothes' from *The Brazen Lyre* (Smith Elder, 1911), and 'The Passing of Sherlock Holmes', *The Strand Magazine*, 1948, reprinted by permission of Maria Fitzgerald.

Ronald Knox: lines from 'Absolute and Abitofhell' in *Essays in Satire* (Sheed & Ward, 1928), and 'Battology' from *In Three Tongues* (Chapman & Hall, 1959), reprinted by permission of A. P. Watt Ltd. on behalf of the Earl of Oxford and Asquith.

Kenneth Koch: 'Variations on a Theme by William Carlos Williams' from *The Collected Poems of Kenneth Koch* (Knopf, 2005), copyright © 2005 by The Kenneth Koch Literary Estate, reprinted by permission of Alfred A. Knopf, a division of Random House, Inc.

Osbert Lancaster: from 'Poet's Corner' in *Draynefleet Revealed* (John Murray, 1949), copyright © Clare Hastings, reprinted by permission of John Murray.

David McCord: 'Baccalaureate' from *Bay Window Ballads* (Scribner, 1935), copyright © 1935 by Charles Scribner's Sons, copyright renewed 1963 by David McCord, reprinted by permission of Scribner, a division of Simon & Schuster, Inc. All rights reserved.

Dwight Macdonald: 'A Brief Statement of Our Case' from *Against the American Grain* (Gollancz, 1963), first published in *The Observer*, 1961: copyright holder not traced.

Julian Maclaren-Ross: 'The Pursuit of Fame' from *The Funny Bone* (Elek, 1956), reprinted by permission of the Andrew Lownie Agency Ltd.

Louis MacNeice: 'Or One Might Write It So: Yeats' and 'Or One Might Write It So: Lawrence' from *I Crossed the Minch* (Longmans, 1938), also published in *Louis MacNeice: Selected Prose* edited by Alan Heuser (OUP, 1990), reprinted by permission of David Higham Associates.

André Maurois: see George D. Painter.

Gwen Melvaine: 'Bell Birds' from *Oz Shrink Lit* (Penguin Australia, 1980), reprinted by permission of Penguin Group (Australia).

H. L. Mencken: from 'The Declaration of Independence in American' in *The American Language: an enquiry into the development of English in the United States* (4e, Knopf, 1936), copyright 1936 by Alfred A. Knopf, Inc. and renewed 1964 by August Mencken and Mercantile-Safe Deposit and Trust Co., reprinted by permission of Alfred A. Knopf, a division of Random House, Inc.

J. B. Miller: 'Harry Potter and the Rolling Stone' from *The Satanic Nurses* (St Martin's Press, 2003), reprinted by permission of the publishers.

Jonathan Miller: 'Early Days at Cambridge' for 'Beyond the Fringe' revue, published in *The Complete Beyond the Fringe* (A. & C. Black, 2003): copyright holder not traced.

J. B. Morton (Beachcomber): 'When We Were Very Silly' from *The Best of Beachcomber* (Heinemann, 1963), copyright © J. B. Morton 1963, reprinted by permission of PFD (www.pfd.co.uk) on behalf of the Estate of J. B. Morton.

Howard Moss: 'Shall I Compare thee to a summer's day?' from 'Modified Sonnets' from *A Swim off the Rocks* (Atheneum, 1976), reprinted by permission of Ellen Evans for the Estate of Howard Moss.

Philip A. Nicholson: 'In the manner of . . .' from *How to be Well Versed in Poetry* edited by E. O. Parrott (Penguin, 1990), copyright © Philip A. Nicholson 1990, reprinted by permission of Campbell Thomson and McLaughlin on behalf of the author.

Flann O'Brien (Myles na Gopaleen): from 'La Traitement Superbe' in *The Best of Myles* (MacGibbon & Kee, 1968), copyright © Flann O'Brien 1968, reprinted by permission of A. M. Heath & Co. Ltd.

Iona and Peter Opie: playground rhymes from *The Lore and Language of Schoolchildren* (OUP, 1959), reprinted by permission of Mrs I. Opie.

George Orwell: review of *Assignment in Utopia* by Eugene Lyons from *The Collected Essays, Journalism and Letters Vol. 1: An Age Like This 1920–1940* edited by Sonia Orwell and Ian Angus (Secker & Warburg, 1961), copyright © George Orwell 1938, copyright © 1968 by Sonia Brownell Orwell and renewed 1996 by Mark Hamilton, reprinted by permission of A. M. Heath & Co. Ltd. Authors' Agents on behalf of Bill Hamilton as the Literary Executor of the Estate of the late Sonia Brownell Orwell and Secker & Warburg Ltd., and of Houghton Mifflin Harcourt Publishing Company.

George D. Painter: from *The Chelsea Way, or Marcel in England: A Proustian Parody* by André Maurois, translated by George D. Painter (Weidenfeld & Nicolson, 1966), English translation copyright © George D. Painter 1966, reprinted by permission of the publishers, an imprint of The Orion Publishing Group, London.

E. O. Parrott: 'The Runnymede Song' from *The Dogsbody Papers* edited by E. O. Parrott (Viking 1988), copyright © E. O. Parrott 1988, reprinted by permission of Campbell Thomson and McLaughlin on behalf of Mrs Tricia Parrott.

S. J. Perelman: 'Waiting for Santy'—a Christmas playlet from *A Child's Garden of Curses* (Heinemann, 1951), originally published in *Crazy Like a Fox* (Heinemann, 1945), copyright © S. J. Perelman 1945, reprinted by permission of PFD (www.pfd.co.uk) on behalf of the Estate of S. J. Perelman.

Noel Petty: 'Dear Father' and 'Lines on the Death of Samuel Johnson, Esq.' from *The Dogsbody Papers* edited by E. O. Parrott (Viking, 1988), reprinted by permission of the author.

Nigel Planer: see Christopher Douglas.

'Pontifex': 'Jenny to Rosetti' from *New Statesman Competitions* edited by William Whitebait (Faber, 1944), copyright © New Statesman Ltd. 2009, reprinted by permission of *New Statesman*. All rights reserved.

Ezra Pound: 'Ancient Music' from *Personae*, copyright © 1926 by Ezra Pound, and from *Collected Shorter Poems* (Faber, 1952), reprinted by permission of the publishers, Faber & Faber Ltd. and New Directions Publishing Corp.

'Pulex': 'Donne and The Flea' from *New Statesman Competitions* edited by William Whitebait (Faber, 1944), copyright © New Statesman Ltd. 2009, reprinted by permission of *New Statesman*. All rights reserved.

Henry Reed: 'Stoutheart on the Southern Railway' first published in *Sense of Humour* edited by Stephen Potter (Reinhardt, 1954), and 'Chard Whitlow' from *A Map of Verona* (Cape, 1946), reprinted by permission of the Royal Literary Fund.

Christopher Reid: 'Letter to Myself' first published in the *New Review*, 1970s, reprinted by permission of the author.

S. C. Roberts: fragment from *New Light on Dr Johnson* edited by Frederick W. Hilles (Yale, 1959): copyright holder not traced.

Charles Robinson: 'To His Far from Coy Mistress', *New Statesman*, 11.7.1975, copyright © New Statesman Ltd. 2009, reprinted by permission of *New Statesman*. All rights reserved.

Carol Rumens: 'A Response to Philip Larkin's "This be the Verse"' from *Blind Spots* (Seren, 2008), reprinted by permission of the author and the publisher.

'Sagittarius': 'Matthew Arnold Writes to *The Listener*' from *Targets* (Cape, 1944), and 'Heil Gottingen' from *Sagittarius Rhyming* (Cape, 1940): copyright holder not traced.

Ethel Talbot Scheffauer: 'Who, or why, or which, or what, Is the Akond of Swat?', *New*

Statesman, copyright © New Statesman Ltd. 2009, reprinted by permission of *New Statesman*. All rights reserved.

W. C. Sellar and R. J. Yeatman: 'Old Saxon Fragment' and 'Beoleopard, or The Witan's Wail' from *1066 and All That* (Methuen, 1930), reprinted by permission of the publishers.

Stanley J. Sharpless: 'The Tale of Miss Hunter Dunn' and 'Dylan Thomas Rewrites *Pride and Prejudice*', *New Statesman*, copyright © New Statesman Ltd. 2009, reprinted by permission of *New Statesman*. All rights reserved.

George Simmers: 'In a High Style' from *The Spectator*, 17.1.2009, reprinted by permission of the author and *The Spectator*.

Posy Simmonds: from *Gemma Bovery* (Cape, 2001), copyright © Posy Simmonds 2001, reprinted by permission of United Agents Ltd. (www.unitedagents.co.uk) on behalf of the author.

Louis Simpson: 'Squeal' from *The Hudson Review*, vol. x, no. 3 (Autumn, 1957), copyright © Louis Simpson 1957, reprinted by permission of *The Hudson Review*.

F. Sinclair: 'The Owl's Reply to Gray', *New Statesman*, copyright © New Statesman Ltd. 2009, reprinted by permission of *New Statesman*. All rights reserved.

Alan Sokal: from 'Transgressing the Boundaries: Toward a Transformative Hermeneutics of Quantum Gravity', *Social Text*, May 1996, p. 217, copyright © Duke University Press, reprinted by permission of the publisher. All rights reserved.

J. C. Squire: 'If Pope Had Written Tennyson's "Break, Break, Break" ', 'If Gray Had Had to Write His Elegy in the Cemetery of Spoon River Instead of that of Stoke Poges', 'The Little Commodore', and 'When I Leapt over Tower Bridge' from *Collected Parodies* (Hodder & Stoughton, 1921), reprinted by permission of Roger Squire.

Dylan Thomas and John Davenport: 'Parachutist' from *The Death of the King's Canary* (Hutchinson, 1976), reprinted by permission of David Higham Associates on behalf of the Estates of Dylan Thomas and John Davenport.

James Thurber: drawings for 'Lochinvar' by Sir Walter Scott from *Fables for Our Time and Famous Poems Illustrated* (Harper, 1940) originally published in *The New Yorker*, 8 April 1939, copyright © 1940 by Rosemary A. Thurber, reprinted by permission of Rosemary A. Thurber and The Barbara Hogeson Agency. All rights reserved.

Hugh Trevor-Roper: 'A Brief Life' from *Letters of Mercurius* (John Murray, 1970), copyright © Hugh Trevor-Roper 1970, reprinted by permission of PFD (www.pfd.co.uk) on behalf of the Estate of Hugh Trevor-Roper.

John Updike: 'Miss Moore at Assembly' from *Collected Poems 1953–1993* (Hamish Hamilton, 1993), copyright © John Updike 1993, 'On the Sidewalk' first published in *The New Yorker*, 1959 and extract from 'Beerbohm and Others' from *Assorted Prose* (Deutsch/Knopf, 1965), copyright © John Updike 1965, renewed 1993, reprinted by permission of the publishers, Alfred A. Knopf, a division of Random House Inc., and Penguin Books Ltd.

Peter Ustinov: 'The Gift of Bad Dialogue', no. 3 of 'With and Without Prejudice', *The Author*, vol. lviii, no. 1 (Autumn 1947), reprinted by permission of the Estate of Peter Ustinov.

G. H. Vallins: 'Mr Smith Tries in Vain to Telephone' first published in *Punch*, reprinted by permission of Punch Ltd.

Keith Waterhouse: 'The Cratchit Factor' from *Fanny Peculiar* (Michael Joseph, 1983), reprinted by permission of David Higham Associates.

Evelyn Waugh: 'The Suicide of Sir Francis Hinsley' and funeral ode from *The Loved One* (Chapman & Hall, 1948/Penguin Classics, 2000), copyright © Evelyn Waugh 1948, reprinted by permission of Penguin Books Ltd. and SLL/Sterling Lord Literistic, Inc. and PFD as agents for Evelyn Waugh.

E. B. White: 'Across the Street and Into the Grill' from *The Second Tree from the Corner* (Hamish Hamilton, 1954), reprinted by permission of Allene M. White for the E. B. White Estate.

Kit Wright: from 'Humpty Dumpty: The Official Biography' in *Poems: 1974–1983* (Hutchinson, 1988), reprinted by permission of the author.

Although every effort has been made to trace and contact copyright holders prior to publication this has not been possible in the cases indicated. If notified, the publisher will be pleased to rectify any errors or omissions at the earliest opportunity.

INDEX OF PARODISTS

INDEX OF THE PARODIED

ANONYMOUS OR REPRESENTATIVE LITERARY MATERIAL

OTHER MATERIAL